CORPORATE BOLD

CORPORATE BOLD

What Every Corporate Professional Must Know!

Written by

101 Corporate Professionals!

iUniverse, Inc.
Bloomington

Corporate Bold
What Every Corporate Professional Must Know!

iUniverse books may be ordered through booksellers or by contacting:

iUniverse
1663 Liberty Drive
Bloomington, IN 47403
www.iuniverse.com
1-800-Authors (1-800-288-4677)

ISBN: 978-1-4620-1513-9 (sc)
ISBN: 978-1-4620-1514-6 (dj)
ISBN: 978-1-4620-1515-3 (ebk)

Library of Congress Control Number: 2011909088

Printed in the United States of America

iUniverse rev. date: 06/23/2011

Authors

Core Author	Hussain Noordin
Co-Authors	
Alex Merchan	Assumption #1
Andreas Wutz	Assumption #1
Bengt Campbell	Assumption #1
E.J. Ackerman	Assumption #1
Heather Vozella	Assumption #1
Holly J. Berk	Assumption #1
James Parnitzke	Assumption #1
Jared Flynn	Assumption #1
Mark Frederick	Assumption #1
Sally Petersen	Assumption #1
Christopher Campbell	Assumption #1
Carlo Caminiti	Assumption #2
Amber J. Laxton	Assumption #2
Carlos Buxton	Assumption #2
Gerald Ratigan	Assumption #2
John D. Lestock	Assumption #2
John Masoudpour	Assumption #2
Kimberly Denney	Assumption #2
Laurent Borne	Assumption #2
Mark Herbert	Assumption #2
Reid Lang	Assumption #2

Rene Zipper	Assumption #2
Roshan Mahtani	Assumption #2
Valerie W. Perlowitz	Assumption #2
Aja Edmond	Assumption #3
Chris Martines	Assumption #3
Jacqueline L. Benitez	Assumption #3
Fran Nahabedian	Assumption #3
Steven Young	Assumption #3
Andrew Broderick	Assumption #3
Maritiza (Tesa) Anderson	Assumption #3
Steve Callisher	Assumption #3
Jean Kim	Assumption #3
Michelle Clauss	Assumption #3
Renee Rhoades	Assumption #3
Ronald V. Bryant	Assumption #3
Sean Lee	Assumption #3
Jessica Z. Hall	Assumption #3
John Jameson	Assumption #3
Ronak Baxi	Assumption #4
Anthony Knierim	Assumption #4
Britt V. Pearson	Assumption #4
Brooke Ann Etzel	Assumption #4
David Jara	Assumption #4
Ericka M. Berti	Assumption #4
Louis Bing	Assumption #4
Ahmad Noordin	Assumption #4

Michael Podemski	Assumption #4
Nina Chavda	Assumption #4
Cherry Worring	Assumption #5
Chris Bradshaw	Assumption #5
Dan Kesselring	Assumption #5
Donna Horowitz	Assumption #5
Donna St. John	Assumption #5
Jeffrey Phillips	Assumption #5
Len Salva	Assumption #5
Lionel Roblin	Assumption #5
Miguel A. Velazquez	Assumption #5
Naseem Malik	Assumption #5
Papi Valmond	Assumption #5
Tomi Davies	Assumption #5
Veronica Paz	Assumption #5
Sonia Clayton	Assumption #5
Wei Fuh	Assumption #5
Bob Gamble	Assumption #6
Brad Wachter	Assumption #6
Shalin Kothari	Assumption #6
Henry Motyka	Assumption #6
John Yavelak	Assumption #6
Melanie Hayes	Assumption #6
Ronald R. Dull	Assumption #6
Sarah J. Peacey	Assumption #6
Shane Cox	Assumption #6

Ali A. Gowani	Assumption #7
Alexander Sultan	Assumption #7
Beth Becker	Assumption #7
Christy Nicholas	Assumption #7
Clare Cooper	Assumption #7
Dawn Mc Rae	Assumption #7
Jawed Valliani	Assumption #7
Louise Carley Lewisson	Assumption #7
Marcie E. Thomas	Assumption #7
Matt Bell	Assumption #7
Matt Shefchik	Assumption #7
Thomas Juli, Ph.D.	Assumption #7
Thomasina Tafur	Assumption #7
Wayne Anderman	Assumption #7
Joan Finley	Assumption #7
Christian Nascimento	Assumption #8
Craig L. Chapman	Assumption #8
Frank T. Mitchell	Assumption #8
Lila Asante-Appiah	Assumption #8
Mario Sanchez Carrion	Assumption #8
Mark Goloboy	Assumption #8
Mike Levy	Assumption #8
Sandra Teague	Assumption #8
Scott Sutker	Assumption #8
Sheila Wyatt	Assumption #8
George Moraetes	Assumption #8
Marcus Cadell	Assumption #8

* * *

Corporate Bold holds all organizations that provide their associates with gainful employment in the highest regard.

No one incident should be considered as the true and final reflection of any organization.

While events in this book may be true; names, gender, location, or other attributes may have been changed, where appropriate, for privacy.

Corporate Bold is a private publication, with no sponsorship or relationship with any Governmental or Non-Governmental Organization or Agency.

* * *

Preface

Two guys walk into a bar. One guy says to the other, "Boy, you know after fifteen years at my job, I actually got laid off today." The second guy answers, "Oh, that's too bad! What are you going to do now?" The first guy then replies, "I don't know, I'm not sure what I'm qualified to do anymore."

Over the years, I've had the pleasure of working with some really talented individuals. From my days working for an iconic entertainment organization, to Fortune® companies, then an international pharmaceutical firm, on to one of the hottest startup Dotcoms of our generation, and many others. I have been truly blessed and lucky to have worked with so many talented individuals. I miss working with many of them and I often think about everything that I learned just by being around them.

That being said, I have often struggled with one question since the very beginning of my career: Why are so many corporate professionals stuck in the same job for so many years, and why are they heartbroken when their organization wants to "breakup" with them? Could it be that they simply don't know what others have already figured out?

Whenever I asked this question, I heard many different answers. Most of them were neatly packaged and rationalized. And yet, I wonder if those types of responses will help the working professionals of tomorrow who are leaning into a corporate structure that is similar to mine. Furthermore, I am finding that there are certain individuals who are already aware of the shift that is taking place in the corporate world. They are following a specific path and applying specific principles to alter their future.

Their path is dynamic, and it rewards them each step of the way. They are, what I have come to know them as, **Corporate Bold.**

Corporate Bold is not about the next up-and-coming industry or job trend. It is not intended to be a guide about how to ask your boss for a raise. And it is certainly not meant to serve as the only roadmap on which you should rely when navigating your particular field or organization.

Corporate Bold is a completely different way of looking at your corporate position; as opposed to viewing it in a more traditional sense. For those who may not be able to deal with the concepts that we are about to discuss, it is likely to cause them anger or discomfort. Yet, for those who are willing to challenge what they know, it may very well change their lives in a significantly positive way, as it has undoubtedly changed mine.

Hussain Noordin

Core-Author, **Corporate Bold.**

Introduction

Imagine yourself at "the career networking event" of the decade. You are standing in the middle of a large conference room, and you are surrounded by 100 corporate professionals, all wanting to speak with you. There is something each one of them would like to share with you personally; something that could change your life in such a positive manner that you may even be compelled to share it with others.

For this event, I—the core-author of this book—will be your host.

What you are about to experience is, quite possibly, something like never before. Never before has such a large collection of individuals co-authored a book in the hopes of providing a roadmap to help you succeed as a corporate professional.

So, before you read this book, you must ask yourself this critical and overarching question: What can 101 thriving corporate professionals teach me that, perhaps, I didn't already know?

My goal will be to introduce you to each co-author when the time is right. For each topic, we will present a few concepts then I will share some personal experiences to get your feet wet. Once we have covered the topic thoroughly, you will then be introduced to professionals who will share their experiences and ideas about that topic. The end-goal is to help you avoid or navigate some of the dead-ends and detours that come as part of working in a corporate environment. What you are about to discover are experiences, strategies, ideas, and stories of successes or failures from 101 corporate professionals.

The co-authors come from many different industries and organizations; some from different countries, backgrounds, or job functions; many work for some of the top organizations from around the globe. However, at some point in their career, they faced a perspective-altering situation that taught them an invaluable lesson and made them **Corporate Bold**.

You will find that the ideas presented in **Corporate Bold** will become more prevalent in the upcoming era where the corporate world will place demands on professional that are far different than those of yesteryear.

While we may generalize or point-out things that you might be doing, and will want to defend to death, the important thing to remember is that this is a learning opportunity. Many individuals will never read this book due to personal pride since they 'know it all' or 'have been-there, done-that.' The reality is that only those who are willing to learn, by challenging their assumptions, will be rewarded. Just open any history book, and you will find it littered with examples of those who challenged their assumptions, which lead them to experience a breakthrough. All we ask is that, as you read, you challenge your past assumptions, and you try to think about how you can best leverage some of the principles that we discuss.

We all have different goals in life, financial or otherwise. Some individuals are entrepreneurs in-the-making while others are building their career in a specific industry or organization. Whatever your goals are, becoming a professional in a corporation environment can the first stepping stone for many individuals today.

We hope to provide a guide on what it takes to become **Corporate Bold**. That is, a framework designed to ensure that you are on the path to success as a corporate professional. You should be able to start thinking about, and applying, some of these principles right away. And when I say, "right away", I mean, right away. For instance, if you are reading this during your lunch break, then you could apply some of these principles as soon as you get back to your desk. You don't have time to waste, and we don't want to waste your time either.

Why, Why, and Why?

You may be asking yourself: Why did so many corporate professional feel the need to co-author **Corporate Bold,** and what is the reason for this type of approach? It's true, bookshelves are cluttered with business, management, and career "how-to" books. So, why bother adding yet another one to the collection?

There are three fundamental reasons why we, as corporate professionals, feel the need to step in at this time. First of all, according to Amazon.com, there are some 90,000 books and materials on the topic of "career", up for sale today. Now, take a moment to ask yourself, of all of the business, management, and career how-to books that you've come across, how many of them have actually "changed your life"? How many of them have given you the necessary tools, ideas, skills, and examples to have a positive impact on your life? After all the hype from the bookstores and bestsellers dies down, how many of them had a **true impact** on you? A true impact would be considered when you could trace a real event in your life that occurred as a result of your reading any one of these other career-related books.

You must ask yourself: Why do so many of those books fail to make an actual difference? We can summate the answer in one word: **applicability**. If you can't apply what you know, what is the value in knowing it? What is the purpose of reading through the bestsellers list each year if you cannot do anything with that knowledge? Their value becomes little more than entertainment on your way to and from work.

Secondly, when a plumber wants to learn a better way to fit pipes in a home, does he go to a carpenter to ask for advice? Probably not. So, as corporate professionals, why are we subjecting ourselves to how-to tips in newspapers and magazines written by someone who may not be able to *truly* relate to what it's like to be a corporate professional? For example, I've stayed up numerous nights because my organization was implementing a system for a 5:00 AM project release the next morning. I often asked myself, could the writer of that weekly career column in my local newspaper actually relate to my experiences?

This is our second reason for publishing **Corporate Bold**. This book is not a collection of a 101 articles from self-help gurus, glued together to make you feel all warm and fuzzy inside. As we mentioned before, each co-author is a real professional who wakes up every morning to perform their corporate duties.

Finally, the third reason is, do you have time to wait for a comprehensive twenty-year-long study that lays out the top five things you should be doing at work today for success tomorrow? You can be sure that, by the time that twenty-year study is done researching, synthesizing, and reporting its information, many of us will be close to retirement, which would make it slightly difficult to apply some of that information. It is not enough to have applicable ideas; we also need them in a timely manner.

We hope that you now understand the goal of **Corporate Bold**, which is to bring you applicable ideas from a very large number of real professionals. As a companion to this book, we encourage you to visit *Corporate Bold* online at, www.CorporateBold.com, to facilitate your ongoing success.

Basic Training

You are probably aware that, in the military, new recruits go through what is known as "Basic Training". Well, consider this your Basic Training because once you're up to speed, your mission of a lifetime will start—right away, that is! Alternatively, you might have already started your corporate journey, so you can take this opportunity to reevaluate the direction you're going as well as reexamine your assumptions and results thus far.

Let me start by asking you this: Do you know the difference between a job and a career? By now you have probably heard the news that, over a lifetime, most people will change their careers three to five times, or more—not their jobs but their careers. The point is that we need to be clear on the distinction between what is considered a job and what is considered a career. What I've discovered is that many individuals are grossly confusing the difference between the two. Beyond this initial confusion, the real problem becomes when people base many of their critical life decisions around a job, not a career. If they do this, they will most likely have to pay a heavy price for this confusion. So, how can you avoid this same mistake? Well, in case you haven't heard, jobs get eliminated, careers don't.

When I ask corporate professionals: What is a job? I usually get some interesting responses. However, their responses are nowhere near as intriguing as when I ask: What is a career? Or, what does "career" mean? This second set of questions usually invokes a detailed and impassioned soliloquy that they are drawing-up on the spot, mind you. Here is a related thought from Albert Einstein, "If you can't explain it simply, you don't understand it well enough." So, in the spirit of Einstein, let's get some **Corporate Bold** definitions out in the open.

Throughout this book, we will be using certain words, in a certain way, to make a point. You can find all the relevant definitions at the end of this book in the Corporate Bold Dictionary. Or, you can find them on our website at www.CorporateBold.com.

Corporate Bold Dictionary Lookup

Job: A task that you perform to get a result.
Career: A series of tasks or jobs around a discipline.

So, now that we have stated what job means in its simplest form, you know that when you show up to work and perform a job, it is only to accomplish some specific goal. Your goal could be to take home a paycheck, learn a skill, coast and burn time for some other reason, etc. While you are trying to accomplish one goal, you may very well have more than one goal that you'd like to accomplish from your job.

A career, then, is the big-picture that comes together over time and is formed by all the different types of jobs you've held in the past or will hold in the future. For example, if you've held three jobs over the last ten years working as the ticketing agent for three different airlines, your career could be in customer service. Should you no longer wish to work in the transportation industry, you could take your customer service career into retail, hospitality, or any other applicable industry.

Are you Cliff? Cliff started working in a corporate environment and showed some competency early-on. Cliff's boss or co-worker told him that he was doing a good job. So, for the next ten years, Cliff **pitched a tent** and hunkered down in a cubicle. One day, Cliff's boss quit, was fired, laid off, or left the company for some reason—permanently. Next thing you know, Cliff is given a slight promotion. I say "slight" because, most of the time, these promotions are just enough to keep professionals like Cliff from leaving the company. Otherwise, who would step-in to do the work that his boss used to do? Or maybe still, Cliff got a new boss, and once again his life went on. This cycle will repeat itself a few times, but by then retirement will be within sight and that's what we are all racing towards, right? You have to ask yourself: What is the quality of this type of a life? This example is certainly an oversimplification of what actually happens but, for many like Cliff, it's not too far from reality.

Most workers who have pitched similar tents in their cubicles are rational, logical, fair-minded, and downright good people. And there are valid reasons to pitch tents at the right place and the right time. However, there are also some patterns that take place outside of "the right place at the right time" category.

These are some of the reasons, which are outside of the "right place at the right time" category, I hear from people who have decided to hunker down in their cubicles:

1. I am fine with what I do, and I don't mind doing it.

2. Gosh, I've been doing this for so long; this is what I do.

3. I'm not really sure what I want to do next so I'm going to do this for a little while longer.

4. They can't let me go, they need me.

I am so tired of watching talented corporate professionals put themselves on the next flight to disaster—all because they did not pay enough serious attention to their career development. Their attitudes are highly detrimental! Mortgages, car loans, student loans, monthly bills—all of these things tend to be part of reality for the average corporate professional these days. For those who have kids and are living on a single income, the problem can intensify many times over.

While some may consider branching off to build passive incomes outside of their corporate life, your corporate life should not be forsaken until you are ready to take that leap. Your current job is what pays the bills, and it will do so until you have established other means of generating income. Given that the corporate life might not be your final destination, it is still your current journey. So, before you quit, get fired, laid off, outsourced, etc; consider practicing the **Corporate Bold** principals first.

Corporate Bold applies to people who are following a specific pattern or process when it comes to their corporate careers. They have a different approach and a different mentality altogether. The interesting thing is that these people are not taking radical approaches in their career development. They are simply challenging some of the core rules about being a corporate professional. They have come to an understanding that there are no hard and fast rules, rather, a short series of ever changing assumptions that must be checked and applied and appropriate. The sooner you learn about these assumptions, the sooner you'll be able to apply them and see the results for yourself. We all make choices about our future. **Corporate Bold** isn't a matter of *if*, rather, it is a matter of *when* you apply these principles or assumptions; so you can sidestep hazardous pitfalls and gain the benefits that a **Corporate Bold** life has to offer.

The Key

Let me ask you this: When you go to work, what do you see yourself as? Ask yourself: When I go to work, what am I? Picture yourself at work over the past year. Take a second and try to answer this question honestly. You might think to yourself that you are a project manager, a secretary, an analyst, a manager, a copywriter, a clerk, etc. What we're missing here, is that these are merely snapshots of you—this is you trapped in a title!

So, really, who are you? I hope that you've answered that you are a **Talent!** You should constantly remind yourself that you are a talent. Many organizations call their "Human Resources" department, the "Human Capital" department. They do this because organizations want to treat you as an asset or, at least, they are aiming to do so. They have systems called "Talent Management Systems" and "Talent Teams" that work to "acquire Talent". And yet, I am amazed at the number of people who are either unaware of their talent or who simply do not believe that they are a Talent!

How do I know this? Simple, because of their behavior at work. I can see it in their response when their boss asks them to research training opportunities or take-on a new project. Their behavior is a direct result of their misconception about who they *really are* at work. They fail to see that their current job is an opportunity for them to develop their talent. We'll talk a little later about what to do when your job no longer helps you develop your talent but, for now, we will define what we mean by "talent".

So, what does it mean to be a **Talent**? A Talent, you and I, are the only ones keeping the organization running. The performance of any organization is a direct indicator of the type of Talent(s) running the organization.

Talents are people, not processes, not technologies, nor anything else. And so, a Talent needs to be nurtured because it must constantly grow and refine itself. Would you say that George Foreman was a talented boxer? Most people could be talked into believing this. Do you think that just because he won a few trophies at boxing, that he didn't have to continue to practice, learn, or grow? Of course not! We all know that talented athletes will constantly push themselves to practice, learn, and grow. What makes you, the corporate professional, think that you don't have to push yourself as well? The answer is simple—somewhere down the line, you stopped thinking about yourself as a Talent. You started to tell yourself that you are "just an employee" (I despise that term, personally).

For example, when I've asked for help in a department store, I've heard the department store employee utter this phrase on more than one occasion, "I don't know; I just work here." Whenever I hear this phrase, I know right away that I'm dealing with an employee, not a Talent. This person does not want to attempt to solve a problem that could act as a learning or growing opportunity in disguise. The reality is that he or she has given up on him or herself, at least for the time being. And I certainly won't think twice before taking my business elsewhere when I realize that I am dealing with someone who has given up.

Message

When you sit around, warming the corporate bench, and actively stop developing your talent, you are putting yourself in an extremely detrimental position.

In fact, here are some of the things you are unintentionally telling your company and your boss:

1. You should probably outsource what I do to an expert who can bring you more value for your dollar.

2. I don't need merit or a pay raise, just keep me in pace with inflation each year, if you want. (By the way, do you know what the current inflation rate is? How close is it to your last salary increase? If the two are close, you will soon find out what you need to start doing and why.)

3. Whatever you do, don't promote me—I am very comfortable with what I do even if you don't need me to do it anymore.

4. This is my station in life. I will be stopping here forever; so you can feel free to push me around because I won't leave on my own.

If these are the types of messages you'd like to pass along to your company or your boss then, at least now, you are aware of it, and you are making a conscious choice to do so.

But, if these are *not* the types of messages you want to send to your company or boss then, perhaps, you should start conveying different messages as soon as possible. Furthermore, you should consider sending your company and boss the type of message that a Talent would send instead.

Quiz

Sometimes it can be difficult to gauge where we stand on the Talent scale. How do you know if you may have completely stopped seeing yourself as a Talent?

Try some of these scenarios on for size:

1. You have officially become a regular in the office lottery pool (thinking in the back of your mind that retirement could start first thing Monday morning).

2. You have a deeper knowledge of sports or entertainment than you do of your industry. (Working for fifteen years filing legal documents at the office does not equate to *knowing* your industry. But, knowing a thing or two about a recently passed bill and how it could impact your boss, does. I can safely say this from personal experience, since one of my former jobs was to file legal documents.)

3. You have not read a book, listened to an audio book, or attended training on a topic that relates to your career in six months or more. (If your company doesn't support your development then they are telling you something. If you don't support your *own* development then you are telling *them* something.)

4. The announcement of outsourcing scares you. (After all, the mortgage payments are due when they are due. Outsourcing means that your company is publicly announcing that business is business, and they hope that you have been developing yourself as a Talent. We will discuss more on outsourcing later.)

5. You have little to no clue where the latest version of your resume is. (Raise your hand if the last time you reviewed your resume was the day that you were upset at your boss or company.)

Look, the intent here isn't to beat anyone down or to be mean, nasty, or cruel. We are trying to illustrate something that is holding so many talented people back, something which bothers me very deeply.

Reality Check

In many companies, for many projects, the senior management often brings in external consultants. Consultants, rumored to be the know-it-alls who are supposed to come and make the problem go away—bare a high reputation for "getting things done." And, for their reputation, they are able to charge a sizable premium. Consultants can do this because your senior management team knows that they don't have a lot of time to dilly-dally around, and they need to meet their business objective within a given timeframe or its game over (possibly for you *and* them). Outwardly, management brings in consultants for their expertise, but inwardly management brings in consultants for their own peace-of-mind.

So why are consultants so sought-after? It is because a consultant acts and behaves as if he or she is a talent (for hire). Their consulting firm acts as the talent pool that will provide a company with "thoroughbred talented warriors" who have "been there" and "done that" and can get the job done.

The general difference between a consultant and a corporate employee is that a consultant is working toward becoming an expert in an industry while the corporate employee is looking to become an expert in his or her own company. For example, a consultant in the insurance industry will have worked with many insurance organizations, not just one, and can bring expertise from throughout the entire industry. The corporate employee will have a general idea about the insurance industry, but he or she is primarily focused on developing a deeper knowledge and relationships within his or her own organization in addition to studying the inner workings of its various departments.

Why do I bring this up? Because you are about to find out why being an expert on your organization had better be a conscious decision on your part.

What I'm about to present to you is a typical scenario that happens in many organizations and will continue to happen in the future. There is a really good chance that you have probably experienced this already.

The scenario: It's Friday afternoon, and your supervisors call you to a departmental meeting. Your department's fearless leader, a VP in many cases, stands before you, yet you notice that not everyone in your department is part of this gathering. Your fearless leader has some new faces standing with him or her, and without waiting too long, he or she turns the floor over to them. Brace yourself because panic, anger, fear, frustration, disappointment, grief—all of these *wonderful* emotions are about to take over your mind. The reason? Within a few seconds you will find out that you and your co-workers are being laid off due to budget-cuts, right-sizing, down-sizing, outsourcing, or some other real business reason, and there is no way around it.

Allow me to share. One morning, I found myself in a departmental meeting at the new company. The situation was much the same as the one I just described. I was sitting with my colleagues as our fearless leader took the front of the room, opening the meeting with the usual pleasantries. He then started with, "As you all know, we recently had a merger, and I have great news for everyone ..." she continued, "Since we now have two departments doing the same thing, senior management has decided to eliminate one of the departments, and our department is the one that is going to stay." I could see that people around me where breathing once again, some were even smiling. Everyone left the room in high spirits. A few short months later, our fearless leader was shown the door, and the department was outsourced to another company.

History has many interesting way of repeating itself. By now, you already know the lay of the land; I'm at a new organization, and I'm taking part in a departmental meeting that has just started. My fearless leader is making my colleagues and myself aware of the reason that some of our co-workers are not present in this meeting is because they are attending another meeting where they are being told that their "roles have been eliminated".

These are only a couple of events in a series of many; however, this is just the reality of being a corporate professional. This is business, and the events that I've described are all true and very routine—so let's get used to them.

I also heard an executive at one of my organizations say that they are *intentionally* turning every business function into a commodity to lower costs for the company. I commend the executive for being honest and upfront about the company's intentions.

After that executive made this comment, I looked around the room to see the reactions of my peers regarding the statement. Frankly, most people were lost in their own world and did not pick-up on the content of the comments. They weren't aware that the executive had just said that our company was *actively looking to replace them* and their departments if it would save the company some money.

Sadly, most of those people had already pitched their permanent tents, and the only thing for them to do now was to come up with reasons why the company could never let them go. They had made the mistake of falling in love with an organization that had no reason to love them back.

A Talent, while human, does not exist nor work out of fear. It isn't that they are immune to the realities of the corporate world. A Talent is well aware and for this reason works from a completely different context and framework. There are some assumptions that a Talent works from. Once you've studied and become familiar with them, you will instantly realize what separates a Talent for every other corporate professional.

You will notice that we call each of these statements as assumptions and not rules. As a corporate professional, we know that our world is highly dynamic. So for us to publish any work as the ultimate guide containing final commandments that all corporate professional must follow to succeed, would be to do a great injustice and act with a lack of integrity with our fellow corporate professionals.

To ensure that our community can synergize from our collective experiences, CorporateBold.com is an ever present resource for all of us to build and share our experiences, progress, and new insights.

The assumptions that we are about to review are at the heart of what it takes to become **Corporate Bold**. We trust that they will lead you in being a thriving Corporate Professional!

Talent Assumptions

Did you know that Talents work under certain assumptions?

Today's Talents are working under the following assumptions:

Assumption #1:
You have to actively change your role.

Assumption #2:
It is your personal responsibility to develop yourself.

Assumption #3:
You can either be managed or you can be mismanaged.

Assumption #4:
You should seek out and work with other talents.

Assumption #5:
Ignore your performance evaluations.

Assumption #6:
Never ask for a merit increase or a promotion.

Assumption #7:
Openly teach what you do at work to anyone willing to learn.

Assumption #8:
Never fall in love with your company.

Keep these assumptions posted some place where you can read them again and again. You must constantly remind yourself of these assumptions. Each day, when you go to work, your actions should be directly in-line with these assumptions.

Assumption #1:
Actively Change Your Role

Let me ask you this; What is the difference between quitting your job and changing your job? Obviously, it's all the difference in the world. Quitting your job usually manifests from negative emotions against your job, your company, or someone at work like a boss or co-worker. Maybe you're just fed-up with having to do other people's work or your ideas are overlooked repeatedly. You know not to let negative emotion take over, but they can despite your best efforts to the contrary. After all, we are human.

There is an excellent book about this subject entitled *Crucial Conversations*, which illustrates how chemicals in our bodies are released once we develop a negative perception about a person or an event. I frequently recommend this book during casual conversations at the office as it is a part of my personal collection. According to book, in such events, we have essentially told ourselves a story, that may or may not be true, but it's too late now and we have to deal with the chemicals that our bodies release into our bloodstreams.

So what happens now? Well, you start to reminisce about the past and more anger builds-up—until—you say to yourself, "**I quit!**" Sometimes, the ranting continues for about another 30 seconds accompanied with some choice foul language to boot. Remember, this is just you talking to yourself.

Luckily, after thinking it over, most of us calm down and talk ourselves out of our decision to quit. We've all done this. We start to think back to why we "need" this job . . . We like the people we work with, the money is okay, the benefits are decent, and who wants to fill-out all the paperwork that goes along with changing jobs? Not you. "Oh for goodness sakes, now I have to start the whole job search process again—this is not the right time to quit," you say to yourself and push on one more day. After all this, how excited do you think you're going to be when you go back to work the next morning?

Which brings me to those who have simply had more than enough and actually quit. Sometimes the quitting process can get ugly, and sometimes people just want to get it over with. Ever hear of someone quitting by sending a text message to their boss then never picking up the phone when the boss calls back? Of course this happens.

Now, think of the last time you got a new job. You very likely gave your two weeks' notice to your, soon to be, former employer. You probably told all of your friends about how wonderful the new opportunity is going to be and how excited you are to start. You may have even "checked out" at your current job already. There is also good chance that you got a bump-up in pay or a la-de-da title or both (my personal favorite). You're now on your high-horse thinking, "Yup, in one week, things are going to be pretty darn good. I will really commit to this new company and do my best. Heck, I should try to go to the bookstore and pick up a book on how-to-do-so-and-so or how-to-be-a-better-so-and-so." You might even go online and start reading things like "10 Big Mistakes People Make When They Do-So-And-So." Those articles are undoubtedly instant confidence boosters, no?

Now the first day or so of your new job can be a bit nerve-wracking. Your boss walks you around the office, and introduces you to lots of new people who have no preconceived notions about you. You get introduced in meetings and your boss adds, "He'll be working on the so-and-so project." In response, you hear, "The so-and-so project? Well how exciting! Welcome aboard, it's a challenging project but I'm sure you're very talented." If you've ever worked for a brand name organization in the past, your boss will showcase you around the block and do some name dropping like, "Yeah, she comes to us from Google and she was with NASA before that!"

For many people, the first few weeks at a new job are almost magical until you reach the end of the first month. I've found that the end of the first month really seems to be the threshold before things change. The reason for this is because you've now really started to understand why you're there and working on that particular project. On the way home one day, you think to yourself, "Was it really *that bad* at my last job?" You know in your heart that there is no going back at this point, and it's not that you don't like your new job—but you understand that for the next few months, you're going to have to do some heavy lifting to get your arms around your new position. But life must go on.

Going back to the difference between quitting your job and changing your job. When you change your job, you have a plan to leave your current position for another position—it's not an accident. This is a key distinction that you must be 100 percent clear about when it comes to quitting or changing your job. The former tends to be done out of negative emotions while the latter fosters a positive energy once completed.

Personally, I would never advise you to quit your job because I don't know you or your life situation well enough to offer such a blanket piece of advice. It would be unethical to do so. What I am advising you to do is to start thinking about changing your current role and to anticipate your future path.

It disgusts me when I see Job Boards marketing big ads suggesting that people should quit their jobs for whatever reason because the Job Board can help them find their ideal job, a utopia or some such. Those ads are nothing short of poor self-serving advice. No ethical organization should ever suggest something like this, just to grow their business. And yet, they do, and they will continue to do so because when a person is frustrated, quitting seems like the quick fix-it solution.

Why Change Your Role?

One of my favorite board games of all time is Monopoly (all rights reserved by Hasbro). Do you know how many times the game of Monopoly has changed its rules over the last fifty years? The exact number of times is Zero! The point here is that a lot of us are playing with the fifty-year-old Monopoly rules in the corporate environment when we all know that the game board in the real corporate environment changes almost daily!

It is not surprisingly to find out why many have simply given up. They have thrown their hands up into the air and said, "Okay, I don't know the rules anymore so I quit."

Look, the jobs of tomorrow have not even been conceived of yet. The Internet, for example, has completely changed the way we live. For thousands of people, their position in the corporate world has been a direct result of the Internet. Twenty-five years ago, for the average Joe, some of our jobs would have seemed like something out of a science fiction movie.

And yet, despite all of our recent advances, many people are still playing with the rules that were designed to work well in the 1950s—when every parent wanted their son and daughter to be a doctor or a lawyer. Needless to say, the rules have changed, and we all need to reexamine our assumptions about the corporate world. Assumption #1, which states that "You have to actively change your role" is the most important assumption, **point blank.**

A former boss of mine, who used to work for a major company, once told me that his former organization had a position for a "Circling Clerk". The "Circling Clerk" had to look at two documents that were exactly alike and, should one of the two documents not match, the clerk was to take a red pen and circle the incorrect document, hence the job title: "Circling Clerk".

It's funny, now, to think that this was a real job and that someone performed this function every day. What do you think this clerk was qualified to do after the organization got a computer system to check the documents for errors? Look, I understand that we all need a paycheck, but every Talent knows that they have to actively change their role *long before* that role is no longer needed in order to keep them relevant to any organization.

If luck is the meeting of preparation and opportunity then you need to work on the preparation part proactively. If there is one assumption you can't afford not to heed, it is this assumption.

When to Change Your Role

The starting point for you is to ask yourself: "How long have I been in my current position?"

How long have you been in your current position?	
Your Answer	Corporate Bold Answer
_____	2-3 years

Those who apply the principles of **Corporate Bold** and consider themselves as a Talent will answer: two years, or three years at the most. It is recommend that you should not say in a position for longer than two years (three at the most) unless, of course, you have a valid reason to stay put—and we will go over these reasons soon. "Staying in a position" means: doing the same things today that you did two years ago and nothing beyond those tasks.

When to Stay Put

So let's talk about when it is ideal to stay in your current position. For many of us, there will likely be times when we will want to pitch a tent in a cubicle or an office. It starts out as a short-term deal, and soon enough you're tempted to pour in a foundation and mix up a batch of mortar to turn your short-term tent into a permanent fort.

There can be valid reasons when pitching a short-term tent. This could be because you're experiencing a life-changing event like going back to school, having children, working on a personal project that needs your focus, etc. All of these reasons have one thing in common—they are all short-term oriented.

The right time to pitch your permanent tent would be if you have a considerable financial stake in an organization. It's important to make this distinction. Your permanent tent must only be pitched in an organization due to your stake in that company and not due to your tenure or title.

When one has a considerable financial stake in an organization they have the option to pitch a permanent tent because their financial consideration separates a particular organization apart from all others.

This, however, does not mean that you should remain in the same position at your permanent company. It is not too uncommon to find that certain individuals pitched a permanent tent in an organization due to a considerable financial consideration; however, they simply stop there and stop treating themselves as a Talent. Soon they find that their organization will seek out ways to downgrade their position or have them removed permanently.

If you want to be demoted at age fifty then that's a personal choice. Your management doesn't want to have to do this, but they will, should you stop treating yourself as a Talent and force them to.

Team Meeting

This assumption is so powerful and true that it has been experienced by many a corporate professional—perhaps even you. I'd like to introduce you to some true Talents. They have personally experienced the value of "actively changing one's role". Not only will they share their personal experiences and insights with you, they will share real, actionable, steps that have worked for them, which you can apply too.

Allow me introduce you to . . .

Contribution by **Alex Merchan**
Marketing Director
Hard Rock International

How do you expect to change your existing role while simultaneously positioning yourself to achieve some of your long-term professional goals? Betting your future away on luck, a job posting, or an existing supervisor to give you that "big break" is not the solution. It's your own responsibility to watch out for your best interests and that includes thinking about where you see yourself down the road. Whether you are just starting your professional career or you are wanting to make a change to a new one, you'll need to know what you want and you'll need to create a specifically defined path for how to get there.

You don't have to have a detailed plan for the next twenty years of your career, but it wouldn't hurt to envision yourself two, five, or even ten years down the road with an idea of what you aspire to accomplish. It's much more likely you'll get somewhere if you have an idea of where you want to go. Start by determining what it is that you want (or don't want) for your next role.

> While in my freshman year of college, I knew that I wanted something "different" for my career than the job postings I had seen listed for the graduating class and something more than what my guidance counselors suggested. I had a passion for business and thoroughly enjoyed the entertainment industry. I didn't want to start a career in an industry that I wasn't going to be passionate about. So how would I pursue my ideal career?
>
> There wasn't a list of my dream jobs out there and I hadn't met anyone who I aspired to be like, but I knew I wanted to work in this industry and

I decided to take an active approach to making it happen.

Once you've determined what your big-picture goals are, it's time to review those goals (or desired position) and do your best to understand what is needed to be qualified for that role. Think about the skills and knowledge needed to get you to that next level. Do you have the experience and skill set necessary? How far are you from seriously qualifying for that spot? If you aspire to reach that position, seriously analyze your skill-set and how you stand-up to achieving that goal. Does your degree and education demonstrate an affinity for the requirements of that position? Are there other skills or requirements necessary for that position—like a specific degree, certification, or language?

I focused on ways to help me develop skills and knowledge that would help me obtain my ideal entertainment industry position. Subscribing to trade publications, reviewing trends, and attending industry seminars helped me start to gain a better understanding of the industry. This requires a lot of personal time and effort. Pursuing courses related to pertinent subject matter and joined interests groups to meet other people with similar interests and great experiences are other methods to better understand a future role. These types of efforts should lead to obtaining key insights and experiences for future success in your field.

In an increasingly competitive environment, employees are finding ways to better prepare themselves for a specific career and are improving the talent pool for existing employers. You can try to fight it or you can ignore it altogether but, in reality, things will continue to get more competitive around you whether you like it or not. You need to differentiate yourself from the rest of the field by obtaining the necessary tools and experience. As you pursue your future career path, you have to be prepared for unexpected challenges. Not all opportunities will "fit" the plan you've developed. This doesn't mean that you need to overlook that opportunity and try for another one. Although you may have certain ideas and goals in mind, be sure to have some flexibility. The first opportunity that comes your way may not be ideal, but it could put you in a better position to reach future goals.

> That same summer, I was fortunate enough to land an unpaid internship for a global company in the music and entertainment industry. That job would allow me to work in an area of interest that I enjoyed. The challenge was that it didn't pay and, in fact, would be an expense for me to commute and spend the better part of twelve weeks there. I was only one of two interns in this position and I was sure that if I didn't make the best of this job, they would find someone else who would. Although it was an ideal learning opportunity, it did come with its own set of challenges. In order to sustain myself, I managed to keep a paid summer job; I worked twenty-five hours a week to cover my expenses and I vowed to focus any free time on developing my career through the internship. This meant that I spent the rest of my summer working for free, but I gained vast amounts of knowledge and firsthand experience. Juggling my time, responsibilities, and priorities was an on-going challenge, but I had to create my own future, and I knew that this would be an investment toward achieving my goals.

Developing the track toward a future role will most likely require a lot of extra hours and effort after a full day at the office, dealing with your personal/family life, and managing just about everything else that occupies your already-busy schedule. In order to truly understand what you want and to gain any type of competitive advantage, you'll need to put in that extra work. If it was easy to pursue an ideal role then everyone would be able to do it.

Make the most of any opportunity and be sure to maintain an open mindset. When looking to develop new skills or learn about a new industry, you may have to "start from the bottom" and, no matter how frustrating this might be, the right attitude and approach can make all the difference.

> While in this summer position, I applied my strengths and enthusiasm, I humbly absorbed what I could from those around me, and I was exposed to and learned more than I would ever have obtained in four years of classroom lectures. I was exposed to real world business situations and I was considered a part of a driven and successful international sales team. Most importantly, I had direct exposure to executives who I learned from and, ultimately, would become colleagues with. My dedication to this internship (where I spent more time and energy than I did for my paid job) solidified my efforts and allowed me to continue setting goals for myself. My hard work and dedication during this one summer lead to many doors opening for me—multiple job opportunities, recommendations, and even a paid job within the industry the following semester. Ultimately, this one experience set me on my way for what's been well over a decade in the industry.

So maybe your current career scenario is not an ideal one and the path towards the role you seek is difficult. That shouldn't be an excuse to keep you from reaching your goals. If you are truly determined to achieve that ideal role, you'll find a way to make the time and put forth the effort in a more productive way toward that future role. Be sure to make the most of it. Whatever your sacrifice, know that it is an investment toward your future.

Contribution by **Andreas Wutz**
Managing Director
brain4charity

Within my career, I've have to cope with several company mergers. Economic environments change. Because of this, I had the chance to try out at least three different strategies for not only surviving but also for pushing my career forward.

Let me describe the strategies I tried:

(1) Submariner: The first company I worked for faced a change of control. As an inexperienced young professional, I tried what I call the "submariner strategy". This means: doing the opposite of what assumption 1 states, meaning, I dove deep in the business water and hoped that nothing changed on the surface. I only survived due to luck and because some parts of my workload was highly specialized. In retrospect, I do not recommend this passive strategy at all.

(2) Actively managing a given change: I worked for another company as the head of sales strategy management. One day, the whole strategic positioning of the company changed due to a new managing director. All sales-driven jobs were not needed anymore and therefore my own department was closed. My team had the choice to wait until somebody told us what would happen to each of us individually or we could move actively toward the new alignment ourselves. We preferred the "actively managing a given change" strategy. During internal-team-workshops, we estimated the potential consequences of the new strategic position for each of us. Then, for each imaginable scenario, we developed alternative reactions. One measurement we used was that we persisted to get an appointment with the new managing director and we present our job skills and our own identified options to be part of the decision-making process in the newly positioned company. The new managing director was impressed by our proactive way of managing the change and he got the chance to know us and our skills. Due to this, most of us were able to be placed in a new position after the company shifted.

(3) Anticipate change: An additional and absolutely self-initiated strategy is to monitor the economic environment (right from global macroeconomics to internal company microcosms) and anticipate the potential effects on your own job. I followed this strategy during the "New Economy" era when IT Jobs were glorified. I reflected on how to best benefit from this environment being employed as a business project manager. My job had been to act, on the business side, as an intermediary between business and IT. I read a lot of books to deepen my knowledge of IT so that I would know how to serve as a project manager on the IT side. This action resulted in a new job as the IT project manager at a new company. This strategy to "anticipate change" requires carefully monitoring your environment and actively changing your role to fit new opportunities.

My conclusion: Actively changing your role is the most promising way to survive and, more importantly, to get you moving forward in your career.

*   *   *

Contribution by **Bengt Campbell**
Vice President
Citigroup

While there are certainly many potential strategies and paths to follow toward success in the corporate world, I believe that it is essential to actively change your role throughout your career. No career path is set in stone and, at times, it may be impacted by forces outside of your own control. However, you must remember that you are the steward of your own future and, as such, you must take the driver's seat and proactively make decisions that will keep you on the road to success!

In today's corporate world it is becoming increasingly uncommon to stay with one company for your entire professional career and many professionals choose to move between companies every few years. I believe that any such move, generally, should be well thought out, planned in advance, and only undertaken after considering if there are equally, or more, attractive opportunities to change roles within the company first.

Perhaps one of the biggest advantages to working for a mid-to-large-sized company is having the ability to pursue and excel in multiple roles internally, before having to leave for another company in pursuit of new challenges and career growth. In large global firms, you will frequently find senior managers who have risen through the ranks and achieved a successful career within the company by completing a multitude of assignments, in various roles, corporate divisions, and perhaps even multiple countries. Beyond the standard progression of taking-on additional responsibilities related to your current role and, with time, hopefully advancing up the corporate ladder; there is some real opportunity to be found by periodically seeking out a new role within the company that aligns you with the product, service, strategy, function, or country/region that is at the core of your company's current focus and success.

For a corporation to thrive in good times, or even survive in tough times, it must constantly adapt to changing market, economic, and competitive conditions. Similarly, for you as an employee to advance in good times or survive potential layoffs during tough times, you must take control of your career and actively change your role to adapt to changing company conditions. I do not doubt that being very good at what you do is a key component of your success and unlocking opportunities for advancement but you must never forget that this only holds true for as long as what you do remains important to your company.

For example, if you are in a front-office revenue generating role, you want to position yourself to deliver the maximum contribution to your company's revenues. If you are in a non-revenue generating middle or back-office role, you want to align yourself with the company's profitable business, product, or strategic priorities. No matter what your role, you should be contributing to the company's bottom line by over-delivering on expense reduction and optimization initiatives.

You want to ensure that you are, and will remain, an asset not only to your company but also to your career. Leverage the performance and career management tools that are available to you including: goal setting, personal development planning, internal and external training, certifications, mentor relationships, and so on. Enhance your abilities by training in transferable skills such as project management, communication, leadership, and management. Assess your own strengths and weaknesses periodically while trying to focus on filling the gaps that will enable you to advance in your career.

Before you accept a new role, you should think about where you see yourself next and how your current role will help you get where you want to go. Once you start the new role, your focus should be on doing your job well and the time you invest in that role should allow you to become great at what you do. You should continue to take-on more responsibilities and grow your skills along with your role. However, if you find that you are no longer being challenged, or if the role is no longer aligned with your company's or your own objectives, it's likely time to move on to the next challenge.

Consider going outside of your comfort zone and seek out a "stretch assignment." Without setting yourself up for failure, you do want to really challenge yourself to demonstrate that you are capable and willing to take on a role that is not only unexpected but also puts you on the fast-track toward advancement. You want to avoid becoming "pigeon-holed," where your experience and skill-set is perceived to be too narrow, as this will limit the opportunities available to you in the future.

With experience in diverse roles comes big picture knowledge that will make you more well-rounded. It's important to understand your company and its business model—the more areas you have worked in, the easier it will be for you to identify how you can best fit-in and contribute. The same concept holds true for having experience with diverse companies, industries, regions, countries, and cultures. As you plan and execute your career, you should certainly consider any opportunity that helps you grow into a well-rounded professional or manager.

Should you just be starting your career, or perhaps ready to follow a new career path, be aware that many companies offer Leadership/Management Development programs. These programs are usually geared towards recent college graduates, or internal individuals with high potential, who are identified as potential future leaders for the company. The company is investing in the program participants by providing them with cross-functional, cross-business, and sometimes international work experience. By rotating the program participants between these multiple assignments, the company is grooming them and helping them develop the very characteristics I've stressed the importance of above.

For the program participant, these Leadership/Management Development programs offer an opportunity to sample different parts of the company while quickly gaining the experience and exposure needed to quickly advance into management. Upon a successful completion of the program, the corporate doors will open and final placement will often land you in a management role much sooner than had you worked your way up to it in a more traditional way. Should a program like this not be available, you can still aim to achieve the same result by actively changing your role, in the same manner, over time.

When you look back at your career, or project forward on your future career plans, you want to see a steady progression of roles, which demonstrate that you have used the time spent in each role to grow and prepare for the next role. You must learn to strike a balance between spending too long or too short a period of time in the same role. You must also adapt to change and plan your moves within, or between, companies in such a way as to position yourself for success. You should never become too comfortable in a role—essentially remaining on cruise control while waiting for someone else to recognize your value and capacity for advancement. It is up to you, and you alone, to develop the skills and pursue the roles that will make you successful.

I have personally followed these principles throughout my career. I have always had the long-term goal of achieving corporate and financial success and I have not been afraid to adjust the plan, over time, of how to get there. As an undergraduate college student, I proactively changed my major to Information Technology to better position myself for employment in the IT industry, which I felt I could achieve the most success. Upon graduating, I accepted an IT position in the higher education industry as it allowed me to gain valuable IT work experience while I was also being sponsored for a graduate degree in Management of Technology. After I completed my graduate work, I was recruited to join a top-twenty Fortune 500 company in the financial services industry.

I joined the company through a Technology Management Development Program and, after only two years and the cross-functional assignments, I was promoted directly to Vice President. When it was time for me to decide on a post-program final placement, I elected to go with an IT role that was at the core of the company's data center optimization and expense reduction strategy. Within a year, I was managing a team and contributing directly to board-of-director-level commitments. After about eighteen month's time, I felt that, while I had done very well in that role, the global economy and company's priorities had shifted and it was time for me to move on.

I wanted to take the next step in my career but I chose to remain with the same company, which allowed me to leverage the corporate experience and transferable skills I had gained while working in multiple areas within the firm. I took on a stretch assignment, leaving the IT field behind (at least for a time), and moved on to manage a corporate operations team focused on business plans and analysis. I was, again, well positioned with my team providing the workforce and expense related decision management information required for the firm's major global headcount and organizational change initiatives.

To date, I attribute much of my corporate success to proactively changing my role and I encourage you to do the same!

*　　*　　*

Contribution by **E.J. Ackerman**
Strategic Technology Executive
Information Services Industry

At a small division of a fortune 500 financial services company, I was hired to design and implement some compliance exception reports to identify potential firm / regulatory violations. This project entailed identifying the firm's regulatory risks, evaluating the data necessary to develop reports to mitigate these risks, and documenting procedures to work the reports on a daily basis. Although this was an important project, I was not selected to lead a more strategic and high profile project, the IT Strategy Project, to define the company's Technological Vision.

The compliance reporting project proceeded as expected and lasted four months. At the conclusion, the new reports were designed, developed, and implemented without issue. The compliance department utilized the reports and management was impressed with our quick delivery of the final reports. Unfortunately, the success of this project was overshadowed by the less than stellar results of the IT Strategy project. Although the management team approved the IT Strategy project deliverables, none of them were actionable and the project ended without an implementation of the recommended solutions. As there were no new projects, my role converted into a maintenance and support role. I was slowly stagnating into a dead-end corporate role.

As the IT Strategy project deliverables stagnated for almost a year, the company hired a new Chief Information Officer (CIO) to redefine the company's technological vision and implement the much-needed new systems. Rumors swirled around the company that a new executive would be starting in a few months and no new projects would be initiated until he started and approved each one. The mood at the office was nervous, as no one knew what to expect.

The new CIO spent most of his first two weeks in meetings, catching up on the status of different projects. About a week after he started, he and I shared an elevator ride. I was nervous, as we had not been formally introduced, but he knew the results of my compliance reporting project and asked me about my thoughts on the technological organization and overall technological vision. After a slight hesitation, I told him why the IT Strategy project failed and listed the steps that needed to be taken to resolve the fundamental issues of the IT Organization. We spoke for less than ten minutes about the current issues and the vision for the future. In hindsight, this was a very risky move as he could have perceived me as a rouge member of the team who was speaking out against the current leadership. There was a fifty percent chance that I would be demoted and permanently assigned to production support tasks.

Fortunately, the new CIO appreciated my candid response and immediately scheduled a two-hour meeting to review my thoughts on every aspect of the technology team, application architecture, current processes, and my three-to-five year vision for the project. He and I worked on a presentation that outlined the issues, organizational changes needed before any technological changes could be initiated, the future application architecture, and a timeline for replacing all of the back-office systems. After several iterations, the recommendations in the presentation were adopted by the various members of the management team and this lead to several changes:

The priority of several projects was modified and resources were shifted so that the most important projects could be completed on-time.

There were several organizational changes made to support the new procedures and processes.

They selected me to lead the most strategic project of the year because of my contributions.

I spent the next two months refining the technological vision and evaluating different systems that could support the back-office operations. This was the role that I loved and I was once again excited to come to the office everyday.

Although my various roles in this process created some animosity from others in the organization, I was driven by the need to change my role in the company. I wanted to participate in the strategic projects that would be the foundation for the organization's application architecture. Stagnating in a maintenance and support role was simply not my vision for where I wanted to be in my career. Even though it was risky to approach the CIO directly, I know it was the right decision.

*   *   *

Contribution by **Heather Vozella**
Marketing Manager
Independent Management Consultant

In my previous role with a Fortune 500 retail company, I continually explored new ideas and ways to improve processes. Managers who I worked for began to see this and repeatedly created positions for me based on the solutions that I was finding and how to improve processes within the company. I always felt that my job as a Marketing Manager was about more than how to bring in revenue for the company. It was also about finding ways to cut costs and improve production in order to increase profits.

It is most important for managers and employees alike to actively take part in evolving or changing their roles to tailor to the needs of the organization. It is especially important, in today's job market, that employees and managers seek out ways to improve work within the organization. Employees should search for ways to focus on their jobs, take ownership of their work, and feel empowered to change their role into one that is more meaningful for the company. After all, industries are constantly changing and employees should be too. Taking ownership and accountability for changing your role can create a new level of business acumen within your organization and show your employer that you are interested in staying with the company and that you are committed to helping them succeed.

My experience working with big companies has taught me that if an employee is not consistently changing his or her role and looking for ways to better himself or herself, he or she may get left behind and have to fight to hang onto his job. Not to mention, these types of employees will find it harder to compete in today's job market without the most up-to-date skills. One example is a manager I knew named Chris. Chris was very good at his job and he continually worked overtime, completed his projects under budget, and had a great working relationship with all of his clients. He was always happy to come to work and if co-workers complained, he always found the silver lining in their stormy clouds.

One day, we all came into work and learned that the company was cutting our department in half. The executive management team told us that we would need to take on additional responsibilities that were not currently in our job descriptions. They also indicated that some of our additional responsibilities may mean that we would need to seek supplemental education or training in order to learn and execute these new responsibilities. For the first time, Chris was not happy.

That afternoon, Chris turned into a different person. He was no longer happy with his work but he continued to do his job that day. However, all of the other employees could see that he was not his same, jovial, self. At the end of the day, I walked into Chris' office to see what the trouble was that caused his change in persona. Chris was very upset stating that he liked his job the way it was: all of his projects in place, his schedules in line, his daily routine outlined, and his happy clients taken care of. He felt that taking on new responsibilities would disrupt all of that and cause his client relationships to suffer, his projects to lag behind, and worst of all, he claimed that he was "too old to go back to school to receive training." I was shocked. Not only was Chris only forty-one years old but I also could not believe that school would be his biggest hurdle because, throughout his career, Chris had leaped over many other tougher, larger, hurdles.

I explained to Chris that school was not such a big deal and not only was he young but he was also in the midst of his career! He should be learning new areas of our industry, new techniques, and new process improvements. School and additional training would give him more techniques and tools to work with, more knowledge, and more information about how to do things better and faster. Nevertheless, Chris was not convinced. He went on and on about how he was "too old" and that our company was "ridiculous" to think that employees would go back to school to receive training in new and different areas of our business.

Months went by and Chris became miserable to work with. Employees and management alike were complaining about his work ethic, his projects lagged behind, and his relationships with his clients suffered tremendously. He refused to learn any of the new techniques that management asked of him, refused to attend school or seminars to receive any additional training, and worse yet, he refused to accept any of the new responsibilities that management requested of him.

After one full year of his co-workers and management trying to convince him to get beyond his way of thinking, Chris was fired. On one hand, employees were relieved to see him go because he had become so miserable to work with. But, on the other hand, they were sad because the once terrific, happy-go-lucky manager, that had become a role model for so many other employees, had crashed under the pressure of having to change with the organization and learn more. Now, not only was Chris without a job, his skills and training lacked the requirements needed to obtain another job in the highly competitive job market. Who knows, if Chris would have been willing to go back to school, get additional training, and acquire the tools needed to improve his skills, he might have stayed with the company.

Chris approached the situation the wrong way. Instead of using the opportunity to learn more and become a role model for other employees who might be afraid to change, he collapsed under the pressure of having to change himself. Instead of showing other employees that he was afraid to change, he could have provided those employees with his experience and showed them that changing their roles is positive—both for the company and for themselves. He could have taught those employees why it is important to learn, to evolve, and to change. Instead, he became negative, isolated, and depressed. Chris could have showed others that it is their responsibility, as employees, to learn more about our industry and our competitors in order to not only improve the work that we do but also to open up their careers to change. This would help them grow as people and it would help them become more competitive in a tough job market. Who knows, by Chris changing to adapt to new roles, he could have even started to change the management department within our company to help other employees.

Actively changing your role and adapting to change shows employers that you understand that change will happen, needs to happen, and should happen. It is important for employees to avoid seeing themselves as victims of change (like Chris did). Rather, their willingness to evolve is an important part of change in order to help their company grow and become more competitive. Employees need to see that training is an integral part of their careers and employers need to understand that they need to provide this training as evidence that they do care about the employees and their future with the company.

At first, changing your role at work might seem a bit challenging. I have actually done it three times in my career and each time, I had to learn new skills by either going back to school or receiving additional training through my employer. In some cases, I had to move into a lesser role in order to move forward more quickly over the long term. All the while, I reminded myself why I was doing any of it: acquiring more skills makes one better prepared, more competitive, and more preferable to employers. It worked and now I am knowledgeable about many areas of marketing versus only being knowledgeable of one.

Throughout my years working in management, I have encouraged my employees to keep an open mind about their career paths, to be open to continuously learning, and to look for new areas of opportunity for their roles to change. I do the same for them; I watch what skills are needed, where areas of improvement are appropriate, and I note the talents that each individual employee brings to the table. I also look for new ways to challenge them and create roles that are suited for them. But, I prefer that they find new areas of opportunity, in which they are curious about, so that they can get excited about learning those new areas. I explain to them that not only will their new skills and additional responsibilities look impressive on their resume but it will also send employers the message that they are open to change. It will help them stand out from the crowd and become a more knowledgeable and well-rounded employee and individual.

*   *   *

Contribution by **Holly J. Berk, PMP**
Strategic Management and Service Quality Assurance
Universal Weather and Aviation

My first, unofficial, mentor was my Aunt Judy. She was well-educated, traveled abroad frequently, and continually evolved in spirit and career. She told me on many occasions that the key to being successful was recognizing that the "only constant in life was change." This statement has become one of my favorite mantras for managing my career.

A career is just a job if it doesn't lead to your next opportunity. Opportunities can not be realized if they go unrecognized or you're not prepared for your next role. You cannot simply assume responsibility for a new role and be successful in it if enhanced skills are not obtained along the way. You must take on tasks that, likely, fall outside of your current position in order to ensure new skills and tools are obtained and mastered.

Therefore, if you want to take control of your career and position yourself for grander, more rewarding challenges, you must acquire new skills by constantly changing your role within your organization or move on to another company, or industry, in order to acquire what is needed for your long-term success.

I joined the workforce in the early 1980's and I rejoined it in the early 1990's, after earning my Bachelors degree; So, I lived and worked through a few economic downturns. These negative experiences have resulted in my creation of, and adherence to, a career management philosophy that enables me to retain employment during even the worst of economic conditions. The foundation for success is to create a reputation for yourself as being a "doer" and to then leverage that expertise into obtaining new skills within an organization.

Opportunities for new challenges are never offered to the "clock-puncher," the "dreamer," or the "one-trick pony." They are offered to the "doer;" the person who gets the task done while maintaining a great attitude and a sincere willingness to assume more responsibility even when operating in unfamiliar territory. It is my contention that any skill of substance can be molded into another useful skill, when necessary. Therefore, when functioning in a new role, one can leverage existing skills by simply modifying them to adhere to the new situation or task.

Some skills are easily leveraged and those are the skills to keep sharp through repetitive application. Skills in this category are your primary skills that demonstrate your competency. Skills such as good facilitation or communication. These skills are enablers for career growth as the pay-off for honing these capabilities will be new projects and position advancement.

However, planning for your desired future position is just as important as leveraging your current skills because you need to ensure that the opportunities you take advantage of today will align with your ultimate goal—being positioned for, and eventually offered, your next desired role within an organization.

Planning for role changes throughout a career takes effort and consideration of what's really important to you. There will be times in your career that you wish to experience personal stability and moving into another role is not congruent with your core need for stability. However, the ramifications of being stagnant can be detrimental to your long-term success and you must consider other options for building new skills while maintaining stability.

One way to accomplish this is to assume a role you are extremely comfortable performing at another company or in a different industry. This may look like a lateral position change or will likely be a demotion in title. However, changes of this nature can also result in immediate visibility and lead to long-term opportunities within the new organization. The key is to out-perform your peers and to recognize that the visibility of your contributions will far exceed the importance of the temporary state of being in a role you are over-qualified to perform at that point in time. The most appropriate use of this method is moving from one industry to another. The challenge will not be in executing the tasks of your new role, it will be learning the new products, services, jargon, acronyms, etc associated with that new industry. Your learning curve will become apparent to management and staff within a short period of time because you will leverage your existing talents to accomplish tasks with confidence and speed.

Now you can prepare for your next internal career move while maintaining a desired level of stability because you can set the pace of your contributions. That is not to say you should hold back when performing any task, it simply means you should maintain a steady pace or you will be quickly pushed into a new role because management will see you are capable of do so.

If personal stability is not a concern for you, you should ease into your new position by adding value in areas that you are extremely comfortable in and confident about. Beyond that, your primary tasks should include: listening, observing, and volunteering. These three skills are often under-utilized and under-estimated by many in the workforce; this is not because we don't believe they are important but because we forget to consciously and consistently apply them to our careers. I believe that if you actively listen, stay aware of what's happening around you, and you are willing to assume responsibility without being asked, you will quickly be identified as a "doer." Once this tag has been placed on you, opportunities will manifest themselves and it will then be your challenge to recognize them.

If you know your end goal—your desired role within an organization—you can position yourself through thoughtful execution with each opportunity that you accept or decline. The key is being true to yourself by knowing what you want for your career and by knowing when you want to obtain it.

*   *   *

Contribution by **James Parnitzke**
Practice Leader Core Technologies
PricewaterhouseCoopers (PwC)

Today's world is getting smaller, flatter, and smarter. The business sector has embraced the notion of "flattened" management structures, which has created a real need for multi-faceted generalists with the agility to respond faster, and more effectively, to the changes in the world around us. Those who will thrive in the new business landscape will need a wider range of experiences and skills. As a talent, you must energize yourself with new skills by constantly changing your role and learning to embrace change.

Many of the old rules about following a certain career path, specialization, and focus (there are exceptions) may not be valid anymore. Old adages may, in fact, prevent you from reaching your true earning potential or finding the kind of rich, rewarding experience. This type of experience can only be earned by embracing a wide variety of roles, which will add meaning and enjoyment to your professional life. If, as they say, "perception is reality," then if you stay too long in one role or position you will (as we used to joke) become part of the fixtures. Or worse yet, you could be perceived as someone who has moved from the income statement to the "fixed asset" section of the balance sheet—this is not good.

In order to avoid this situation, you need to ask yourself these bigger questions on a regular basis:

How can I escape this paradox and grow my personal brand across traditional organizational boundaries?

How can I enrich my personal and professional life and make it more rewarding?

How can I become a sought-after resource—rather than chasing opportunity—a person who my peers and colleagues seek-out for advice— a trusted partner and advisor?

What roles should I assume in order to fulfill my personal objectives?

The answers have, most likely, always been right in front of you. The hard part is actually doing the very things many of us find uncomfortable or uneasy. Learning and growth, unfortunately, mean acquiring new skills, relationships, and competencies so that our reach always seems to exceed our grasp—this is change and it makes most of us very uncomfortable. Conquering this fear by actively seeking new roles will result in a far deeper understanding of others through continuous learning.

Most of us learned in business school to use the balanced scorecard as a planning and management tool in order to align business activities with the strategy of the organization. This practice will improve internal and external communications while simultaneously monitoring performance against these goals (source: Robert Kaplan and David Norton of the Harvard Business School).

We have all, probably actively, participated in performance evaluations using the same principals expressed in individual terms. You may have seen this same idea expressed as Management by Objective or Exception, for example. Yet, how much time and thought have you actually invested in this as a personal guide or framework for your own career? Maybe if you begin to think about it in these terms and personalize the concept, it would provide enough motivation for you to take the right type of actions in your career. These actions will help you actively manage the uncomfortable changes that a truly balanced career demands.

So, take the four following perspectives and think about them the next time you become uneasy about changing and what the real impact will be on your future.

Learning and Growth

Continuous improvement and learning requires an intimate involvement with several aspects of your business. It also requires the assumption of different roles to optimize your personal development. For example, if you are a technologist and you really want to grow and learn, get actively involved with the Marketing function to gain a deeper understanding of the real needs for translating the raw data, you have provided, into usable information products. Use those slow office days (even after hours) to learn about operational roles outside of your niche and then use this information to leverage a move into this new discipline when the opportunity arises. Engage the local community or use teaching opportunities to learn how to successfully convey complex subject matter to lay-persons in order to improve your communications skills. This is difficult, I know, but it is also an invaluable way to learn.

Internal (Business) Processes

How well do understand the processes that create and deliver real value to the customer? Do you really know where to focus the activities and key processes required for you (and others in your organization) to excel at providing this value? Get out of your office (and your position if you can) so that you can discover for yourself what operations management really is all about. Find out how the customer service representatives are handling the customers in the call center. Find out how research and development is driving innovation into new products and services. This is a real opportunity to better understand the role of others in your organization and it just might make you think twice before introducing some "bonehead" idea without having a deep knowledge of how things really work first.

Customer Perspective

This perspective defines the value applied to satisfying customers. Understanding how sales and business development create value should include active participation with real-live customers in a role that will improve operational excellence, deepen customer intimacy, or promote product leadership. If you are in an internal function (like accounting or marketing), it really is an eye-opening experience to get out in the field by taking on a business development role. If you are able to do so, you will see how hard it really is to achieve successful outcomes in a consistent and repeatable manner. I think everyone should have some life experience in selling tangible and intangible products to customers because selling really is where everything in business begins. Take the time (as painful as it may be) to take on a role like this and learn as much as you can. The rewards will be significant and they will represent a solid set of skills that you will use throughout your entire career.

Financial Perspective

Examine the personal implementation and execution of your strategy as a contributor to the bottom-line relationship with your organization. This relationship represents the tangible outcomes (results) of your efforts typically represented (source: Kaplan and Norton) as rapid growth, sustainability, and harvest cycles. So you must carefully judge where you are within this cycle and you must forecast your next role in order to leverage your talent into optimizing your personal financial growth.

During periods of rapid growth you may have to expend precious political capital in the fight for scarce resources and funding. Yet, by assuming a more sustainable role, your position will become more defensive with very different priorities and financial implications than that of rapid growth periods. Whereas "harvesting" means to use the relationships that you have carefully cultivated during your career in order to move on to a new endeavor. Finally, in your new role, the cycle repeats itself.

Above all, always use the concepts found in the balanced scorecard to forecast your next role. Do not be afraid to actively seek out and change roles in order to fulfill or balance your career and meet your personal objectives. Use this concept as a guide or map to achieve a balanced approach to your life's work. In the end, the rewards you will reap, for carefully seeking out and doing the very things you're not comfortable with, will enrich your professional and personal life. The experiences you will gain across a wide variety of roles will prepare you so that when you're called-on to make a difference, you will be ready.

*　　*　　*

Contribution by **Jared Flynn**
Director, Workforce Planning and Analytics
Safeco Insurance

While working for a Fortune 200 financial services organization, I had the opportunity to take a short-term, high potential, rotational assignment. At the conclusion of the assignment, I had the option to go back to my previous niche or join a new function that was emerging out of this high-profile assignment. I opted to go back to the comfort and security of my previous field. It felt good to be an expert and I looked forward to enjoying the kudos that come from being a consistently strong performer.

Shortly after communicating my decision to my employer, I was summoned to the C-suite to meet with the EVP responsible for the business unit. She asked me what led to my decision. Then, she transitioned the conversation into a discussion of exercise and fitness. She inquired about my gym routine by asking, "Do you work on developing your strongest muscles or your weakest muscles?" Before I could respond, she said, "You should work on your weak muscles to maintain balance and avoid injury." She then translated this idea to apply to my professional life. "We already know you have strong muscles," she stated referring to my previous field. She explained that the company needed balanced corporate "athletes" that could perform in a variety of roles. She "suggested" that I take a day to rethink my decision and to consider how I could develop my weak muscles.

As I left the C-suite, I was livid. I knew what she was doing. How dare she force me to take the other job! I had made the decision I thought was in my best interest. Now that decision was being trumped for the convenience of the company. The next day, I begrudgingly sent a note stating that "after thinking things over, I wanted to accept her challenge and develop my weak muscles." Looking back, this was the best decision of my entire career.

While I had skills that were in demand, I was essentially a niche player. Having been a consultant in the field and having experience on the corporate side, I thought that I had a diverse skill set. What I failed to realize was that career progression is not solely based on proficiency in one field. Modern corporations need flexible talent that can plug-and-play in multiple roles. That flexibility is learned and demonstrated by taking on new assignments and challenges.

Four years after my "weak muscles" conversation, I had established myself in the new function, I was hired away by a competitor, and I had progressed through several levels of management. My new company was acquired and began an extensive talent review process. Going into the review, I was confident because I knew my chances of landing a "go-forward" role were greatly improved due to my ability to plug-and-play in multiple functions.

When you can contribute in multiple functions, you have options. When you face periods of recession, downsizing, or an acquisition, it's good to be well-rounded. You must actively change your role in order to develop and demonstrate flexibility.

*   *   *

Contribution by **Mark Frederick**
Manager, Business Account Services
Puget Sound Energy

The key to any kind of development, personal or organizational, is having a central vision of yourself and where you want to be.

In a down-sized world with shrinking budgets and growing challenges, there is not enough time or resources for an organization to create this vision for their employees. Thus, workplaces become competitive arenas with an equal opportunity to outshine others or fade away into the darkness.

Those who choose the latter option are the ones most often found behind the curve on the career track and the org chart. Their profile is one of studied diligence, at best, and wasted opportunity, at worst. They may also feel that their commitment to their present role will somehow magically raise their profile and that opportunity will come knocking on their cubicle wall. Of course, in reality, that just doesn't happen.

On the opposite side of this arena are those with a vision. Now, are they the smartest or the most educated people in the arena? Maybe they are, maybe they are not. It doesn't matter because they have marshaled their resources and put together a plan based on a vision of themselves and the arena that they play in.

This sounds great but it really isn't easy. It requires an honest assessment of skill sets (personal and professional) and past performance. What did past success and failure look like? How did skills and behavior contribute to both and what did one look like when it happened?

In many ways, this is not unlike the process of shinjo. Shinjo is the Japanese term, derived from Confucianism, for the "stripping away of illusions through honest self-reflection." In ancient Japan, it was utilized by the samurai as a method to prepare themselves for combat or any major undertaking. A person who had undergone this process was ready to fulfill their destiny with complete focus whether it be success in battle or death in the field, they had no regrets. Subsequently, this often led to success over their opponents who were not as mentally prepared.

The modern workplace may not be as deadly but these principles still apply. For example, in 1995 I was the terminal operations coordinator for an international shipping company in Seattle. On paper, it looked like I was responsible for hundreds of thousands of dollars in transportation equipment as well as the efficient flow of cargo to and from the harbor. Yet, in reality, the position was not as exciting as I had expected it to be.

My job involved union grievances, cranky equipment, and even crankier people. I was a long way away from my undergrad days studying the Spanish Armada and the meaning of history—I could feel it in my bones. My future there would have been one of growth through seniority by trying to outlive my competition. I was looking for creativity and inspiration so I ditched the whole thing for an internet start-up company specializing in international currency trading. I didn't know what to expect and I didn't have a plan but I thought all I needed was a dream.

Not unexpectedly, the company didn't take off. We couldn't attract enough customers to make-up for the one's that left after they made money and we didn't have the resources to build a good account management and retention program. I was left wondering what to do next.

This time around, however, I took the time to reassess myself and my true motivations by applying the concept of shinjo. What did I want and what was I willing to do to make it happen? I reviewed my education and professional experience to find out what motivated me, what turned me off, and what I was capable of. I drew up a list, comparing positives to negatives, and what I found was that I was not an operations-professional but, rather, I was a person that was motivated by monetary success and creativity—the very two things that my past profession did not provide for me.

Lacking the credentials and experience needed to fulfill my goal, I had to make a plan for my professional reformation. Step one was to get the credentials. I understood the value of differentiation early on, so I chose a university in Europe (Belgium to be precise) that offered a two-year masters degree in marketing. Having earned previous graduate credits in the US, I parlayed it into a one-year program instead, so that the rest of my time could be used for networking and travel.

That turned out to be the best experience of my life and the best move that I ever made professionally. Apart from learning a lot in an international environment and making some good connections and great friends, I also met my future wife and had an experience that many people only dream about.

After returning to the US, I was armed with a new mission in life as well as the knowledge that one's role in life is a story that can and should only be told by the person living it. I eventually ended up in two successful Dotcoms where I was able to work with creative people in an energetic atmosphere while being rewarded for the things that I love to do.

*   *   *

Contribution by **Sally Petersen**
Principal Consultant
MAD Consulting

"Crazy Job Hopper," was the title bestowed upon me by one of my brilliant colleagues at a national Fortune 100 bank. This particular leader has remained in the same department for ten years and the same position for seven years. He claims that he stays in his role for economic stability and because he loves his work. Yet, I can't help but to think, are his reasons enough to stay competitive given the current challenges in the marketplace?

In today's business environment, I believe that you must continually reinvent yourself, redesign your role, and refine your strengths each and everyday. What do you offer that separates you from others in today's competitive marketplace?

This is one of the never-ending great debates: are you a specialist or a generalist? If you don't actively change your role, you inevitably become a specialist. If you allow yourself to be labeled as a specialist, you inadvertently pigeon-hole yourself into one role, one department, and one industry (similar to my co-worker mentioned above). However, if you choose to actively change your role and pursue new opportunities and experiences, you become a generalist . . . a jack of all trades . . . a corporate work culture chameleon.

At one point in time, the role of a specialist was sought after by many. All prominent and knowledgeable business executives wanted to be the master of their trade. However, that approach to personal development is becoming less and less admirable for a few reasons.

First, the market place demands versatility. Being able to change and having the ability to quickly adapt is mandatory in today's culture. Since moving into the technological era, business moves fast than ever and decisions are made quite quickly. By broadening your skill set, you automatically prepare yourself to map over to other roles and opportunities as needed. This allows you to keep pace with the ever-changing market.

Second, social networking is everything in today's world. By taking on new assignments or expanding your knowledge on a particular topic, you also broaden your social network. At one time, social networking was considered a strictly "social" activity . . . drinks after work, taking a client to the ball game, etc. However, networking has taken on an entirely different meaning today. The more people you and engage with, the more you learn about business, about the world, and about yourself. By actively changing your role, you will instinctively expand your social network, which will ultimately provide you with more knowledge, cultural diversity, and personal adaptability.

Third, nothing stays the same. This is especially relevant in today's world where unemployment is high and career opportunities are low. Organizations routinely down-sized and positions are eliminated daily, making the competition fierce among the unemployed. The more you grow your personal skill set and expand your work experience, the better you are positioned to map over to other opportunities.

With that being said, you are the only one that controls your future. Your manager, boss, spouse, or mentor might help you find your way but, ultimately, you are responsible for your own growth . . . personally, socially, and intellectually. The more you have to offer a potential employer, client, or business associate, the better chance you will have at making an impact.

*　　*　　*

Contribution by **Christopher L. Campbell**
Current Job Title: Product Manager, Cloud & Datacenter
Current Organization: Multinational Technology Firm

Do the role you want in addition to the role you have. It goes without saying that you first need to do your day job. You need to excel at your current tasks. It doesn't matter how great you can be at your future role if you can't do your current role well. Doing it well shows commitment.

It's important to evaluate your knowledge and credentials. Some positions may require you attain a degree or certification that no amount of experience or work ethic will give you. A VP once told me that you can never be too overqualified. Making the commitment to improve your credentials may be time consuming but can also pay big dividends in the end. It will also set you apart from your counterparts that haven't made that kind of investment. If you're moving from a technical role to a management role or a role with operational and strategic implications, know your strengths and weaknesses and build on them. What made you an indispensible engineer won't necessarily make you a great strategic thinker or people manager. Don't focus on the things you're good at. Focus on the things you're not good at and build those skills.

Find and create projects on your team that will showcase your talents within the company. In addition, make sure others know the awesome job you're doing. Market yourself! If you don't sell your talents to others who is going to do it for you? If you don't make any effort to show others you're ready for more responsibility then you're destined to languish in your existing role. I have a friend that graduated from a major college in New York with a dual Bachelor of Science degree in Management and Finance. 15 years later he is still a Personal Banker. Within a five year period and with no degree (I got my degree later) I started as a Level 1 Engineer and made it to Technical Relations Manager. 10 years later with an undergraduate degree, multiple certifications and halfway through my MBA I'm now a Product Manager. Know what you want and actively work towards it. If you intend to move up the corporate ladder, any role you work towards should give you the following three things: international exposure, people or project management experience and profit and loss responsibilities. You may not be able to get all three initially but work on adding at least one of these responsibilities in your next role. As Bob Marley once said "Anything you want, you have to work really hard to gain".

Assumption #2:
Develop the Talent

Constant development must take place in order for a Talent to actively change roles. Take a look at the Talent Model below; this is what needs to happen in order for you to have a constantly successful career. The model is a blend of experience and education. Both elements are important, and you should not neglect either one of them. Should you deviate from this model, there is a good chance that you will feel frustration during your career development.

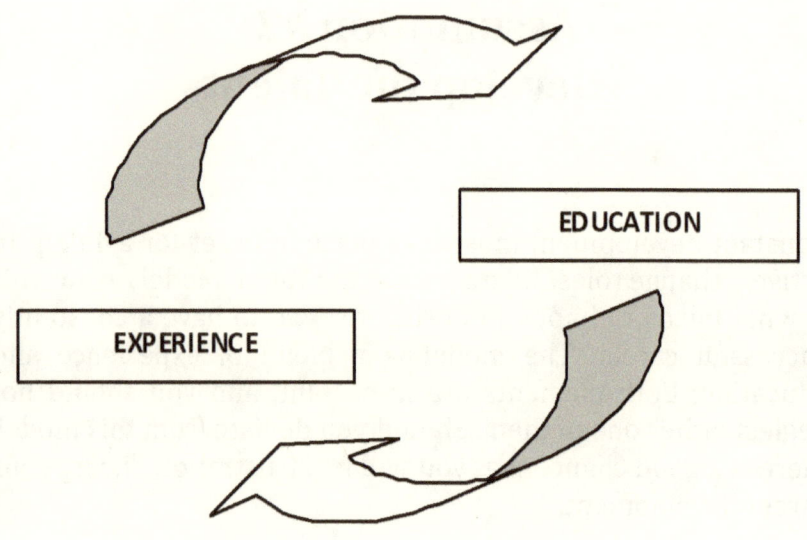

EDUCATION

EXPERIENCE

Talent Model

This is a how the Talent Model works and how it can be used by anyone as a measuring tool in terms of their career development. Let's say, you find a job as a filing clerk at an accounting firm. You are now working on the experience aspect of the model. In order for you to move forward in your career, you will now have to apply the education aspect of the model as well.

Following the model's guidelines, you realized that you are experiencing career limitations, and you decide to go for an undergraduate degree in Accounting. Once you have earned your degree, you have successfully applied the education aspect of the model. Thus, you will find that your firm and other similar firms are now interested in you to perform higher-value tasks for a higher compensation. Voilá, your career starts to move forward once again!

Nevertheless, after about two years or so, you realize that you are feeling career frustrations once again. You feel like you're not "going anywhere." You feel like you're a hamster running on a wheel. When you search for other jobs, most positions you find are similar to your current role. So you ask yourself, "Why should I change my current position for a similar position?" And more likely than not, there is no good reason to change. You don't need to go out and get a new job—you need to find a new role.

When you review the Talent Model once again, you realize that your current role has allowed you to focus on the experience side for the past two years; however, it's time to balance the scale out with some more education.

You now have the choice: Study and become a CPA, pursue an MBA, or acquire a Masters degree in Information Systems, Finance, or Accounting. You could even seek-out some other form of education entirely. The point is that you can use this opportunity to change the focus of your career, if you'd like. For instance, you could try to go for a Series 7 certification and move out of the accounting world. This is, of course, an oversimplified example and life can be a bit more complex than that, depending on personal situations. Over time, you will find that as you change roles and add education, you'll be rewarded for your efforts each and every time.

It is only when you stop following the model that you have put yourself in a very dangerous situation. If you stop following the Talent Model, you will find that you have no option but to pitch a tent. You must actively guard against this situation, and take it upon yourself to develop your career.

Fortunately, I've had some very caring bosses over the years, but it was never their job to map-out my life for me. It is your individual responsibility to develop yourself. You are a Talent. Thus, you must cultivate your Talent. Somewhere in the back of your mind, you've always known this to be true, so don't gamble with your life. You only have a certain amount of time to be proactive so that you are not forced to cling to your job or become **Trapped (by a system)** (see Corporate Bold dictionary in the back of the book for definition).

Look, the Talents of this world just can't imagine a quality career without the application of this Talent Model.

Talent Traps

The primary job of a good coach is to make you aware of some of the potential hurdles that you might encounter. So let's get right to some of the traps awaiting your arrival. While we go through the traps, keep in mind that all of these traps are self-made! What this means is that, although you may or may not be aware of it, you are the one who will allow these traps to develop and ultimately cause yourself to fall into them.

Number one on the hot-list of Talent traps is being Trapped (by a system). This is an *extremely* common trap. Here is how it works: At your work, you are asked to take a role in building, maintaining, monitoring, or administrating a system or process. This could be any kind of a system or process at your company. It could be the billing system, the filing system, or the new employee hiring process. Regardless, you have been identified as the go-to person for this system or process.

One positive thing about this situation is that, for a short period of time, you have an opportunity to learn something new or apply your knowledge to refine an existing system or process. You might even have some pretty good job security, for the moment. In meetings, your name and the system or process' name are used interchangeably. You are the one keeping the system or process functioning, and this makes you look pretty darn good to everyone else in your office.

The trap here is, until and unless your company moves to a new system or finds someone else to take over, you are not going anywhere. You are, in essence, Trapped (by a system). And when the workload gets to be too much, your boss will try to find someone who can help out. Yet, unless you can easily and permanently transfer your knowledge to that person, you are still the go-to person and you are trapped.

Alright, now let's say that you decide to teach someone else how to run the system so that your boss doesn't have to be totally dependent on you to run it. The conventional thinking would go something like this, "If I give away my knowledge of the system or process, I am also giving away my job security." Just look at the pharmaceutical industry, for example, where the patients help keep the drug producing companies from having to give away their competitive advantage. However, the exact opposite is true of a corporate professional. If you can't give away or transfer your knowledge, you management will eventually try to find some outside company or solution to take the complicated process or system off their plates. And with that—goes your job security. At that point, you essentially have no exit strategy. If you don't pass your knowledge on to someone else, then you are Trapped (by a system).

Here is a very common scenario. It's Monday morning and you're at work. You think about the potential career-ending move of mentoring a teammate about your system, and you decide to hang-in-there and do nothing for the time being—with no solid plan for the future. Late Thursday evening, your boss comes out of a meeting and tells you that management has decided to replace or outsource the system that you are currently trapped by. You will, of course, have a lead role in removing the old system. Then you either have to start looking for another job or you have to bring in a new system so that you can end up being trapped all over again.

This trap is so common that you can probably name multiple individuals in your company who are Trapped (by a system) at this very moment—is your name on that list? Are you wondering if this has ever happened to me? You bet it has!

I recall being trapped as a "one-man-show". I learned the hard way that the more I worked to show off my abilities in hopes of a promotion, the more and more trapped I became in my role. When my annual review came around, I asked my manager how he saw my career developing over the next few years. After a brief blank stare, he rambled a lot of words that didn't really say very much. It became clear that my manager had no reason to promote me. Why should my manager take on that risk when I was already doing such a good job?

That being said, you shouldn't shy away from being the Go-To person for a system or process. Stepping-up as the Go-To person is a great way to showcase your Talents. However, you should always keep the thought in the back of your mind that you will want to transfer your knowledge to someone else in the future. When you work with this frame of mind, you can preplan for your next position.

Now that we've covered being Trapped (by a system), are you ready to find out the second trap? Great! The second trap occurs when you have changed roles at work, but you are **not mentally ready to leave your old role**. Let me explain this further because this usually happens after you have changed your role within one organization instead of moving to a new company.

Here is an over-simplified example of the second trap in action. Imagine that you are a really good sales representative in Dallas, Texas. Your company reviews your performance and decides to promote you to a sales manager position for the entire Southwestern region. "Great," you say, until you start seeing the sales numbers from Dallas each week. The second trap begins to take shape when you continually scrutinize the person performing your old job. In your imagination, you are still performing the Dallas sales representative's job. **Mentally, you have not left your old job**.

In *Your First 90 Days*, a Harvard Press book, they confirm that this is the #1 problem for every new manager. A new manager **must** mentally and physically leave his or her old role in order to be successful in a new role. This, obviously, does not apply only to managers. It applies to you and me as well—the Talents.

One of the reasons why this may happen is because we performed so flawlessly in our previous role. After a few false starts in our new role, it is likely that we digress back to our previous role where we excelled and were considered an *All-Star*. So the message here is to move on to your new role and to embrace it wholeheartedly. By allowing yourself to be exposed to uncomfortable and challenging elements, you will grow as a thriving corporate professional.

Let's get right into the third trap: **Martyr-Me**. There is very likely at least one person in your organization that you can standup and point to who falls into this trap (but please don't actually point—they may not know why you're pointing at them). Martyr-Me is when you think to yourself, "boy my company really needs me and I must sacrifice myself for the good of the company or project . . . If I don't, then the whole company will just shutdown." If you have not fallen into the Martyr-Me trap, or haven't seen someone fall into this one, then you probably think that I am exaggerating. I'm not.

Martyrs honestly believe that their company's future rests on their shoulders. "If I don't do this then who will?" They often exclaim. "I'm the only one who can do this and the company needs me" is a common theme heard from Martyrs. However, something rather miraculous happens when Martyrs go on vacation. While a Martyr is out on vacation, all the problems and emergencies that were happening will more or less subside for the time being. Then, the moment the Martyr comes back from vacation—boom—the floodgates open once again. So, why do we care about these types of professionals?

Martyrs are hard workers who do their best to contribute to the organization's success. When they start to internally tell themselves that they are best performers and most valued in their organization, they can become complainers. They are not interested in being the police or traffic cop at your workplace; they are interested in being the authority on "what everyone else is doing wrong." They'll tell you that accounting doesn't do a good job of process expenses correctly and that the whole IT department is being run by a bunch of misfits.

These corporate professionals tend to be top-notch complainers. Martyrs tend to whine about co-workers, other departments, and other you-name-it. We need to be careful so that we do not turn into to complainers like these individuals. As a thriving corporate profession, we must ensure that we do not set a tone as being complainers.

Now that you know all three traps, watch for them and correct them as needed. It is only okay to be Trapped (by a system) if you need to coast at work or you want routine type tasks for a short period of time. Always be sure to leave your old job, mentally, when you move on to your next job. Lastly, your ability to perform with a positive attitude is a critical element in your success.

Path of Opportunity

So far, we've painted a very rosy picture for a Talent, and with good reason too! The benefits of being a Talent are so prevalent that it becomes nearly impossible to ignore them. To help you move forward in your path to success here is a model that can help you navigate through your **Path of Opportunity**.

This is how the Path of Opportunity works: The next time you go back to work, treat yourself as a Talent. Hold yourself to a higher standard because you know that you are there to solve your organization's problems. By doing so, you will develop yourself into a problem solving and accountable individual. After you do this, what you will quickly find out is that not very many people around you consider themselves as a Talent. In fact, you might even experience some negative emotions related to your co-workers who refuse to see themselves as Talented, and who are simply occupying space.

You will have to learn to ignore others. It's difficult but you have to make sure that you stay focused on yourself and not anyone else. Pretty soon, you will find that others will start to seek out your advice because they consider you a leader within your team, department, or organization.

The reality is that you are stepping up to the plate and others are showing you some gaps in the organization that they need your help with. These gaps are really opportunities in disguise. And, by now, you can almost step back and see the multiple gaps throughout your team, department, or organization. This is your Path of Opportunity. The question that now remains is: Which one will make you look like a hero and teach you the most? Pick your battles based on what you think you can handle.

Take a look at the Path of Opportunity illustration that follows, it visually summates the process. Start by trying to pinpoint where you are in the process. Are you at step 1, 2, or 3? Perhaps you have completed one cycle of the path and are headed for round two. If you find that you are not able to pinpoint yourself on the illustration then start by moving toward step 1.

Path of Opportunity illustration:

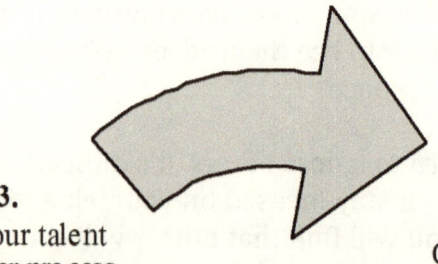

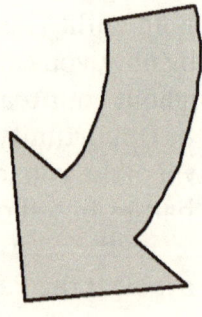

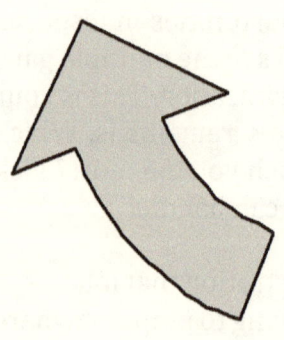

3.
Take your talent
to another process
or position and
start over.

1.
Others see you as
a Talent and bring
you their
problems.

2.
You solve the
problems that
have high impact
and learn from
them.

Team Meeting

This may not be the first time you've heard the idea about continuously developing yourself professionally. Yet, it's amazing how many corporate professionals fail to do just that, and the price of failure can be quite high. We are all busy; however, we must make time do what needs to be done, even if it is in slow increments.

There is a special group of Talented professionals whom I'd like you to meet. These professionals know the value of developing one's talent first-hand.

Please allow me to introduce you to . . .

Contribution by **Carlo Caminiti**
Manager
Hewlett-Packard

Be a salesperson and a politician!

Today's organizations are eliminating more and more layers of formal management. I have found that in today's organizations, you must be able to play both "team member" and "team leader" roles—sometimes simultaneously.

It is important to actively learn skills that will benefit you in both scenarios. Sometimes referred to in corporate lingo as "soft skills," it would seem like these skills are less important than knowing finance or how to build web pages, for instance; but in my experience, no matter what your career goal is, be prepared to enhance these skills—the salesperson and the politician.

Becoming a salesperson is the starting point for positively influencing others by doing what you believe in and showcasing your value and ideas to the organization.

Learning to play like a politician is a helpful skill to manage the degree of uncertainty that is generated by not having everything under control. It will also help you understand how things work in the organization.

As an example, in many of the multimillion dollar projects that I worked on at Fortune 50 companies, my "project resources" were not my subordinates and my sponsor was rarely my direct manager. Rather, teams are built out of peers from my or others' teams. This means that to get things done, you need to juggle between "demanding action" and "influencing action." Likewise, feedback on results is not achieved through a direct interaction between myself and my boss, but rather through a network of individuals making my skills as a salesperson and a politician all the more important.

A former boss of mine used to say, "you have to create your next job, yourself" and another one affirmed that "when a job is formally posted, it's too late." While this might not be true everywhere, the art of influencing, powered by the ability to positively sell your skills and achievements, are tools that will allow you to do just that—proactively identify opportunities before they pass you by.

*   *   *

Contribution by **Amber J. Laxton**
Manager of Student Accounts
DePaul University Continuing and Professional
Education

In any organization, employers value employees who are eager to learn new techniques and practices that can be applied immediately on the job. These employees not only develop their own personal capacity, but also contribute to the success and longevity of his/her organization. While it is no longer the case that the individual is personally responsible for developing him/herself, it is certainly the individual's responsibility to demonstrate a desire to learn. It is, therefore, in the employer's best interest to acknowledge that desire and assist employees in professional development opportunities. As an end result, the expansion of practical knowledge of an employee will contribute to the competitiveness of that organization.

In the last 25 years or so, the concept of continuing education—also referred to as lifelong learning, professional development, and adult education—has become a necessity to a competitive resume. Employers are looking more and more for professional credentials attached to a person's name. Not only do these acronyms imply achievement of a nationally or internationally recognized certification, it suggests a person who values learning and intends to acquire more knowledge in the future. It suggests a person who takes his/her career seriously and wants to continuously learn new revelations in that particular field.

If employers look for these designations as a prerequisite to many professional jobs, then why would it be their responsibility to aid in further development? Once a certification has been obtained, many professional organizations require certification maintenance, which may include additional continuing education and training programs. It is now in that organization's best interest to assist the employee in maintaining a valued designation—a large contributor to the reason that person was hired—that is highly regarded and respected by peers and colleagues.

With globalization and the fast-paced changes in technology, an organization is only as competitive as the employees it bears. Keeping staff knowledgeable and keeping them leaders in a field is quintessential to business in the 21st Century.

In my current position in a continuing and professional education unit at a Chicago university, we fully recognize the needs of local businesses to educate and expand the knowledge of its employees. We work with companies to manager third-party billing, and also to conduct customized onsite visits to organizations to train groups of employees. A large percentage of our students responded to a survey indicating that they decided to take a continuing education course for career development, and many were enticed to do so through conversations and encouragement from their employer. Continuing education programs are not traditional in the sense that they are non-credit may not be covered using financial aid. That being the case, students often rely on a third-party payer, which often is their employer. In continuing education, just as it is in business, what is most important is staying ahead of the game.

*　　*　　*

Contribution by **Carlos Buxton**
Business Consultant
State Street Corporation

I was interested in IT all throughout college, and thereafter as my chosen professional field ranging over several other industries including resources, manufacturing, insurance, and financial services. I was involved in numerous IT initiative cycles like Y2K, ERP implementations, business process re-engineering, capability outsourcing/off-shoring, and other related "flavors of the week." Throughout all of those times, the key driver behind my Talent has been the acquisition of knowledge the specific technologies, processes, and applications. Keeping oneself current in the emerging technologies and processes of one's field is absolutely essential for all disciplines.

I have met many excellent people in the field, both contractors and corporate employees alike, whose knowledge in specific areas made them extremely valuable assets to their companies. Unfortunately, I have also seen many of the same individuals make the mistake of assuming that such cycles will sustain their careers forever, and therefore they neglect their training and development for the "next" evolution. Technology evolves as new advances supersede "older" ones. Thus, processes change and adapt to the marketplace. Because of this fact, the professionals who did not continue their education and training suddenly found themselves obsolete because they lacked the proper tools and knowledge to effectively and efficiently cope with change.

The only constant in life is that it continuously changes, and there is always a new experience around the corner. One must learn to adapt and face the challenges of a new day, or they will end up going the way of the dinosaurs.

This is particularly true in IT because of the ever-shortening, emerging-technology maturation curves. However, this is also true for every other professional discipline, as outsourcing has amply demonstrated in the 20th century. The initiative to keep oneself current, or the willingness to learn new skills, is an increasingly important quality that all managers value in the workplace—I know I do.

*　　*　　*

Contribution by **Gerald Ratigan**
Internal Audit Manager
Cooper Industries

Do you have the tools to achieve your personal success?

I challenge you to build your professional tool belt. Successful employees possess distinguishing characteristics that set them apart from everyone else. What sets you apart?

It does not matter what your current job or position is within your organization. The fact is no one will take as much interest and responsibility for your development then you should. You need to look out for number one. Most organizations do not possess the expertise in talent development of its employees to help them reach their personal best. Some companies have formal and structured training programs; oftentimes these programs are only offered to select individuals. In any case, you should take ultimate responsibility to develop tools to achieve your long term goals and objectives. These tools will require you to seek both internal and external resources. As part of your development plan you should focus in on three areas to obtain immediate results.

First, ask for feedback. Tomorrow, set up a meeting with your immediate supervisor to obtain their opinion of your performance, leadership style, and ultimate potential. This is the most critical relationship you have at work. Find out what skills matter most to them and agree to develop steps you can implement to be an exceptional performer. You should also obtain feedback from your current and former peers as well as the people you manage. Obtaining different perspectives on your job performance is a key tactic in identifying your strengths and weaknesses. The data you obtain from these encounters can then be studied and action plans can be developed to address deficiencies. In my opinion, most people are afraid of conflict and are scared to seek out the feedback that could unlock the key to achieving their ultimate potential. Why wait until an annual performance meeting when behaviors that could have been identified and corrected earlier in the year are now communicated as significant negative annual review points. It is no secret that your boss assesses your advancement potential. Unless he/she believes you possess the necessary tools to be promoted, you will continue to stay in your current position. Without insight into their assessment, you have no impact on influencing this key decision maker. Additionally, to be a high achiever I recommend you schedule regular follow-ups with the people that provided your original feedback in order to monitor results. Consequently, you will know what efforts are working and what is not.

Second, step into the water hose to educate yourself on your company. Many people have compared learning new things to an overwhelming feeling similar to being in front of a fire engine hose shooting out hundreds of gallons of water every minute. Don't be afraid. Learn everything you can about your company's history, policies and procedures, corporate culture, and departments that have effective teams. Research is required to find out which tools are valued most by your current organization. These tools may not be on your priority list at first, but without them your advancement and promotions will be limited. One way to uncover these tools is to interview and observe the high performers in your company. Old timers that have been with the company for a long period could also be valuable to you in your information seeking process. Create and test hypothesis to find out what tools are most valuable and can achieve the results your boss and department care about most.

Third, build your emotional intelligence. Some companies will offer internal trainings to improve your communication skills; however, it usually is general and not the type you can utilize immediately in your day-to-day job. Most, if not all, is forgot the moment you leave the training session. To complement this effort you should seek out training seminars or clubs that allow you the ability to practice problematic areas in your communication ability. Also, don't wait on your company to present training opportunities, as it is usually in their best interest and a financial incentive to make sure you remain competent to perform only your current job requirements. That is why it is the utmost importance for you to seek out and create your own development plan. This plan should be documented and negotiated with your boss to create accountability.

Finally, I recommend that you perform regular tool check-ups to determine whether your existing skills are best being utilized. This check-up should be performed at least annually. The earlier you can address deficient tools and set goals to improve them, the faster you will achieve your goals. This evaluation could result in a change of position, company, or even career. Specifically, you need to re-examine your tool belt, but not to see if you have the right ones to do your current job. The examination will help you see if you have are building the skills and experiences that will help you obtain and become successful in your dream job.

*   *   *

Contribution by **John D. Lestock**
Payroll Tax Accountant
Starbucks Coffee Company

On March 30, 2007, I became a Certified Employee Benefit Specialist (CEBS). It took me nearly eight years, but after successfully passing ten exams, I succeeded in earning my certification. Why did it take me so long? There were many reasons, but a big reason was the fact that I paid for most of the courses by myself for quite a few years. So, using my own money, I needed to pace myself in order to maintain my ability to budget for the costs without "breaking the bank," so to speak.

When I initially started taking the exams, I did it because my employer paid for the full cost of the exams—books and testing fees. They even provided up to two paid days off for studying and taking an exam. Hewitt Associates valued the CEBS certification and provided generous incentives to encourage its employees (or "associates" to use Hewitt terminology) to take the exams. After completing two exams, I quit Hewitt to work at a new startup down the street from the company's operations in The Woodlands, Texas. This new startup, Exult, was creating a new market in the outsourcing industry dealing with HR BPO, or human resources business process outsourcing.

The opportunity to work for Exult was too good to pass up, but the company was limited in regards to the kind of benefits it could provide to its employees compared to the benefits Hewitt offered its employees. Specifically, Exult didn't pay for CEBS exams. Granted, the company had an education reimbursement program, but due to budget constraints, it was extremely difficult to convince managers to approve the expenses. And, since Exult was footing the bill, the company would have required me to turn over any textbooks and materials since they would have been considered to be materials purchased by Exult. I didn't agree with that policy. So, I had a choice: either depend on Exult to help me pay for my CEBS exams following their policy, or take the initiative myself and pay for them with my own money and use my own vacation time to study and take the exams. Given the restrictive education reimbursement policy the company had (they technically had education reimbursement benefits, but they didn't really encourage their employees to actually use them), I knew I couldn't depend on Exult to help me continue on in the CEBS program; however, the idea of throwing away two completed exams and all the work that went into passing them didn't sit well with me.

I had found success with the CEBS program, and I really wanted to continue taking the exams and obtaining my certification. At the time, I had always depended on my employer to provide me with company-sponsored training and financial support for any formal classes and exams I took outside of work. I learned very quickly in my short career after college to not depend entirely on my employer for such things. Company-sponsored training was helpful, but too many times the training was tailored to the specific needs and proprietary systems of the company. Any kind of financial assistance for outside coursework required formal approval from management. If there were budget constraints or management didn't feel that either my contributions to the company's success or the nature of the coursework itself justified the expenditure, my outside coursework wasn't approved for reimbursement. I faced a similar situation with Exult.

I decided to pay for the CEBS exams myself. I knew I needed something to supplement my work experience. My undergraduate degree was solid, but I knew I needed more to demonstrate to my current employer that I've developed myself beyond college. Work experience was helpful, but it wasn't enough. I needed more formal knowledge. I needed to develop and expand my knowledge. I needed something to fall back on in case I had to look for another job.

Years later, Exult was acquired by Hewitt, and I became a Hewitt associate again. However, my position at Exult was eliminated since it was a duplicate function performed by another person at

Hewitt's corporate headquarters in Lincolnshire, Illinois. So, I had to look for another job within Hewitt and outside of the company. At Exult, I was a payroll tax accountant. When I interviewed for jobs at Hewitt, I interviewed for pension analyst roles. Those positions were vastly different from my own current job. Yet, because I had continued taking CEBS exams and was only about three exams away from obtaining my certification, I was able to demonstrate my versatility and personal initiative during the job interview. I had formal outside coursework to supplement my work experience, which proved to be quite valuable given that I was interviewing for roles completely different from my current role. I succeeded in getting the pension analyst role and worked at Hewitt for another year before I quit again. This time, I had to quit because my wife and I were relocating to Seattle, Washington for our new jobs at Starbucks Coffee Company.

I had interviewed for a payroll tax accountant role at Starbucks, and it was my continued dedication to the CEBS program as well as the variety of roles comprising my work experience that helped me to successfully land the job with Starbucks. Once at Starbucks, I completed the final two exams I needed to obtain my CEBS certification. I also completed two payroll certification exams. Granted, the company paid for those payroll exams through the company's tuition reimbursement program, but had they not paid for those exams I would have still taken them. I would have paid for them with my own money.

Those payroll certifications were very important to me, just as the CEBS certification was important to me. I needed the formal training. I needed the knowledge that came from studying for those exams. There were just certain topics that I would have never encountered had I depended solely on company-sponsored training or on-the-job training. I may have been prepared for doing the work in my current roles, but without the formal coursework I would have never been prepared to take on new responsibilities, or transition to new roles within the company, or even to look for jobs outside of the company. I would never have been able to transition from a defined contribution plan accountant at Hewitt Associates to a payroll tax accountant at Exult, and then to a retirement plan analyst at Hewitt Associates followed by a payroll tax accountant at Starbucks Coffee Company without taking any formal coursework and passing certification exams. And, I couldn't depend solely on any one particular employer to provide this for me. At some point, I had to take ownership for my own self-development and continue on with my coursework using my own money and vacation time. The investment was definitely worthwhile.

*   *   *

Contribution by **John Masoudpour**
Senior Financial Associate
Wall Street Firm

Self-improvement—the desire to better oneself in a specific way—is a fundamental component to a successful career. It relies on several ingredients, most notably: self-awareness, curiosity, motivation, and hard work. Combined and put into practice, these ingredients can ensure a career marked by growth and achievement rather than stagnation and discontent.

Self-improvement can be achieved in several steps. The first step—recognizing the need for improvement—is the hardest for many, yet also the most fundamental. It requires acknowledging that we are deficient in one or more areas; being self-aware; and having a healthy sense of confidence. This last point is what often trips many people up.

Often times, human beings occupy the extremes of the confidence spectrum and struggle to find a healthy equilibrium. This is especially true in the corporate world, where one is surrounded by extraordinarily bright and talented individuals. Here, overconfidence is a survival tool many of us employ. Faced with the choice to believe that we are just as good, if not better, than those around us, or that we are inferior to them, we choose the former. And herein begins the mistaken development of a sense of overconfidence. Not only is this development mistaken, it also may be dangerous. To co-workers and management, even a whiff of overconfidence is unappealing, and, for oneself, overconfidence is unproductive. It inhibits any desire for self-improvement, which is the ultimate goal.

Once the need for improvement is recognized, then comes step two—determining where improvement is needed. Sometimes areas of weakness are obvious, but other times they are not. When that is the case, use feedback from managers and annual review reports as indications of where improvement is needed. This might jog your memory as to assignments and projects that you did not feel comfortable doing because you doubted your knowledge on the subject.

Finally comes step three—do something! You have endured a great deal of self-analysis and discovered one or more areas of weakness. Now it is your job to fill that gap in your knowledge, to educate yourself, to broaden your skill set, to minimize that weakness, or even make that weakness, strength. So take a class, do some research, meet with experts in the field. Do whatever it takes. Keep at it until you see progress, and when you do, then move on to the next area in need of development. Herein lies the beauty of self-improvement—the work is never done. There is always some way in which we can better ourselves and those who recognize this fact and do something about it are guaranteed to be more successful. Those who do not are doomed.

If you don't believe me, meet Nelson. Fresh out of college, he landed a finance job in a Fortune 500 company. In his first year, Nelson performed his job but struggled a bit. He was not making deadlines, submitted reports with erred calculations, and could not manage expectations for himself. Nelson's colleagues and superiors quickly noticed his deficiencies and recommended that he undergo training in order to improve his professional and financial skills. Nelson, however, ignored this suggestion and continued with his job, just barely making it by. Focused solely on getting promoted, Nelson viewed any activities outside of his work a waste of time. Unfortunately for Nelson, that meant he missed the very important point that getting promoted was contingent on performing well. Thus, performing well, in his case, was contingent on receiving training.

Nelson continued "getting by" for some time. He went overseas and worked for the company's international office, but even there, Nelson exhibited the same poor performance. So, his manager on the international project suggested professional training, but Nelson again ignored the advice. When he returned to the U.S., the management in Nelson's group had changed and he had a fresh opportunity to prove himself. But since Nelson never developed his skills, he had nothing to show except for the same series of mistakes he'd made in the past. Management remarked on Nelson's inabilities and started to lose confidence. Soon no one entrusted Nelson with any projects, fearful that his work would be rife with errors and that the time it would take to fix his work was not worth involving him at all. A typical case of overconfidence, Nelson blamed his lessening responsibilities and diminishing opportunities on poor management. Finally, after six months of pretending to work, while really doing nothing—not even taking those training classes that were offered to him—Nelson was fired.

While it's unfortunate that Nelson was fired from his job, the saddest part of his story is that he never learned his lesson. And since he never learned his lesson then, it's very possible that Nelson is going through the exact same experience all over again.

As with Nelson's case, orientations and training sessions may help the majority of people get by in their jobs, but they are not responsible for the promotion and success of the best and the brightest. Those individuals do well in the workplace because they bring initiative to the table. They do not wait for their superiors to tell them they need to seek training; they go after it themselves. They are constantly analyzing their own abilities—strengths and weaknesses—and considering how to leverage the former while developing the latter. They accept personal responsibility for their growth. They take classes to stay current in their field of expertise. They challenge themselves to learn something new every day. They have confidence that they can get through and learn from anything and everything they experience. Finally, they remain flexible and constantly adaptable. So, starting today, challenge yourself to improve your mind and abilities. It is no simple task, but the benefits are limitless.

*   *   *

Contribution by **Kimberly Denney**
Sr. Director, Advanced Technology
Edwards Life-sciences

In 2001, while working for a Johnson and Johnson (JNJ) operating company, I had the opportunity to attend a dinner meeting featuring a keynote address from JoAnn Heffernan-Heisen. By 1999, JNJ had more than 190 operating companies and more than 97,000 employees. At that time, JoAnn was the highest ranking woman at JNJ serving as the Worldwide Vice President and Chief Information Officer. The theme of her talk was, "owning your development plan." She touched on several aspects, and three questions that she asked her audience that evening sparked my imagination and fueled my desire to take those important first steps in taking the responsibility to develop myself. The first question she asked us was if we had taken steps to further our education. She asked if we had volunteered for stretch assignments, and the third question she asked was if we had cultivated mentors. The advice she shared that evening served as a profound turning point in my career. Her words resonated even greater with me because I could relate to her experience working in mostly male-led companies as a working mother.

Up to that point, I actually felt pretty satisfied with my career. I had received fairly steady promotions moving from field sales representative to training manager to an expatriation assignment in Europe as a Director of training. However, I knew that I wanted to move my career away from the management of shared services toward positions that would come with real responsibility. And, I realized that I had no clear vision how to move beyond my first sales management position. I was now competing with a number of talented sales managers. Outside of the performance of my division, I was not sure how I could set myself apart, be noticed, and seriously considered for advancement.

When she asked that first question regarding how many of us had pursued advanced degrees, I think I may have blushed. I had a Bachelor's degree in Business earned 17 years earlier. I had given some thought over the years about going back to school, but I had not taken any real action toward pursuing an MBA. After all, I was working as a field sales manager, traveling 50% of the time during the week, and I had two small children at home. That evening, I recognized those were the excuses holding me back. Several months later, following discussions with my management, I received full financial assistance to enroll in an executive MBA program. I dedicated virtually every Saturday for the next two years toward completing an advanced degree in International Business. This was an invigorating experience for me that restored my confidence that I could set lofty targets and achieve them.

Her second question served as another trigger point when she asked how many of us had volunteered to lead a project or important activity outside of our own area of expertise. Reflecting on her question, I realized that up until that point, I had largely worked on what was in my area of responsibility and specialization. I had not really taken on a significant stretch assignment. Her advice stayed with me, and I again spoke proactively with my manager to ask him to help me be considered for a future project. About a year later, I got my opportunity to be part of a small project team focused on creating a customer segmentation strategy for our US business.

Interestingly, like me, most of the team had no tangible knowledge or prior experience in this area. We spent a lot of time and effort in defining the scope of the project for our stakeholders and the primary project owner –our Company President. I spent the better part of a year working on this project. By the time it was finalized, I had been promoted to Regional Marketing Director. Importantly, I had the opportunity to implement the new program and its tools on a National basis. The win for me in taking on this stretch assignment was that I now had a vehicle that broadened my exposure to senior management and provided me with numerous opportunities to present to expanded and diverse audiences.

The third question that JoAnn raised was when she asked us whether we had identified and cultivated a mentor. Most companies do not formalize mentorship programs. If you are serious about your career, you will need to take personal responsibility to identify your mentors and proactively cultivate relationships with them. I recognized that taking responsibility to identify and sign up my own mentors was one of my biggest mental hurdles. I had been holding on to a false belief that executives in my company or in other companies would be too busy to mentor me. It took a lot of effort for me to initially work up the confidence to reach out unannounced and uninvited to a corporate officer of the company, a company president, and other senior executives. What I learned from making that effort is that most of them were pleasantly surprised and even flattered that I was asking them for this assistance. They are busy people, of course, but I found that I could with persistence schedule time with them. Even 15 minutes over coffee became an extremely beneficial interaction.

During the time I was working on the customer segmentation project, I found that my company President was often available around 7:30am in his office. I arranged to meet him several times informally. Sometimes, I updated him on the status of the project and current activities in the field which I knew were of interest for him. Other times, I asked for his advice on moving my career forward. In the end, he took a personal interest in helping me advance my career by sharing my profile with other company presidents. His support resulted in my eventual move and promotion to another JNJ operating company. Since then, I have established several other mentoring relationships which have been instrumental in shaping my career.

Today, I continue to own my own development. I consistently seek out and accept new, challenging assignments that stretch me and open new doors in my career. Now, I am also trying to pay it forward by mentoring others. Hopefully, like the spark that JoAnn ignited for me, I will also spark a turning point for others who are early in their careers or navigating through some turbulent times.

*   *   *

Contribution by **Laurent Borne**
Consultant
McKinsey and Company

"Hey Boss, can you help me with my statistics exercise?" This is what I heard from a technician on my team back in 2003. Intrigued, I asked about the exercise. I was very surprised but delighted by the answer. "I am following your advice and trying to build up my skills independently of the company." A few months before this discussion, he and I had had a career discussion where he was asking what it would take for him to get a larger role, where he could contribute more and also why the company was not doing more to develop him. My answer was simple: "Don't wait for someone else. Teach yourself the skills you need to acquire to go where you want." My advice had then been received coldly, to say the least.

I have always advocated and practiced self training since I was given the very same advice I gave my technician early in my career. The first time I met a senior executive from a previous employer—an automotive supplier—at a welcome breakfast for new hires, I asked him how to maximize my opportunities. His answer was shocking to me as a recent graduate from a top engineering school: "learn, learn and learn. More importantly teach yourself the skills you need or may need. Don't wait for someone to decide for you or to send you to "right" training. Be proactive, this is the best way to keep bringing something to the table." I had just spent five tough years learning about math, physics and other sciences to discover it was not enough! That couldn't be true!

Despite my original skepticism, I have religiously followed this advice ever since teaching myself on my own time everything I thought I needed and more, from a foreign language to some advanced computer skills. Cynics could say, it's only to leapfrog others, foster my career, and please whomever one needs to get promotion. Maybe that's the case. But it does not change that this is effective in many ways for career development and is a win-win deal for both the individual and the organization. The former advances his career while the latter gets continuously expanding skills at little costs, other than the ones related to the career promotion.

Self training is usually very effective at developing skills. One must invest one's free time to do it. So, chances are, the individual will try to maximize the return on investment. Is it always the case when one attends a corporate training? I seriously doubt it as my experience both as a trainee and a trainer has shown me.

Learning new skills also makes me feel good in my day-to-day job. Who hasn't been promoted to a larger role based on skills that did wonder in the previous one but had nothing to do with the new position requirements? How many organizations simply tell their individuals "figure out!" I have already held many different positions in different geographic locations, in many different functions, and many different levels of responsibilities, executing and inspiring a group of people to go the extra miles. For most of them, I certainly would not have had the required skills to get started on a good footing had it not been for my self teaching. Indeed, I was told more often than not to . . . "figure out!" Self teaching may not guarantee success but at least it avoids setting oneself up for failure!

And this is where self learning is powerful: as you display skills that are unexpected from managers and peers, you can be put on short lists of candidates for jobs you usually would have never been considered to do. In every one of my appraisals during my career, one skill was always mentioned: versatility. My ability to jump from a finance problem to an operation discussion or from a very tactical question to a more strategic one, to work with senior executives or operators alike, has opened up opportunities for me in various fields. And yet, I know for a fact that no one has ever taught me this versatility.

Self-training is easier than ever and mostly is only a matter of will. Many new media make it possible, fairly cheap, and pretty effective. Books, podcast, webcast, forum suggests that time is really the only scarce resource required. And by the way, any new position should also be considered from the point of view of what the individual will learn. If only the company has interests in the new assignment, then the deal is not sustainable.

Concerning my technician, he kept on training himself and attending night classes about tools and techniques that only engineers would learn during a formal five year college education. He left his comfort zone, signing up for projects and assignments that would lead him to applying them in his daily activities. About a year after our exercise, my Chief Engineer asked me about an open engineering supervisor position. I gave my technician's name, asking my chief engineer not to see him as a technician but "instead to interview him as any other candidate for the job." Two weeks later, despite competition from engineers with degrees from good schools, he was offered the job. As I congratulated him, he simply told me with a blink of the eyes that he had had a good statistics professor!

*   *   *

Contribution by **Mark Herbert**
Principal
New Paradigms, LLC

You Own Your Career

It is interesting to me in this age of "empowerment" and engagement that there is still discussion around who is responsible for managing the individual employee's career.

I remember starting my career with a Fortune 100 organization in the late 70's. I was bright and capable and proceeded with the assumption that I would spend my career with that organization eventually advancing to a corporate Vice Presidency.

I spent the first part of my career there recruiting some of the top schools in the country and hiring people to feed our voracious appetite for talent. It was exciting and fun. Then the bottom dropped out. I spent almost six months playing a major role in reducing the workforce, including eliminating the jobs of people who had been with the organization a very long time.

Shortly after that, I found myself in a discussion with my boss. She shared with me that I was what the corporation considered a high talent individual. She also shared with me that realistically the likelihood I would advance to a management role in that location was unlikely. I was by far the youngest and most "inexperienced" member of the team. With her support I accepted a transfer to another division 3000 miles away in a very different setting; it was, however, a management role.

My new boss had a frank discussion with me. He told me my role was going to last two to three years before I was ready to move on. He was right, but that assignment broadened my experience tremendously. The situation became even more interesting when a little less than three years later I got a call from the executive from my old location wanting me to consider a promotion and transfer to a satellite location supporting that division. I accepted and effectively leapfrogged my old peer group. I was now my ex boss's peer.

History had a way of repeating itself and six months into it we received instructions to essentially shut the location down—once again I was in the layoff business. We literally laid off people who had spent their entire career with the organization. The average tenure was over 25 years.

I was also stranded. I accepted a transfer to the host division to work for the location executive who I had worked closely with on negotiating the union contacts and other key activities. I thought we had a good rapport and it was a promotional opportunity. I actually received a stock award from the corporation for my efforts. Less than six months into it I recognized that my new boss and I were totally incompatible. He literally told me, "I have never seen anyone get so far with so little talent in my career." I was devastated. I had been promoted six times in less than nine years.

I talked to previous supervisors and found out to my surprise that although they disagreed with his assessment because of politics they would not intervene. They would assist me in finding another role outside the corporation, but not internally.

I accepted a position in another smaller organization on the West Coast. At this time, I began thinking that the corporate life didn't really fulfill me the way it should; something was missing. I really wanted to try consulting. I needed to build a "portfolio."

In the almost six years I spent with that organization, I took on as many challenging assignments, training, and as much education as I could handle.

In 1993 the business stalled and we were back in the layoff business. After a couple of rounds of reductions and some pretty frank discussions with my boss about having no interest in being his successor, I was pretty sure I was on the "list."

One morning my boss came to me pretty visibly distraught and said we needed to meet at 2:00pm. I went out at lunch and rented an office in an executive suite arrangement. When I met with my boss at 2:00pm he shared with me that my position was indeed being eliminated. He asked if I knew what I might do and I told him that I had rented an office for my brand new consulting firm that afternoon. He was stunned. He said he had no idea I was planning that, and I shared that I had been preparing myself for that role for over five years. The severance package would give me a "bridge" to get started.

Since 1993 I have successfully moved back and forth between C level positions and consulting. I have had an opportunity to work with clients and organizations all over the world, representing multiple business sectors. I have had a blast and have no regrets.

My C level employers saw my business acumen and entrepreneurial abilities as an asset. They weren't always as happy with my complete lack of dependence.

There are a couple of takeaways that I would like for people to get from my experience:

Your "career" is something that you look back on when it is over. Have a plan and a structure, but be sure it is your plan and your structure.

I would never work for an employer that I didn't consider being a "partner" in my career and who is willing to share in my responsibility for development, for the ultimate accountability for your career is your own. The flip side of empowerment is personal responsibility and accountability.

Every time you change jobs, whether voluntarily or involuntarily you are presented with a new opportunity; it is up to you to decide what to do with it. When in doubt always remember: "When you are getting run out of town, get up in front, and make it look like a parade!"

* * *

Contribution by **Reid Lang**
Strategy and Operations Consultant
Deloitte Consulting LLP

"Work is either fun or drudgery. It depends on your attitude." This quote is from Colleen C. Barrett, President and Chief Operating Officer of Southwest Airlines Company. Even though this is so simple in thought, it is harder to put in to action and I don't feel most people do. But, I deem this to be the key to leading a successful career and forging through the walls along your developmental path.

I graduated with a degree in Mechanical Engineering four years ago and received a job offer from a consulting firm that is a competitor to my current company. Let's use XYZ Consulting as a placeholder name for this consulting firm. I knew I didn't want to be a practicing engineer so a career in consulting was just what I was looking for. I was extremely excited to work for XYZ Consulting. I heard such great stories of project opportunities, how great the people were, and the travel perks involved to name a few. I do agree that all of that is true, but what I didn't know is that it would be my responsibility to develop myself and get the opportunities that I wanted. It's fair to say that I spent the first year disinterested in the type of work I was doing. This made me quickly realize how important it was to differentiate myself.

After my first year, I was in between projects and I was searching for the next when one happened to approach me. The project was in the finance group at XYZ Consulting, where I had no experience, but was something that I wanted to learn more about. This was a project role that I did not want to let slip by and, fortunately, my overwhelming interest was well received; I was selected for the role. This was the beginning of an incredible journey for the next two years that helped me grow far beyond what I anticipated in my first three years out of undergrad.

What did I experience during these three years? I was responsible for deployment of a financial performance management tool for a group of retail stores at a $40B company; I lead user acceptance testing for a group of retail store General Managers, Territory Directors, Corporate Directors, and VP's; I was granted enrollment in a selective finance training program; I was granted a transfer into the XYZ Consulting finance group; I achieved top peer group rating in the XYZ Consulting finance group.

These are just a few of what I was able to accomplish at XYZ Consulting. How was I able to accomplish these things and work in the finance area with no background there? That can be easily summed up. It was by being enthusiastic with my role(s) and striving to be the person that everyone wanted to work with. I will give you some examples on how this can be accomplished:

First, always be willing and excited to take on any task, even if it is printing and collating papers, because you won't get more responsibilities if you can't handle the basics.

Secondly, communicate and build relationships with everyone on your team because this helps you understand what makes each person "tick," and you may find out an interesting network connection a colleague may have that you want to call on in the future.

Thirdly, be willing to help out and work extra hours with the team, when it's required of course, as these are the opportunities to get to know your colleagues under a whole new light; it shows them that you are one they can trust and count on

Lastly, always be positive, even if it's 3:00 AM and your team is still in the office.

I realize that the above aren't all ideal, but these are examples of opportunities to make yourself visible and show your dedication as someone that is irreplaceable in your company. Companies are more apt to spend the time training and developing employees they enjoy working with and have a true interest in expanding themselves over someone who feels they are at the "head of the class" because they have an MBA from Harvard.

Now that you have established the foundation in building your "personal brand" at your organization, you have the green light to be open with your manager about your goals and expectations for where you want to be in a month, year, five years, etc. Your management team will be engaged and listen to your aspirations, because you have proven your value. Companies do not want to lose people like this, so they will do all they can to position you for where you want to be in the future. But, you must take the initiative to communicate your aspirations or you will never move vertically within your organization.

I know it sounds simple and questionable, but no matter what you are doing, embrace it and others will take notice. Never allow skill or knowledge gaps to impede your progress. You will earn the respect of others as they witness your fun spirit and dedication you have for your job. Management will ensure to keep you happy and work with you to fill in those gaps, as they want to retain their top employees. So, ask yourself if you have fun with your work and if your annual reviews say "very positive employee and someone everyone enjoys working with."

*   *   *

Contribution by **Rene Zipper**
General Manager
Hill-Rom

Personal Development touches all areas of our lives. It is my belief that everyone should be on a quest to grow every day. In my twenty four years as a professional salesperson, I have always felt that if a person does not take personal responsibility to build his/her talent beyond what is required by the organization that he/she is a part of, then he/she will not have any special qualities that would set them apart from their peers.

While all of the companies that I have worked for have provided excellent training, it was my belief that this was not enough. Corporate America today is a competitive landscape. Failing to take personal responsibility for both your own personal development and professional development will assure that you will be average at best.

Wherever you stand today, there is always an extra step you can take to better yourself. For example, on a professional basis, you may want Six Sigma certification, you may want to reach the next level of Microsoft Excel training or you may want to enhance your presentation skills by learning more about Microsoft PowerPoint. Some companies or superiors will ask you what additional training or skills you would like to acquire. Generally, this question is geared toward professional development. Even so, these companies are rare. More often than not, if you do not pursue avenues for growth, they are not going to facilitate your growth plan.

Throughout my career, many of my associates have been shocked to learn that I continue to take the extra time to pursue both personal and professional growth. They find it hard to believe that I do anything more than what my company expects of me, and they are even more shocked that I oftentimes pay for these opportunities with my personal funds.

One example where I took personal responsibility for my professional growth is when I hired someone to give me private Spanish lessons weekly in my home. Living in South Florida, fluency in Spanish is a huge asset. The expense appeared to be great when looked at in a vacuum; however, this was an investment in me and this is an investment that will pay off handsomely throughout my entire future. One result of my efforts to develop myself is that I am almost always the "Go To" person for issues like the sales funnel, spread sheets, presentations, etc. Not only is this great during my tenure with a company, it is even more valuable personally because I am that much more marketable.

Managers always look at my constant efforts to be a better individual as a plus. They see me as someone who stands out. They see my efforts and much of this is what I call the difference between being an "A" player and a "B" player. Personal development never goes to waste. Be the one that takes the initiative to read the newest book, subscribes to your industry's journals, or joins a networking club that relates to your business. Take a goal setting seminar, or public speaking course. Do something new or different that will set you apart from your peers. With the Internet being available twenty four hours a day, seven days a week, the offerings are endless.

The question you should always be asking yourself is, "what is in my armamentarium?" If you wait for your boss to ask you to do something that enhances your development it is probably too late. We can all do more to be a better individual, employee, spouse or parent? Personal as well as professional development is your responsibility. You owe it to yourself and your company to become the best you can be. The investment in yourself is the best investment you will ever make.

*   *   *

Contribution by **Roshan Mahtani**
Director
Jewels and Time
Formerly: Senior Internal Auditor,
Royal Caribbean Cruise Lines;
Associate, KPMG

If you're content with sitting in your cubicle and doing your current job, this may not be the book for you. But then again, if you think your company will keep you around when you keep doing the same thing day-in and day-out, or if you are currently looking for a job and think you can relax once you've got it, you might need a reality check. Today more than ever, companies are going to find ways to make fewer people do more work. Companies need to figure out how to make more money and spend less. Companies we once thought were infallible are falling apart. Jobs we thought were bullet proof are being axed.

Now if you are wondering what you can do to make sure you have a paycheck coming in, let me answer you: get better. You must keep an eye on the market you are a part of and find out what new technologies or methodologies exist. It is up to you to find ways to provide more value to your society. I don't say, 'more value to your company' because sometimes companies fail and maybe there's nothing you can do about it, but if you are the most efficient, most productive, most connected person in your field, whatever it is, you will be in demand. But rest assured, just because you are the best today doesn't mean you will be the best tomorrow, so you have to continue to learn.

From my experience, when you are an employee of one of the "big four" accounting firms or a consulting firm it is not at all uncommon for your coworkers or even your managers to be "hired away" because an outside company (generally a client) desires their skill set. Clients will commonly drop hints that they would hire you or even outright tell you they want you to be a part of their team. Being on the receiving end of this is great. But what if you're already a part of that company that's hiring someone from a "big four" or a consulting firm? What does that tell you?

It's easy to take it personally. It's easy to surrender and let it happen. But it's best to look at the situation from an outsider's perspective and try to understand why. Generally, a company doesn't need consultants if they have the skills to achieve whatever task they set out to do in-house. They are after the skill set, and generally, these companies want the projects they set out to do, done yesterday. So if you want to keep moving (or by today's standards, simply stick around) you better not wait for your boss to tell you about a project and what it needs to get done. You need to be looking at the organization's problems and be thinking of ways to solve them. You also need to be looking at what you can be doing to obtain new skills and furthering your current skills. You cannot depend on your company to help you do this. If you do, you're simply asking them to hire it from outside firms, or worse yet, you may be asking them to get rid of you all together.

It's not hard to commit yourself to furthering your skills. Granted, it's not easy to maintain the discipline to keep at it. What's hard is figuring out, 'what's next'. At first you may want to learn the tools that will help you achieve more; simple training to help you use and create simple databases are a good start (in today's market, I already assume you are already an advanced user of spreadsheets and word processors). You may want to learn how to become better connected because who you know matters. Go out and read *How to Win Friends and Influence People* if you haven't already. You may even want to go out there and learn how to better manage your finances because you can focus more at work when you have a financial plan in place. All of these are great ways to start, but what becomes challenging is figuring out what's on the cutting edge. What can you learn to help an organization gain a competitive advantage? To do that I recommend continuously doing three things:

Make sure you know what's new in your profession. When graduates coming out of universities know a better way to do your job, you're in trouble. Joining your alumni group and seeing what classes they are offering in the Major related to your current profession is effective.

Become a content expert in your industry. This is different than knowing your profession; you may be a financial analyst, but if you work for a shipping company, you should be learning all about those ships. The simple application of your profession to this industry is not enough; you should be finding out ways to best apply those skills. Trade publications are a good way of doing this.

Keep an eye on the competition. Being original is great, but sometimes the competition can inspire you or simply botch the implementation of something you can do better. You will not only have to keep your eye on current events, you will have to work on becoming connected to people that know what's going on in the industry.

Whatever you do, don't merely be content with sitting there in your cubicle. There's no telling how long your current skills will be in demand, or worse yet, how long the company that houses your cubicle will be around.

*　　*　　*

Contribution by **Valerie W. Perlowitz**
Senior Vice President and Director, Corporate
Development
ATSC

The thought of self-development can conjure up a touchy-feely sensation that most people don't like. Think of transcendental meditation or falling backward into a group to show that you trust them not to let you fall. While this can be meaningful to some, it is not the way to grow professionally throughout your career. The other extreme are those who believe all they ever need to know is what they learned in college. While there are some rules that no matter how you try to change them, they are hard and fast, learning and self-development is key to how successful you will be in the future and can not be ignored.

So what is self-development and how do you go about doing it? Development is defined as the process of growing and expanding. Self-development then is the growth of personal attributes that will lead to success. You have many facets of yourself that need to be developed in order to be a well rounded individual. Your work life is only one piece of the pie and you certainly can not be dependent on a boss or organization to lay out a plan for you. While there may be some career guidance for the organization you work for (i.e. how you get promoted to the next level), you need to fully understand what you want out of your career and plan for that in everything you do. My motto is "keep the end in mind" for all decisions that you make. If you understand where you want to be at the end of your career, then it is easy to assess how the decisions you make about jobs you take on, career changes and even outside activities, will affect your end game.

What components do you need to focus on to develop yourself to be the most successful you can be? There are two sides—business and personal. On the business side, the obvious is gaining the skills necessary to do your current job well; however, what do you need to advance your career? One place to focus is the professional associations that serve your industry. Be sure to do your homework to determine which organizations best suit your industry and your career goals. Early on in my career, I joined a lot of organizations in order to get exposed to the community. What I did not do was determine which organization was best for me at that time in my career. I spent a lot of time going to meetings, but never achieved the full depth of experience had I done my homework first. I have been able to salvage that work later in my career. My business roles have changed and I have been able to leverage those folks to introduce me to their networks. This still does not make up for all the lost time I spent with organizations that did not assist my professional development. Once you determine where you want to be involved, quickly implement yourself into that organization.

Getting involved in these organizations from a networking perspective helps you to understand where your industry is heading and what you need to do to stay in front of it. More than just attending monthly meetings, a good way to develop your professional network is to get involved with committees in the organization. What you need to remember is that once you commit to a committee, you must carry through on that commitment. Make sure that you understand the time required by the committee; determine if you can commit to that amount of time, while still being able to perform your day-to-day activities at the highest level. There were many times when I participated in committees where people who were overextended would not be able to perform their activity in support of the organization. While this may not be mission critical, if you are on the program committee and you fail to obtain the speaker for that month, you have let your committee members, as well as the entire organization down.

Another way to leverage your time with the organization is to be conscious of what it takes to become a Board member. Generally, the more you participate and become well known, the more you will be asked to take on additional responsibilities, including a Board position. Many organizations have volunteer Boards where you can gain experience in a management setting outside of your work environment. Board experience will also expose you to some people that have been working in your industry longer than you. These people are good to know and one may turn out to be a mentor. Find multiple associations where you can spend your time and you will greatly assist your career opportunities.

Another business side of your development comes from continually learning. Attending seminars, webinars, and even reading trade magazines are good to understand the core of your business. You don't want to forget the other side of the business development is general reading of books about different aspects of where you want to take your career. For example, if you are a technical person and want to get into a management role, reading a book on managing effective teams can be one way to learn your next set of skills. Ideally if you could position yourself to take what you learn and apply to your daily activities by taking on a new assignment, you will be able to translate what you read into actionable activities. This can also open up the opportunity to get a mentor in this area to assist you in the development of that particular skill set. One way to find a mentor is through your trade association, as was discussed earlier. A good mentor will develop plans with you that will help guide you to your next level. A good mentor-protégé relationship is a two way street. Mentors take on protégés to give back some of the knowledge gained, but they too want to learn. Be sure to share your approaches as a give and take during your relationship.

On the personal side, what are the activities that you love to do outside of work? Are there organizations that coordinate those activities? There are organizations to join in order to keep you well-rounded. Successful people are multi-dimensional in their make-up, so it is important to feed all parts of your persona. The same approach will apply here as it did with the trade organizations. Commit yourself to the extent you can and always be looking at how this experience will assist in shaping your future.

Development is a very personal thing, but one that can not be put aside for another day. As you traverse down the career path, always keep the end in mind and be flexible to new opportunities that come your way. Taking a proactive approach to what happens to you and your career is paramount in your keys to success.

*   *   *

Assumption #3:
Be Managed or Mismanaged

Wow! This concept can be a real eye-opener for so many reasons. You go to work, and day in and day out you find that no matter how hard you try, you feel mentally exhausted. This is a clear sign that you are being mismanaged.

When a Talent goes to work, the Talent must leave work, just about every single day, on a high note. You may be working on a tough project, but if you go home on a high note after a hard day's work, you will feel GREAT! You will feel energized. You will feel that you've made a solid and valuable contribution to your organization by further honing your skills.

However, when you go home feeling tired, beaten up, exhausted, etc., or if the night before work the next morning seems like a prolonging death sentence, then this is a red flag. And if you let this go on for too much longer, I suspect you will experience health issues. This is one thing I really did not want to learn from experience, but I hope that you are clever enough to learn from my experience.

If fact, we are going to be so bold as to suggest that if you are experiencing any type of health issues today, you should double check your work as the source. You might be thinking, well, how can the rash on my elbow be caused by my job? Think again! You are being mismanaged and this is causing undo stress on your body.

When I say mismanaged, I mean specifically that your boss is unable to understand your working style or your strengths and repeatedly assigns you to projects in neither areas where you excel nor where you have an interest. We are all different with our own likes and dislikes; however, when we are continuously assigned to projects and tasks that we find nothing short of drudgery, we are being mismanaged.

Being mismanaged is a choice. If you feel that you are being mismanaged, take back your control and don't stand for it another second! Allow me introduce you to . . .

Contribution by **Aja Edmond**
Business Development and Marketing Associate
Global Financial Services Firm

You are only mismanaged if you allow yourself to be. Regardless of who your manager is, or his/her ability (or inability) to commit to your professional development. You are ultimately responsible for establishing clear career goals and then maximizing your role and your success at your firm to the best of your own ability so that you can meet those goals. Technically, you are your own manager.

When I joined my current organization I had a different set of professional interests and goals than my peers. I saw this role as an opportunity to build a broad set of skills that would help me become competitive for an MBA program and prepare me for my long-term career aspirations in brand and strategic management. In contrast, many of my peers' career goals were more closely aligned with the firm; they were committed to the investment management industry and hoped to remain with and rise up the ranks of the organization. The big problem I had to overcome was how to stay true to my interests while still adding value to my firm. After about six months into my new role, I feared that unless I became more active in managing my own experience at this firm, I would be unhappy and at a significant disadvantage competitively (relative to my peers). I realized that I needed to do two things to overcome this problem.

First, I needed to closely align myself with individuals who were dedicated to nurturing talent and bringing out the best in people. In other words, I immediately recognized the need to be "properly managed" so that I could not only thrive in my current role but also get the skills and experiences I deemed relevant to my future career plans. When a colleague in my group left the firm to pursue other opportunities, I asked to support his old manager. I had observed this manager and how he acted with junior associates in our group, including my old colleague. I felt that this manager would not only respect and appreciate my distinct skills and interests but would also push me to excel by capitalizing on my unique traits. This manager was actively involved in my professional development and I largely credit him for many of my achievements at this firm. At the very beginning, I communicated to him my skills, strengths, weaknesses, professional interests and career goals. Because I was honest and upfront and kept an open dialogue with him, he was able to open up doors for me to showcase my talent. This manager trusted me to solve problems for clients in my own particular way, which subsequently, resulted in my contributions being directly responsible for significant business deals. I took the initiative to identify someone who could efficiently and effectively manage me, and it paid off.

Second, I needed to seek additional opportunities inside and outside of my current role to gain greater exposure to projects that would round out my skill set, provide me with different types of challenges and allow me to serve the firm in a greater capacity. A major component of "managing my own experience" was to ensure that what I lacked in the basic job description of my current role, I made up for in other areas. At my current organization I became actively involved in a number of employee networking groups and, after some time, ended up holding leadership positions within these groups. The risk of me becoming unmotivated in my current role was high, given that I had plans to leave the firm to pursue higher education and a career within a different industry. These outside leadership positions kept me energized and excited because they allowed me to accomplish my dual goals of being committed to the success of the firm while subsequently preparing for my future after I left the firm.

Moreover, these extracurricular activities prepared me to take on the significant challenge of becoming a leader amongst my peers. I was appointed to act as liaison between my peers and our senior management team; establish our program's yearly business plan; and oversee the professional development, training and recruiting of my peers. I was able to face this new set of challenges within my role by leveraging the skills I developed from my involvement in extracurricular activities. Because I put the time and effort into managing myself, I ended up overseeing situations where I was managing other people, projects and events within the firm.

One of the most interesting things I have learned about the fine line between being managed or mismanaged is that your manager is not responsible for your professional development, progression in your role and your overall career success. In fact, he/she can only properly manage you unless you have a clear sense of what you want to achieve and communicate those goals to them. From my personal experience, despite having a good or bad manager, the individuals who take matters into their own hands and show enthusiasm about their own professional development are the ones who ultimately succeed.

*   *   *

Contribution by **Chris Martines**
Financial and Operational Senior Auditor
Circuit City

I once took a position at a company based solely on the interview and conversation that I had with the person who would become my new manager. My previous employer had a string of poor managers, directors and Vice Presidents that made me believe that my responsibilities should only include the enhancement of that company and the advancement of those individuals, but nothing for myself. Everything my manager presented in the interview was the opposite; he cared about the work rather then kissing up the corporate ladder, wanted his team to succeed through challenging tasks that would help advance my skills as well as his own career, and was overtly a genuine individual. He left our company after two months to take a position with our direct competitor.

I was surprised when my manager left the company suddenly, but the signs had been there the two months prior because, unfortunately, most of what he had told me in the interview wasn't true. Sure, unlike my previous employers, he was a good person to have a conversation with, but was poor when it came to managing a team. He cared more about his own growth, taking all the assignments that were challenging for himself and giving very little work to the team. There were days when I spent little to no time doing actual work. I've always had trouble hiding my boredom at work, usually jumping around the office hoping to find work because there are only so many articles to read on CNN and ESPN. One day, I asked another associate on the team if she needed help or had some work that I could take off her hands. She handed me a couple of files to analyze and said, "here, these should only take half the day but you can make yourself look busy with them for two days." This was the culture that the manager had created.

That manager taught me an important lesson, rely on yourself before others. Management, like motivation, should come from within. I understand that this may sound like a fortune cookie or one of those ridiculous motivational posters you see in an employee's cubicle, but it's the truth. If you want strong management, which in essence is direction and purpose for your work, you need to take it upon yourself to do it because there are very few others that will take the time to do so. I was at that company for two months, and I could barely tell you how our financial systems worked; however, I could break down the top 10 defenses in the NFL better than John Madden. I then took it upon myself to learn how the audit department and the company operated. I read previous audit reports and all supporting documentation including planning memos, scope memo, audit programs, etc. I did everything I could to help myself make an impact in the department rather then waiting for somebody to hand me a challenging task.

Eventually there was a reorganization that placed my team with a new manager and a director who had been with the company for years. On the first day of the reorganization, the director called me into his office and told me that he was impressed with my work and progress over the past couple months. He bluntly told me that after my first two months he questioned whether I would last with the company because, under my previous manager, he saw no passion, direction, or motivation. He wasn't a fool, he knew that my past manager cared more about himself than his team and promised that attitude would change under his direction, but he wanted to see employees change their attitude first. Because I had taken it upon myself to learn the audit department, understand the company, and essentially find myself work, I impressed the director more than other team members who were satisfied with writing emails all day.

I've had managers that were inconsiderate, others that were condescending or abrasive, and one that took credit for my work, despite my objections to my director. Overall, it took me six years, three companies, and nine managers to find my first good manager. After a year of working with him, the company was liquidated. But, if I hadn't learned to manage and motivate myself, I would have been let go a year before that.

* * *

Contribution by **Jacqueline L. Benitez**
Compensation Analyst
Trustmark

In my previous role with an IT/Finance company, I became involved with the recruiting function. When the individual who did our recruiting left the company, she left me in the midst of searching for someone to fill an entry-level accountant position.

The job was already posted on the job boards and a recruiting company had already been identified to assist us with the search as well.

As I reviewed the requirements for the role and the resumes that we had received, I started to wonder why the intern who had been in that department for the last two years was not offered this role.

I sought out the advice of my manager thinking there was a reason for this decision. She was unaware of anything and we decided we would investigate this a little more. Our thinking was why should we incur expenses on recruiting and training when we already had someone internal who knew the business, the people, the systems, and the processes?

I had a conversation with the intern and it went something like this:

Jackie: Have you seen the accountant position that we have open?

[name]: Yes

Jackie: Are you interested in the role? Are you interested in staying with the company?

[name]: Yes, but I'm not done with school and will finish in May. Yes, I'm interested in staying with the company.

Jackie: Why haven't you expressed an interest?

[name]: Well, my manager hasn't said anything or offered me the position. I'm also not done with school; I didn't think they would hire me for the position since I cannot work full-time right now. It will be another three months.

Jackie: Ok, well, if you are interested, I'd like to talk with your manager about your interest in the role.

[name]: Yeah, that would be great!

The conversation with the accounting manager went something like this:

Jackie: Have we thought about offering this role to [name]?

Accounting Manager: Oh, that hadn't come up.

Jackie: Is [name] performing satisfactorily?

Accounting Manager: Yes, he has been with us for the last two years and has done a good job. I have not had any issues.

Jackie: I guess I'm trying to understand why we wouldn't have offered the position to him.

Accounting Manager: Well, I was waiting for him to express an interest.

Jackie: I did ask him and he is interested; however, his concern was whether we could wait for him to go full-time until he finishes school.

Accounting Manager: Yes, of course we can wait. He is already helping me with a lot of things that he would be responsible for anyway.

[name] was hired and to date is still a full-time employee of the organization.

*   *   *

Contribution by **Fran Nahabedian**
Director—Business Development
Netconcepts, LLC

Overachieving is a good thing . . . but you must manage it.

I have always been an overachiever at work. This mostly comes from not finishing college and feeling like I had to do more than everyone else. Now, don't get me wrong . . . I love my work and I'm passionate about success, and that has served me pretty well. I've had, and am still having, an amazing career.

But, being an overachiever is a mindset and personality trait that can push you into circumstances where, if not properly managed, can lead to no-win situations. I can cite a number of times where my overachieving nature led me to great rewards, promotions, and salary increases. But it's the no-win situations that can be a downward spiral resulting in insomnia, headaches, depression, and in my case, cancer.

For a multitude of reasons, including geography, salary, and sincere desire to stay in my chosen line of work, I accepted a position at a company with very poor leadership. As a family-owned business, it grew from an entrepreneurial spirit to a size where the culture was holding the company back from further growth. After six months on the job, and a new COO was hired, the inevitable reduction in force happened. My position, however, was considered the "new company direction," and my job was saved.

Well, in the new and leaner company, I was asked to lead a team of people that were all good employees, but didn't have a place yet within the new organization. The overachiever in me said "Sure, I can do this and we'll build something to support whatever the organization needs." The reality was that finding opportunities for these employees to shine was not an easy task. Their skills were designed for the former organization and, for more than a year, I tried to fit them in somewhere both individually and collectively. Each review I had with my boss was great, but I knew that without some direction and focus from above, this department of misfits was going south quickly.

What I saw and experienced during that time was life-changing. The morale of the group declined dramatically over time. Each success was celebrated with two steps backward. My overachiever side took complete ownership for the problems; I tried very hard to fix them without any support or direction from HR or my management. I saw the signs but did not have the authority to force an issue.

I was both mismanaging my team, and being mismanaged . . . a no-win situation. As things grew worse, sick time increased and my own health suffered to the point where I was diagnosed with breast cancer.

During my illness and recovery, I learned that the majority of cancer patients do not have a history of cancer in their families. I certainly did not; however, I learned that stress can be directly linked to the disease.

In the end, my overachieving and taking ownership for the departmental problems led to me leaving the company, which I can say now was the best thing that could have happened to me. I can also report that my cancer is more than five years in remission. After careful selection, I found a great fit for my next career move.

Bottom line: Be sure that you are enjoying your work and that your leadership has a focus and direction for you. If they don't have one, figure one out for yourself and talk to your boss about it. If your boss can't articulate a direction then you may want to consider looking elsewhere. You are responsible for managing your work life and your health.

*   *   *

Contribution by **Steven Young**
Operations Project Consultant
Bank of America

Early in my career, I worked for a major telecommunications company in Chicago, IL. I became friends with a coworker, Bob Augusta. Bob and I worked for a manager named Rich Summers. Rich was the type of manager who wanted to make sure his employees were able to learn, grow, and contribute to the group. He made the daily work environment a place to look forward to. In return, if Rich ever needed something from Bob or me, we would go out of our way to make sure we did it for him.

I worked for Rich for about two and a half years before I decided it was time to make a move. I was fortunate to find a management position within the company, but Bob decided to stay behind. He loved the current environment and couldn't imagine working for anyone besides Rich. Bob was always the first to arrive in the morning and enjoyed talking about work with anyone. Little did anyone know what was about to happen next.

Within six months after I moved into my management position, we found out the work my previous group performed was moving to a Indianapolis, IN. Rich and Bob had to make a decision to either move to the new city, stay in Chicago and hope to find a new position within the company, or take a severance and leave the company entirely. Rich was close to retirement so he decided to take the severance. Bob was younger; he needed to work but he didn't want to move to a new city so he moved to a new position within the company. He was nervous but he went into the new position with a positive attitude.

Two months went by and I noticed I hadn't heard from Bob for several weeks. I called his department to check on him, but I was told he hadn't been in the office in a week. Bob wasn't the type to miss work, so I called his home phone and he answered. Bob and I talked for a while and he began to share with me the reason he was at home.

Bob was going through a major change of management styles. Bob described his new manager as the complete opposite of Rich. The new environment wasn't friendly, so he didn't feel comfortable there. He didn't feel as though his ideas were well received, and didn't feel he was being given the opportunity to learn or grow in his new position. In turn, Bob started showing up late for work, then not showing up for work at all and becoming sick when his weekend away from work was almost over.

I decided to help Bob by motivating him and encouraging him to make the most of his current situation while taking action to change the situation as soon as possible. I did this by helping him update his resume to show his skills and accomplishments. Also, because the position I took was a management position, I could see job openings that Bob wasn't able to see. I began sending him jobs that fit his skill set and his desires. Now, armed with a plan, Bob was able to look past some of the issues in the office because he knew it was only temporary. Bob knew a bad management style would not hold him back from the things he desired most. He had learned a valuable lesson.

*   *   *

Contribution by **Andrew Broderick**
Senior Java Web Developer
Thomson Reuters

I could write an entire book on this subject, as it has become very close to my heart. Management, and mismanagement, have defined my experience of being a corporate professional.

Having worked as a senior programmer and web developer at over a dozen companies in the US and three companies in the UK, I can categorically say this with every ounce of conviction in me: **A non-toxic, emotional environment is not just the most important benefit of working at a particular company, it is also the second, third, and fourth most important.**

Let's start at the beginning of my career. I had previously interned at a government-run physics laboratory in the UK. It was an extension of academia, and as such was a very laid-back environment. I then graduated summa cum laude with a Bachelor's degree in Computer Science, and was about to enter the world of commercial software development.

Company # 1: I landed at a small custom software development company, in the days just before the Internet blazed a trail through our collective worlds and redefined the way we live. The work was reasonably challenging and enjoyable. But the problem was, I could never get enough done for them. My performance reviews always said that my throughput of getting software written was not fast enough. I was complimented on the quality of my work, in fact, it was the best of anyone on the team, but that didn't seem to matter. All they could see was what their narrow definition of a good employee allowed them to see. They didn't see all that I have to offer as a person. Needless to say, that job did not end well.

Company # 2: In the next job, I was again hired to do programming. However, they soon found that I had a talent for technical writing. At first, this was an avenue to some much-needed success and recognition. But, a year went by and I was still doing writing. I love programming, not writing user manuals. Of course adaptability is key and professionals should adapt to whatever their role entails, but in this case a niche became a rut. What is the difference between a rut and a grave? The size!

Tensions mounted over time, as I was kept from doing what I love (or even splitting my time between writing and programming). I have much to offer in both departments, but this particular manager's toxic personality would not allow him to see the whole person that I am and tap into my unique strengths and gifts.

This wore thin on my soul, and I began a focused plan to build new software development skills, and find a better position. After six months of learning new technologies, I began to look again. I soon found my next job, and this time the story was very different.

Company #3: I was given a senior development role, with a wide range of creative latitude, and lots of interesting problems to solve. I was finally in programmer paradise! However, that wasn't the end of it. I was also recognized and appreciated: Regular compliments on my work, small things like beer on Fridays, and bigger things like company-sponsored overnight Christmas parties where they would rent out a section of a hotel, and even bigger things, like cash bonuses for meeting particular goals. All of this went towards making me feel valued, important, and integral to the organization. Notice I didn't say integral to the goals of the organization? That's right—to an employee, the main emotional need is to belong, not meet goals. Is it any wonder that the word 'organization' is so close to the word 'organism'? People need to feel that they are part of a family. The warmth is infectious, and is shared among peers. Once that happens, you will never have trouble getting people to be productive.

So, how was this achieved? What book, program or seminar did the boss and founder of this company read to bring this about? He didn't. He knew it instinctively, because it was an extension of who he was as a person. (Organizations usually take on the personalities of their founders). He was a warm, genuine, giving person. He had business goals alright—big goals, many of which had already been achieved even though the company was still in its mid-growth phase. But, he worked to live, rather than living to work.

As a result of his being free on the inside, he was able to see the full spectrum of what others had to offer, both in terms of their skills and in terms of their personalities. He put equal, if not even greater, emphasis on a person's cheeriness, genuineness, and ability to relate to the rest of the team than he did on skills. This is most important, because skills can be learned; warmth and the ability to connect cannot.

When many people connect, on a personal as well as a professional level, the whole is greater than the sum of its parts and the joy of being part of such an environment cannot be overstated. This is just as true of churches, families, clubs, and just about any other gathering of human beings you can name. We are born with an innate need for connection.

So, if there is a secret sauce recipe for good management, this is it: foster a team of genuine warmth, caring and connection, and all else will follow.

The basic tension in business, as in life, is the old conundrum of a 'human being' versus a 'human doing'. If a person only finds their value in performance and is driven on the inside, she will expect the same of her employees. The environment will feel harsh, and people will feel timid and on edge around her. The climate then becomes one of fear, and people perform only because they fear the consequences (stated or not) of not performing. This kind of climate becomes a perfect breeding ground for office politics, favors for favors, and backstabbing in order to climb the ladder. Once these take root, the emotional negativity and oppressiveness of the environment is complete. The best talent will then leave.

Conversely, if she is free to "be," i.e. she knows she is valuable just because she is, she will be able to express the warmth and freedom this brings to her inner being in the workplace. Everyone around her will pick up on it, and people will be affirmed and appreciated. Knowing they are appreciated just for being there, people will then give their very best, just because they want to. People want to build, achieve, and impress. It's built into our nature. We just need to plant in fertile soil, so to speak. In a healthy emotional environment, people achieve because the good manager recognizes their strengths and sees what makes them tick as people. When people feel recognized and affirmed for who they are, good performance is recognized regularly, and a role that fits who they are, there is no limit to what people can achieve.

*　　*　　*

Contribution by **Maritiza (Tesa) Anderson**
Marketing Analyst
County of Los Angeles Department of Parks and Recreation

One of my first jobs was with one of the largest sports conglomerate in the world. I was hired as a Public Relations Assistant. The organization was a well oiled machine, where everyone was empowered and expected to excel in their respective roles. My manager could be defined as a person who allowed his employees to self actualize within their job description. He had been a staple within the company for over 30 years. Upon being hired, he expressed his desire for me was to grow, excel and assume greater responsibilities.

As a successful and well respected manager, I recognized that it would be in my best interest professionally, to emulate his success strategies and business acumen. I remembered everyone's name, their interests and subtleties of their behavior. What an effective tool! Before long, I was rotating to various departments and gaining exposure and competency. My manager noticed my enthusiasm and my ability to thrive in short period of time.

After my first year of employment, my manager asked me to train a new hire. Although I wasn't sure I was prepared, my manager had complete confidence in me. While training the new hire, I provided him an overview of the organization, his role, responsibilities and what was expected of him. He thrived.

Unbeknownst to me, this individual had relationships with powerful people in sports television. While having lunch one day, he inquired about my career goals. I expressed to him that I had aspirations to work in television production. Little did I know, his father was a sports legend and one of the most highly regarded sports commentators in the industry.

Upon meeting his father, I was humbled and in awe. He was genuine and down-to-earth. He thanked me for the inordinate amount of support and kindness that I had shown his son. I had no idea that my accomplishments impressed him to the point, that he made a call of my behalf to the Vice President of Sports Production for a major network and secured a three month assignment for me to work at the Olympics. I was flabbergasted and confused because I already had a position with an organization that provided growth opportunities.

When I returned to the office, my manager had already been briefed on the opportunity that had been presented to me. He supportively said, "your old job will be waiting for you when your assignment ends." I was speechless. I went on to have a successful career in sports and entertainment television.

I recognize how good managers can inspire employees to thrive and succeed even if it means they move on to other organizations.

*   *   *

Contribution by **Steve Callisher**
Director of Human Resources
TDK

My first experience working for a Japanese company was a very enlightening one. I learned several things, developed a new perspective on corporate culture and talent management, and discovered that there are good and bad bosses in different cultures and that language differences turn out to be, for the most part a non-factor (though culture differences can be critical).

The experience at the company taught me the importance of developing relationships and establishing trust before evaluating details of a business issue and proposals, and that group decision making, though often slow and cumbersome, can lead to deeper analysis and more likelihood of acceptance of the final decision. As Americans we have grown accustomed to entering into business relationships which are often quite superficial and we often instead rely on our attorneys to then protect our interests. In contrast, a Japanese businessman will not contemplate the details of a proposal unless time was previously spent establishing a relationship and developing a feeling of trust.

I had four bosses during my seven year stint with the best one being the first who had only limited English speaking capability while the last boss, who was fully bilingual, proved to be the worst boss. My first boss believed in my capabilities in playing a key role in acquiring talent and despite often difficult and challenging circumstances also empowered me to take the appropriate actions to assure that we did everything within reason to retain and develop all the critical within our organization. When it came to our American staff, my role was the "keeper of the culture" to make sure that all our organizational activities would preserve those values that had lead to our success. My boss would show confidence in my abilities, support me in my role and provide me with rewards and recognition commensurate with my results. He understood that as an American with strong Human

Resources capabilities, I'd be in the best position to be sensitive to the needs of our employees, advise managers on critical job satisfaction concerns, and resolve conflicts.

In contrast, my last Japanese boss, with his strong command of the English language, would overestimate his understanding of the American culture and what it took to manage effectively. He believed he already knew all the answers and I believe therefore downplayed my role as a significant advisor who really understood the pulse of the organization. As a result he made decisions which diminished my role in talent acquisition and handcuffed me from taking certain actions which would have served to enhance employee development and improve moral and employee retention. Ultimately he used an economic downturn as an excuse to eliminate my position. I left the organization and not long after though several others left on there own.

*   *   *

Contribution by **Jean Kim**
Business Intelligence Analyst
Fortune® 100 Insurance Company

When you are being managed properly, you will thrive at work. When you are being mismanaged you will see a pattern of lack of energy, feeling unmotivated, and fatigued. Over time, you may even develop health related issues. Learn to see the signs because your goal should always be to thrive in your role.

There are subtle differences between being a great manager and being a great leader. Many times the same person cannot be a strategic thought partner and course corrector. If you are lucky enough, you get to work for someone who possesses both sets of qualities. I had stepped away from the management role to focus on my family and school. I joined a Fortune 100 company working in the technology enterprise portfolio management office (ePMO). At the time, the concept of an ePMO in technology was relatively new which resulted in wide shifts in direction and sudden changes in leadership. I came in with a unique perspective; I understood what it felt like to manage and to be managed.

For the first two years, I was able to work under a relatively new manager. It was a little bumpy at the start but as an employee I always felt supported, protected, heard, and directed. He took the time to get to know his staff, understand their strengths, help them get training to boost their strengths and ultimately position them, either within his team or out, into roles that benefited the person and benefited the company. His motivation was centered on building talent: to better each employee and benefit the company (even if it meant losing an employee to another group). All this happened despite changing corporate priorities and challenging client situations. Our team collaborated with leadership on defining our role, defining our engagement with clients, and defining the strategic roadmap for the division. Communication was free-flowing from top down to bottom up. It was a safe environment and I was thriving. It was exciting to go to work.

At this point, our team merged with another under a new leader. I've been through this type of transition many times before (as a manager and employee) and it always takes time to feel comfortable. However, I did not expect that nearly two years later I would still be as unmotivated as I was during transition. Our new leadership operated in a much different manner. It was clear that we were operating without any vision or mission. Each leg of the division did what was in their best interest, not understanding impacts to the rest of the division. We were a divided house. Where I had felt supported before, I felt abandoned. Where I could rely on my leadership to point me in the right direction before, I felt isolated.

Typical signs of depression started hitting, which for me manifests itself as midnight snacking, sleeplessness, and weight gain. The work had not changed and the team was the same, what was the variable? I was still well respected and became the lead analyst. Soon enough, I personally noticed a decline in the quality of my work. My clients began expressing concern to me directly; they had noticed a shift in my behaviors and output. As the lead analyst, I was also hearing from other clients expressing their concern and frustration with the sudden shift. Work became a burden. The job became increasingly frustrating. Collaboration started falling apart. And, as the lead, everyone (from the top and bottom) looked to me to fix it. As a group, we decided to function even tighter as a unit, to work around leadership wherever possible. As the lead analyst, we put together improvement plans with leadership once we identified the support gaps the team felt. Making all this work requires strong participation and tact on all sides.

I'd like to say that everything worked out for the best; but, in this situation it did not. Hindsight is 20/20 and I now know that despite all the other changes we faced, the team was simply not thriving under this new leadership style. Ultimately, about half of the team switched departments on their own accord, including myself. I am not suggesting that if you do not like your manager, quit right away. I am suggesting recognize when your job becomes unbearable and take the necessary actions to make it better. Try to partner with your current manager to make solid changes and give it some time. You might have to take the risk of effectively communicating what the problems are and be prepared to give suggestions for improvement. If things do not improve for you, it may make sense to look for that next opportunity. As a manager, recognize these signs in your staff. Take the time to work with those who are struggling, understand their strengths and their personal goals. Position your people to be successful whether in your team or out. Be the connector. If you are grooming the new crop of leaders for the organization, it is much better received than having a large, out of control, organization. Talents will seek you out rather than you seeking talents.

* * *

Contribution by **Michelle Clauss, SPHR**
Former Senior HR Business Partner
Financial Services Industry

I worked for a major financial institution in the Chicago area for 10 years. When I started with the company, I worked for a manager who created an environment where her team was energized, motivated, and empowered. We had team spirit, open communication, and were encouraged to take risks, and continually challenge ourselves. During those years that I reported to her, I was promoted a number of times, and thoroughly enjoyed working there. I continued to thrive under her leadership, and I actually looked forward to coming to work everyday. I was one of those lucky ones that truly loved their job and their co-workers.

There was a change in management during the last nine months that I was employed there. Our new senior manager was creative and strategic, yet she was not an effective manager. She lacked integrity, didn't promote a collaborative work climate, and withheld information. As much as I tried to be positive, I found myself turning into someone that I wasn't. I was no longer confident in my abilities, I lacked energy and enthusiasm, and my self-esteem was being shattered. On Sunday nights, I began to dread the thought of going to work the next morning. I felt my team slowly drifting away from me.

This went on for about two months, until I realized that I had to do something to ensure that my team and I were going to be challenged and motivated for the next few months (our jobs were being eliminated within the next three to four months). I decided to accept responsibility for my reactions to her behavior and then took the initiative to make some changes. I realized my team was depending on me to be supportive, create positive energy, and to be upbeat. I couldn't let them down.

I began to laugh more, smile more, and I took the extra time to listen to their concerns. I convinced them to further their training and education in order to be more valuable to an employer. They began to come to me for advice and wisdom, which is something they had been doing prior to the management changes. To enhance my self-esteem, I signed up for business related seminars, updated my resume, and begin to network with other professionals.

I was determined to leave on a positive note, not just for my own self-respect, but also for my team. If I could go out with integrity and class, then they could learn something from my experience.

*   *   *

Contribution by **Renee Rhoades**
IT Consultant
Financial Services Industry

A few years ago I was recruited by a large, international financial services company and relocated to a new state. I was very excited to start my new role at the new company. The organization seemed well-organized and focused on their goals. My team welcomed me with open arms. All my fellow employees seemed to be very intelligent, motivated, and capable of accomplishing just about anything. And best of all, my manager was great with people. I worked long and hard because I wanted to, not because I was required to. I believed in what I was doing and, from what I was hearing back from others, I was adding value. I felt like I had the ability to rise in this new organization.

And then the company announced reorganization to my division and I was moved to another building in a different part of the city and was now reporting to a new manager. I had long ago learned that meeting a new situation with a positive attitude was always the way to influence one's path. So, with a smile on my face, I packed my cube, and faced the new role head on.

At first, things seemed fine. The new manager and my one new co-worker seemed happy to welcome me aboard. The first indications that something was not right occurred when I started to learn of new assignments through the co-worker rather than my manager. When I questioned the situation my co-worker explained that she and the manager were best friends outside of the company so sometimes they discussed work during their extra-curricular activities. I wasn't really comfortable with this but, again, I clung to my positive attitude and agreed to chalk this up to simply a different culture with the new team to which I would need to adjust.

But things continued to get worse. My co-worker was routinely not effectively managing her time which was requiring me to work longer and longer hours each week to cover the slack. (Our manager held us jointly responsible for the completion and quality of all the work in our area.)

Over time, my level of general discomfort with my work environment continued to increase. I would sit in my car in the parking lot for 20-30 minutes each morning avoiding entering the building. Once I was in the office, I was constantly edgy and unsettled. Things with my manager and co-worker were so unpredictable that I was also becoming paranoid.

By that time I was no longer taking care of myself. I was eating poorly, living primarily on drive-thru. I was working well over 60 hours a week to cover my responsibilities as well as those not handled by my co-worker. I was getting hardly any sleep because of the long hours and the mental exhaustion associated with the dysfunctional situation. That was causing me to grow increasingly more and more resentful toward not only my manager and co-worker but other employees and the company as well. My developmental aspirations changed from that of continued advancement and growing responsibilities into simply escaping the situation. I was starting to use more and more sick time and personal time just to avoid spending another 10-12 hours a day in the truly toxic situation. And my normally bubbly, vivacious personality turned into one of anger and sullenness. And worst of all, I was losing my confidence in my abilities.

Again, being a positive person by nature, I tried everything to make my manager and co-worker happy. I was convinced that if I just worked harder or smarter I could ultimately make the manager happy and I could again thrive in the organization and feel that sense of accomplishment that had been missing for so long. I tried speaking with the manager one-on-one, speaking with the co-worker one-on-one, and offered to teach the co-worker how I managed my own time. I even went so far as to escalate the situation to upper management and eventually HR. But sadly, nothing worked. After all that, I finally had the realization I could not make the manager a better manager. The only thing I could control was my own actions. I finally accepted that for whatever reason—culture, personal style, communication issues, etc.—this manager and I were just not right for each other. The only real solution to the situation for all involved was a change. Unfortunately, the company had a hiring freeze on at the time and they were not backfilling open positions so the internal posting process was not an option. So, after a great deal of soul searching, I chose to leave the company and I've never regretted it. Looking back, it was the best thing I've ever done personally and professionally.

*   *   *

Contribution by **Ronald V. Bryant (Ron)**
Former Principal and Account Executive
Hewitt Associates

Management "happens" to all of us, but in my experience, it is largely in our control to make that management beneficial to us and our organizations. I've had many managers in my 26 years at Hewitt Associates, and I've always felt it was my responsibility to help them be successful in managing me.

For most of my years at Hewitt, I thrived because I had managers who understood me and how to manage me for maximum effectiveness. What did those successful managers know about me? They knew that while I wanted to be well-aligned to the objectives of my teams and to the goals of the organization, I also wanted room to be creative in my job for the purpose of making everyone around me more successful. They knew that I could be trusted with the big things (like leading some of our largest client accounts) and the little things (completing company required reports in a timely manner). They knew I was a team player and a leader.

While my managers would have learned these things about me over time, I didn't sit back and wait for that to happen. Instead, I actively communicated what I needed from my managers in order to thrive, and then I made sure that I backed that up with actions that allowed them to manage me as I needed to be managed. For example, I made sure they were always well-informed about the work I was doing, giving them more information than I thought they needed, and then repeatedly asking them how I could better tailor the volume and type of information for their management needs. I took this responsibility my whole career, even as I reached senior levels in the organization where employees often want less management.

Sometimes working with my manger in this way led to questions that would not have been asked had I not been so proactive, and sometimes those questions created additional work for me. But in the end, I usually felt those questions aided in my development as a consultant, and they helped my manager be an integral part of my team, resulting in better results and higher degrees of trust.

What did I avoid by actively managing how I was managed?—micro-management. This is a common form of mismanagement, and one that—when I did experience it during my career—significantly hurt my motivation for accomplishing my goals. It made me feel like I wasn't trusted and it put me in a box that didn't allow me to give my best to the firm. Instead, I found myself paying attention to the wrong things. For example, I began wondering why I had to do certain activities that appeared to me to be adding no value to the firm, or working with my manager to get back to a management approach that would allow me to exceed expectations. Of course, I complied with all requests from these managers, no matter how I felt about the work required. Only then did I have a solid foundation from which to try and change those management elements that I didn't find beneficial to accomplishing our collective goals.

I want to briefly touch on another form of mismanagement that you can avoid by working with your manager: under-management. I never experienced under-management myself, but I've certainly seen it happen. I've watched managers who are somewhat disengaged from the work activities of an employee during performance review time with surprising messages, leaving the employee confused and lacking trust in their manager. I have helped many employees work though these situations. It takes a lot of work to make the manager/employee relationship work again and often it doesn't.

I believe most of your managers want to be good managers. Don't leave it all up to them. Give them the help they need to be a successful manager of you.

*   *   *

Contribution by **Sean Lee**
Consultant
Former Vice President, Finance Controllership
American Express

Toward the end of my first career with American Express, after about 10 years with the organization, I was given the opportunity to take on a new role as Vice President in the Finance Controllership. My motivation to take on this role included the money and title, that I would be only 3 levels below the CEO of the company, and that I so desperately wanted to work for my pending leader; he appeared to me to be a prime time player and one that I felt had my best interests in mind.

After three years as a Director in the International Organization and a year of solid performance, taking direction from, we'll call him GC, I was basically no longer being challenged; yet, He was probably the greatest leader, mentor, and coach I have ever had. I had been smart and lucky enough to hire the best talented people and was now in a position to let the group run itself. Don't get me wrong, there was plenty to do and more business to bring in, but I felt comfortable that the other leaders in the group were ready to move on and up, so we promoted one of my managers into the Director position as I transitioned into my new role. One of the many things that I attribute to our success was to a set of management techniques, some brought over from our European office that we used frequently to ensure we had our finger on the pulse of the group. Some of these were "out of the book", like Myers-Briggs and a number of other behavioral tests; thus, we all knew where we stood with each other.

One of the techniques that I really enjoyed was something we called, "Start, Stop, Continue." This allowed my team to anonymously provide feedback to me and to receive it themselves from their direct reports. This exercise basically asked my direct reports to include things they wanted me to start doing, things I should stop doing, and things I should continue doing. The key for me was that after some difficult conversations with GC about my leadership style in the first year of this position, I learned, finally, to accept constructive criticism and professional feedback. This was a difficult journey at best, but I finally got it and in doing so, my team prospered, my leaders prospered, and I prospered. The secret here, for me at least, was that my boss, GC, was never afraid to call it like he saw it; regardless of my shortcomings, he rewarded me and made sure I understood it was okay to make mistakes, as long as I learned from them. Cliché, I know, but it had a profound effect on me then and will for the rest of my life. At this point, GC's management style and the style I applied to my group, gave me a strong sense of worth, internal confidence, and feelings of accomplishment. I was at an all time high in my career and there was no where else to go but up.

It was now time for me to move into a new role. The ball got rolling a few months earlier … first my new SVP was a customer of the International group and because of our success, we were able to provide his organization with a world class set of products that opened the door to bigger and better solutions. I was invited to a meeting that was "VP Only" to present to the Finance organization and the CFO at the time. The Canadian LFO (Local Financial Officer) went before me and was one of the best presenters I had ever seen, which made for a tough act to follow. I was nervous as you can imagine, but was prepared. Frankly, I knocked them dead. Our presentation and ideas went over so well, that the SVP later said something to me about my "New VP title" hinting that I had done a good job and was on my way up. Well, ultimately, things never move as quickly as you would like them to, but eventually he was asked to create a new organization reporting directly to the Company's new CFO and brought me on day one.

At this point, my new SVP managed me well, playing to my strong suits and equally stroking my ego. He provided me with everything I needed; money, budget, resources and the collaboration was never better, he involved me in all decisions, making sure that I always felt like the decisions "we" made, were "my" idea. He let me create a technology roadmap for the organization as a whole, build a team three-times the size of my previous one, and let me surround myself with experts. Things could not have been better. Along the way, however, there were hints of things to come that I should have picked up on.

I probably noticed his quirks, thinking back, but disregarded them because we had so much work to do. For instance, he would call me at all hours seven days a week. At first I thought, "Wow, he really values my input and needs me involved for every decision" and he also seemed to take an interest in me as a friend, creating a more personal relationship between us which I valued. His explanation was that he wanted to make sure we were always on the same page, which I agreed with. Additionally, and just as frustrating, whenever he asked for me to create a presentation or material for him on what we were doing, every single first, second, and third version was scrapped and started again. He made me believe that it was me, not understanding what he wanted, because he was being perfectly clear; however, in reality, I learned much later he didn't really have a clue of what he wanted. So I spent a tremendous amount of time working and reworking his ideas into visual material he could use to present at the top levels.

Anyway, things were moving along and quickly we built a world class organization and set of tools that allowed the Finance organization to exchange ideas, information, and have immediate access to the companies financials anywhere, anytime. Because we were on the cutting edge and trying to impress at all levels, we moved very, very quickly to implement a number of solutions. At this stage, we should have trenched-in and started producing our prototypes, but our SVP wanted to keep moving forward with new ideas. We found that for every new idea, there came with it a timeline that was far shorter than we could agree to, but there was always a reason why it was "critical" to have it ready sooner than it should be. So we consistently went above and beyond and developed his ideas into workable solutions and tools, but always had to take short cuts to get it ready for the next big meeting or presentation. As we moved forward, we left behind a suite of applications that required more maintenance than necessary and though we went to great pain to make sure this was understood, we later realized that our warnings went unheard.

My management style, though at times controversial, was to become very close to my team members. We all spent most of our time together both at the office and outside of it, spending weekends playing volleyball or having barbeques, etc. We were a very close team professionally and personally and while at times I was asked whether that was really the right approach or not, I can say with confidence that for that team and at that time, based on what we faced together in terms of long hours and hard work, it was the only approach. I gave so much of myself to the team and to the company that, in return, I got the same back from each and every one of them.

Ultimately, we were frustrated and though we protested, we always moved "quick and dirty" into production to meet his timelines. Eventually, he got so involved, he started talking and working with our developers directly, always apologizing later when we found out and asked that the practice be stopped. I recall that his explanations ranged from "I'm just trying to help out" to "I couldn't reach you on the phone for five minutes, so I had no choice." After many 48 hour marathons during the monthly close and many sleepless nights, my team, though spent, felt like we had exceeded expectations and had succeeded in building something never before seen at the corporate level. We spent the next year or so traveling the world, conducting town halls, training sessions, and building momentum for the next round of development and budgets. Eventually, we had an active base of about 5,000 Finance users worldwide and, though we were exhausted and rundown, things couldn't have been better.

As time went on, new leadership was brought into the organization and our SVP was forced to report to the new company controller rather than the CFO. The new controller was brought in from the automotive industry and had never worked in Financial Services before, so we believed that through collaboration and over communication, we would turn him into a strong advocate for the team and systems we were building and maintaining.

We participated in a myriad of team building events and brainstorming sessions, but our SVP was never able to really gain the new controllers confidence and trust. I can't say exactly what the issue was, but I remember some discussions where my team felt that our SVP was not managing the new controller very well; his first and only instinct was to do whatever the controller asked for and rather than push back when necessary or spend more time explaining our strategic vision, we started focusing on "electronic suggestion boxes", "traffic light reporting", and other things that took us away from our core strengths. We shifted direction so many times it seemed, that our creative director actually created a cartoon strip that was hung up on our walls, which depicted our SVP asking for a "moon rock", our finding a way to get to the moon for the rock, then returning with it only to find out that a "moon rock" was never asked for in the first place.

At this point, the team started to unravel and moral and motivation was at an all time low. I was not sleeping; I was stressed out, and my team members were calling in sick more than ever. My team spent more time than ever in meetings, discussing their issues and speculating what could possibly happen next; thus, our productivity took a dive. At one point, stress was so high that a fight broke out between two members in the office while I was in Sydney Australia, which later had to be settled in court.

Anyway, after three reorganizations in six months, the new controller decided that the team we had created belonged in the technologies organization rather than finance, and the applications and tools we had built should come from outside vendors. I spent the next few months when it was decided we were to be disbanded, finding my team members new jobs. I take great pride in the fact that all but one found new positions internally or with external companies. I poured every ounce of energy and passion I had left into writing their final reviews, providing references, phone calls, and campaigning on their behalves. I eventually moved on to a new position and later left the company to build a pair of startup companies. I will always remember the team and the time with great fondness. I'm still in touch with a great number of them and hope that at some point in the future, we'll all get the chance to work together again.

Upon reflection, none of us had really applied perfect management styles; I'm not sure that you can for every situation. It's easy to say that you can adopt a methodology or follow a model, but the real world just doesn't allow you to take a consistent approach all of the time. In hind sight, there are a number of things we all should have done differently, but I think in the middle of battle, you have to rely on your instincts more than anything else. We did what we needed to do and I'll always be a strong believer that you never go behind your leader's back or speak badly to anyone about them. We could have gone around or above our SVP to try and change things, but we chose to try and minimize the politics and became straight-up with our peers, direct reports, and leaders. We always did whatever we could to make our leader look good. Perhaps we should have been more in tune with the political climate at the time and focused more on keeping our jobs by marching to the beat of whatever drum was beating, but I think if you asked any of my team members today, they would not be as satisfied with what they accomplished if we had done it any other way.

*   *   *

Contribution by **Jessica Z. Hall**
Marketing Analyst
Fortune® 500 Retailer

My foray into the corporate world began at the age of 17. And over the years I was exposed to every aspect of the business. Even before becoming full-time, some of my co-workers (all around my age) looked to me when the bosses were out or unavailable since I was the longest-tenured employee. I became extremely proficient on the company's industry. I represented the company at networking events or trade-shows speaking knowledgeably with prospects about how our industry, specifically our company, could help them achieve their goals.

I honestly loved my job, liked my bosses and most of my co-workers, and felt competent. My ideas were heard, considered, and frequently implemented in some shape or form. When the bosses either didn't like my idea or were concerned about potential problems I defended and argued my position fiercely without hesitation. I didn't worry about being "punished" for speaking up.

As the cliché goes, good things must always come to an end. My last year was rocky for many reasons, but the main reason for my unhappiness was that I had little opportunity for growth and many of my proposed projects were put on hold. For two years, I was the marketing department. There was so much more that the company could have accomplished, but fear of change—and failure—prevented us from moving forward. There was more interest in closing sales from customer inquiries than proactively marketing to gain new business.

As this started happening, I found that I wasn't sleeping well, didn't look forward to work, and was more agitated. I stopped caring. I stopped fighting the way I had in the past. I would now just put in my two cents quickly and quietly. Then I'd just do what the boss asked. It wasn't until after I left that I realized that most of these were symptoms of my stress and unhappiness.

Without having a manager dedicated to marketing, unafraid of change, and able to mentor me, I was going nowhere fast. Thankfully, I realized this and soon took a position at a larger organization with opportunity for advancement.

About two years into my new role, I again started noticing the same symptoms that I experienced in the last year of my first job. My answer this time was not to jump ship. First I told my boss that I wanted more responsibility because I wasn't sufficiently challenged. I found ways to prove myself. I knew that if it didn't work, I would then look for another position in another department. I was promoted.

My mistake at my first job was that I didn't communicate. I didn't give my manager an opportunity to show me how I could continue to grow within the company. It's important to realize that you are in charge of your own destiny. Without an insightful boss, only you will know when you're unchallenged or your skills are not being maximized to their full potential.

The sooner you learn how the symptoms of unhappiness manifest in you, the better. Once you find that you're not being managed effectively, reflect on the cause and the possible solutions. Then talk to your boss. If you don't speak up, your boss may think you're content to keep doing what you're doing. Maybe your boss is concerned that you're smarter and wants to keep you down (yes, it happens). Or there isn't room for growth or the organization doesn't view your projects as a priority.

Figure out how your mismanagement can be solved. Talk with your boss or maybe with your supervisor's boss. (Give your boss a chance before going above their head—there's almost as much politics in corporate America as in the government.) Once you've exhausted all possibilities, start looking for another job. Don't take too long to recognize and attempt to solve the problem. Otherwise you may be tempted to jump ship without having another job. And that can worsen your symptoms.

*   *   *

Contribution by **John Jameson**
Talent Sourcer
General Growth Properties

The Interviewer Evaluation Model: Ensuring a Best Fit

It doesn't matter whether you're working at a local grocery store or a leading Fortune 500 firm, the manager and team that you work with on a daily basis impacts your job performance and satisfaction. Knowing how you like to be managed or led is critical to finding a good fit. During your job search, it seems only right that you would invest an hour or more developing criteria to find that perfect fit, doesn't it? The way to do all this is to use the Interviewer Evaluation Model. We will review how to do so through a four step Interviewer Evaluation Model.

- List who influenced your personal growth and why

- Develop interview questions to qualify the potential manager and team

- Identify opportunities to ask qualifying questions

- Conduct research and leverage your network

Step One—Reflecting on Influential People

In order to evaluate a potential manager and team you will want to know both who had a positive influence on your experience and what it was about those people that enabled growth and made them a pleasure to work with. This is the first step of The Interviewer Evaluation Model. Begin by going back to the beginning and make a list of the managers, coaches, mentors, teachers, and even parents that have had the greatest impact on your development and growth. Don't worry about making the list overly comprehensive; just include those who have stood above the rest. Aim for quality, not quantity. You should have at least three names and less than ten. The next step is to list what you liked about that person. It can be character and personality traits, values, similar goals, skills, or a simply a management style that maximized your strengths. They may have been trustworthy, listened well, flexible, or had a good sense of humor. Anything that you liked about working with and for that person is fair game. The goal here is to develop a short list of traits that you can develop into interview questions and keep a keen eye out for during the interview. Now that you've identified what you're looking for you are ready to move to the next step and develop questions.

Sample Influencer Evaluation

Psychology Teacher	Easy going, flexible, made class fun, fair, etc.
Older Sister	Connects me with others, listens well, inspirational, etc.
Former Manager	Challenged with new work, led by example, friendly, etc.

Step Two—Develop Interviewer Questions

The second step of The Interviewer Evaluation Model is to develop questions that will qualify the people you meet with as a fit and is developed from knowing what you liked about the people who have influenced your growth. Asking the right questions will not only qualify the interviewer and give you clues to their management style, but help you to understand their needs, and in turn, provide opportunities to highlight your qualifications. Good team focused questions will help you to evaluate the value that is placed on teamwork. Provided below are sample management ability and team dynamics qualifying questions.

Sample Management and Leadership Probing Questions

Have you coached an employee through a difficult assignment to success despite obstacles?

How do you recognize your team members? Share with me a recent example.

Can you describe the qualities you have seen in one of your most successful employees? Why do you perceive them as successful? Describe how this individual has communicated with you?

Describe the characteristics of an employee that has not worked well with you? What would you have liked to have seen from this person to turn your relationship around?

How regularly would you meet with the person who accepts this role?

If there was one thing you could change about your working/ leadership style what would it be?

Do you have a mentor and what qualities about that mentor do you most admire?

Does the company offer leadership/management training? Have your team members participated?

Sample Team Dynamics Questions

- What are the strengths/weaknesses of your current team?

- What dynamics make your team function successfully?

- Tell me about a challenge that your team has overcome?

- How does your team celebrate noteworthy accomplishments?

- Does your team spend time together outside of work?

- Tell me about a time your team fell short of meeting a goal? How did they respond?

Asking them open ended questions allows you to get a sense of their personality and learn to recognize non-verbal cues because more than 90% of all communication is nonverbal. If you can develop two or three questions for both the manager(s) and team members you meet with, you are on your way to qualifying the interviewer.

Step Three—Identify Opportunities to Ask Questions

The third step in The Interviewer Evaluation Model is to realize when to ask your interviewer qualifying questions. Ask qualifying questions too early in the interview and you may be perceived as pushy, a potentially high maintenance employee, or trying to control the interview. There are several appropriate opportunities in which to ask these questions; these moments are determined on a case-by-case basis.

Recognizing when to ask manager qualifying questions is a critical skill to develop and can occur at various points during the interview. You will often have more than one opportunity to ask qualifying questions so don't feel the need to ask them all at once. The safest time to ask is usually towards the end of an interview when you are asked if you have questions. Being asked if you have questions is an indication that the interviewer has decided whether or not you are a fit. If they hadn't decided, they would continue to ask you more questions. If it happens early in the interview it means that you have either knocked it out of the park or not done enough to sell your transferable skills and explain why you are the ideal candidate. Ineffective interviewers tend to make a judgment in the first five to ten minutes of an interview and spend the rest of the time asking questions that validate their initial impressions which is why it is critical to get off to a good start.

A second appropriate time to qualify the manager is when they begin to sell the opportunity to you. Being able to identify this opportunity can be challenging because interviewers will enthusiastically talk about what they do and how great the company is prior to qualifying you.

You may leave an interview unsure whether or not the future manager and team would be a good fit. When this is the case, a follow up thank you email is still important, but it is not the appropriate time to ask manager-qualifying questions. Provide references, meet more team members on a second round interview, and do what is needed to secure an offer so that you at least have a choice. On more than one occasion I have had candidates request a follow-up meeting with either myself or a hiring manager to ensure that accepting an offer is the right decision. It is an extra step in the process and your potential employer's initial reaction may not be pleasant (because they want you to say yes now), but you are demonstrating that it is an important decision, you take career decisions seriously, and they will respect your request. A post-offer follow up meeting is the last in person opportunity you'll have to qualify the entire package.

If you're still not sure after the follow up meeting but you are confident in the company and opportunity, inquire about the opportunity to work on cross-functional teams or participate in mentoring programs. Also, keep in mind that frequently your needs as an employee may be met by more than one manager, team member, or mentor, and therefore, you will want to get a sense of how the team works and the company culture. However, you will have a relationship with your manager and work with this person on a daily basis so be sure to take the necessary steps and ask the right questions to determine a good fit.

Step Four—Research your Prospective Team

The fourth and final step in our model is conducting research on your prospective team by leveraging your network and technology. Many professionals don't entirely grasp the value of networking until they personally experience the value add. Having a network of trusted contacts and possessing the ability to manage it through technology can create job opportunities, friendships, and allow you to research your potential manager and team. Management styles and team dynamics vary from company to company and team to team so it's important to not only research the company, but the team that you'll potential work with. Here are a few tips to leverage technology and your network to help make an informed decision:

Join LinkedIn, Plaxo, Xing, or another professional networking site. Each can be a valuable resource that provides the intelligence you'll need to make an informed decision. Here are a few tips to effectively research your future team:

Do you have any mutual connections? If so, has your contact reported to the prospective manager or can they speak to the prospective manager's capabilities or refer you to someone who can? Use Six Degrees of Separation to gain insight.

- Conduct an online search of everyone you've met

- Recognize Red Flags

Does their profile reflect longevity in a management role at any firm? A manager that changes companies every two or three years is an indication that they may not be an effective manager.

Many professionals now have recommendations of their work visible online. Beware of a prospective manager that has a large professional online network with many connections and no visible recommendations.

Your manager and team will have a profound impact on your job satisfaction. Employees leave jobs because they are mismanaged more often than they do for a more lucrative opportunity. If asked, most professionals will tell you that they'd rather work at an average firm and have a great boss and team, than work a prestigious firm and have an ineffective manager or dysfunctional team. Incorporating the model into your interviewing preparation will help ensure job satisfaction prior to starting any job. Be safe, conduct research, ask the right questions, and watch your career take off!

*   *   *

Assumption #4:
Find Other Talents

Either you are working with other Talents or you are not. When you work with other Talents, you will learn and grow to be the best. You will see other great Talents in action and how they tackle problems, thereby, helping you rise up to their caliber. Other Talents can act as mentors for you and you should actively seek out Talents in your organization or outside of your organization to work with.

It is critical that we all learn from those who are masters in their field. We should find others who are talented so we can learn from them to enhance our own knowledge. For example, if you want to be great at golf, would you choose to practice five times a week with your mechanic or once a week with Phil Mickelson? You can work with anyone, so why not work with the best so you can learn to become the best?

I once worked with a great Talent outside of my organization on a non-profit project. I was able to learn so much from him just by working one Saturday a week that it made my resume shine above others. I saw direct financial gain just by working with this Talent and by what I was able to learn from him. When your work environment lacks people who are Talents, you put yourself at a risk of turning into someone who no longer sees him or herself as a Talent.

You should know a powerful secret. Talents thrive when they work with other Talents. They feed energy off one another and build a synergy that is beneficial to everyone. Take a look at your work. Do you know of someone who fits the Talent mold? Look closer, chances are that when you see a burst in their performance on a project, it is because they are working with another Talent on that project.

I recall one of my first big projects at an organization to work with an external consultant. I can honestly say today that I was pretty shaky about the whole project from the get-go. I had very few ideas on how the whole thing would come together in such a short amount of time. Some of the tasks were far more challenges than I had ever experienced before, and it was my neck on the line. The night before, I kept thinking to myself. "It's just a job and if you get fired, you'll find another one—just hang in there." To this day I remember how stressed out I had become physically walking into the office that morning.

At about 9:00 am, my boss instructed the consultant and myself to go off and work in a conference room where no one would bother us for the rest of the day. The morning was very foggy for the both of us. We kept working through the problem and I learned that the consultant was only going to be there for that one day. If we didn't complete the project today, then I would have to finish the rest on my own.

Sometime around 2:00 pm something amazing started to happen. The fog was starting to lift, and fast. We were starting to apply some innovative solutions to our problems. If I got stuck, the consultant was able to pull through and vice versa. My energy level was so high that I remember it till this day. I was, as I mentioned earlier, thriving. At 4:30pm we had delivered the entire project. Going home that night, I felt as if I had conquered the world. Everyone, including my boss, was amazed at the progress. I was able to live off that high for nearly a month.

I share my experience because I have actively seen my personal performance and motivation go through the roof time and again when I have worked with other Talents. When I've worked with other Talents, in my team, perhaps someone external or in a different department, the results showed. You will be able to point this out in your life each time when you work with a Talent and deliver something—you will feel a sense of exhilaration; a mental high that will make you feel as if you are the "King of the Jungle."

Now remember the opposite is true as well. When you work with someone who is not a Talent, you will feel drained and tired, both mentally and physically. You will go to work and find that you are constantly drained, even if you do a great job. This is a signal for you to recognize and do something about it. If this is due to a team member, then you may have to try to understand what their motivation for coming to work is? Don't be surprised if you learn that they have been warming the same corporate bench for years and simply lack motivation. There is a reason and you're just going to have to accept that they have pitched their tent and, unless there is a flood, they are not going anywhere.

I will reemphasize that you, as a Talent, cannot worry about others and should do your best not to harbor any unsavory feelings toward your co-workers. We all have different motivations for coming in to work.

Talent Tools

You can be the most skilled carpenter, yet without your tools—hopefully the right tools to do the job—you cannot perform. Talents are all about performing to produce results, even if those results are just a perception. This means that as you start to become a talent at work, you look for certain elements that will elevate your performance.

You as a Talent will want to seek out the following two types of roles within your organization. You will first want to find a **knowledge broker** and, secondly, you'll want to find a **historian**. If you feel you can play these roles yourself, even better. In my experience, I have found that playing both roles can be challenging, especially if you are new to the organization.

Before we go further, let's do a quick lookup of the corporate dictionary.

Corporate Bold Dictionary Lookup

Dinosaur: Someone at your work who has been around for a long time, who has stopped seeing him/herself as a Talent, and is usually willingly **Trapped (by a system)**.

Historian: Someone at your work who has been around long enough and likes to tell you old company war stories.

Knowledge Broker: Someone with deep insights into the workings of an organization and knows where to find certain types of information around your company.

We'll be utilizing these terms very shortly.

Let's take a quick minute here to clear up any false assumptions about what we are going to discuss. You are not using other people as pawns in your own chess game to succeed or move forward. I hope we are very clear on this. A Talent is not in the business of using other people for personal gain. We are in the business of becoming exceptional resources for our organization.

Now, let's begin. When you go out to buy a house, it's a common practice to visit a real estate broker. After all, they've been doing this for years and can help you with some of the pitfalls associated with purchasing a house. When you start your corporate journey in a new organization, you too will need someone similar. I'm not talking about a mentor (while they are great resources as well). Instead, you'll want to find yourself a knowledge broker.

This person or groups of people have, one way or the other, figured out what is going on around your organization. You see, at their most atomic level, knowledge brokers are just that, they broker knowledge. They get pieces of information from all over your organization and are able to put them in their context, explaining why something is happening in the sales department and who is responsible for it. Anything you want to know today? Great, the knowledge broker can take your question and give you an answer or guide you as to where you can get the answer.

Knowledge brokers are not gossipers, there is a difference. While a knowledge broker may gossip, the broker is primarily on a never ending fact finding mission. Their knowledge tends to be based on facts, usually from multiple sources. Their knowledge may not be 100% correct all the time, but they are the closest to real-time information in your organization as you are going to get. Knowledge brokers usually know why something is the way it is or can find that out for you.

The interesting thing about knowledge brokers is that they have multiple links inside the organization. They may know a few key people within the organization that keeps them well supplied with, well, knowledge. Many knowledge brokers can call a member of senior leadership directly. They are also in communication with people at the low end of the corporate ladder, such as the maintenance guy. Knowledge brokers do not care about titles or salaries; they care about one thing—knowledge.

Get to know a knowledge broker or two across your organization. Identify them and test their knowledge. They will be quick to clue you in. No one person can know everything about a very large organization all the time; knowledge brokers deal with different types of information. One knowledge broker might know about systems, while another may know about people or processes. The thing to remember here is that if you are working in a large organization, you will want to try to find multiple knowledge brokers.

The knowledge broker deal is a two-way street. You must reciprocate. You will not go too far in your relationship with a knowledge broker, unless you supply them with some knowledge. You don't have to supply any juicy insider information; even the most mundane piece of information is good enough. This is because whatever information you supply the knowledge broker, he or she, will check it against his or her internal database of information. So, caution, do not make things up. The knowledge broker will know—they may not call you out on it—but they'll know that you cannot be trusted.

Many people will make a career out of being a knowledge broker at an organization. They are very important and it is because of their backdoor channel that information flows and things can get done. In my case, things did not get done; a knowledge broker cautioned me about spending too much time on a project because someone down the line was aiming to kill the project dead on its tracks. Personally, I value knowledge brokers deeply because of my past experiences.

Next, you will want to locate a historian. Spotting historians is pretty easy—they tell war stories about your organization. What I mean is that a historian is someone who has been around your company for a long time. "Long time" is a relative term. If your company has only been around for six years, then four years could be considered a "long time"; however, if your company has been around since after WWII then a good historian has probably been around for fifteen or twenty years.

Let's quickly talk about why historians so important. Working with a historian is not required—working with a knowledge broker is—let me affirm this loud and clear. Historians can tell you about big-picture shifts that have taken place at your company over the years. They will be able to tell you about the culture and what has been tried in the pasts and did or didn't work.

I have found that good historians are those who are, or were, former managers within the organization. If you find a historian who was never been a manager, you might be working with someone who is a historian in the making or an outdated knowledge broker.

It was through a historian that I once found out that I had just come into the organization after the largest shakeup in its history. This bit of information clued me in when I saw a group of talented co-workers exhibiting low morale. The historian was kind enough to give me a tour of how the company came about and shared many war stories. I was quickly able to consume those stories and make references to them in my meetings to articulate my point of view. Wouldn't you know it—an instant success!

Contribution by **Ronak Baxi**
VP of Finance
Leading Manufacturing Organization

Finding other talents is very important and for me it has really paid off. But you can't wait around, because sometimes you have to go find them yourself. We all must work daily to become the Talents that we are. I recall earlier in my career when I was building myself as a Talent and found another Talent who taught me skills that I've been able to leverage in my successful journey.

My 1st year at an internship with this well known organization was spent mostly to build myself and to learn how to build a database for the finance department. Upon returning the 2nd year, the organization moved me into a role that was far more challenging, because they recognized my talents. They recognized that I was there to help solve their problems and willing to push myself as well. In my new role, I came across another talent who took my data-processing skills to a whole new level. Working with complex data was not my career path; however, I took it upon myself to spend time and to learn what I could from him.

What I learned in my short time with the Talent has been something that I've carried with me throughout my career. I've received multiple recognitions because I've been able to automate work that previously took hours or days, to under 10 minutes. This is the real power of finding and working with other Talents. These are the types of results you can expect.

The fact is that I would not have been able to understand what this Talent was teaching me without going through the learning from my previous year's work. I simply would have missed out on all of the knowledge. That's why I said earlier that you must work to build yourself up as a Talent, so when you come across another Talent you are able to gain from their experience.

*   *   *

Contribution by **Anthony Knierim**
Pipeline Generation Expert / People Champion
Accenture

Strengths based psychology is a very important and critical part of succeeding in any organization. What are you good at? Tasks and thought processes that come easily to us are a gift. One should focus in discovering these strengths/gifts and work on them in your world of those strengths. Our co-workers have their own set of strengths and together we can accomplish much more by each of us working to recognize our strengths and not only utilizing at maximum, but aligning teams to have workers strengths complimenting one another.

The idea is to have teams aligned in a fashion where the members of the team all know their specific identified strengths; For in knowing their key strengths, we can then begin to maximize the utilization of combining multiple strengths and start reducing the focus on some of the weaknesses in which one can spend too much time trying to make just, "sub par." Seek out the talents and strengths in others and in areas where you have weakness, so you have more time to focus on your strengths. One can work diligently on improving a weakness to make it just average, but what type of recognition do you get for an average performance? One can spend that same amount of time in focusing on their strengths to make that strength shine as a significant anchor of team productivity/output. In having teams aligned in this fashion, you can see how having each member work on primarily focusing on individual strengths could show far greater productivity in goals and objectives.

People are stimulated far more when asked to do things in areas where they know that they have strengths in delivering. Identifying strengths in others and increasing the amount of focus and demand in those areas will keep team members stimulated with a high level of interest, as well as productivity in the amount of work given. This is different from constantly asking one to perform work and tasks in areas that one might be weak in. Organizing teams to this type of "strength based psychology" will not only increase productivity, but also have an incredible impact on team morale. People are excited to engage in work when the majority of their work is in areas aligned to their strengths, and be rewarded for performing well in these strong areas.

Seek out others with talents that will compliment your weakness; look at how your strengths can be paired with others for greater synergy in the workplace. Taking this proactive approach to better yourself and the productivity of a team/organization will be noticed as well as create a better work environment with increased morale and engagement. Now, go put your strengths to work!

*   *   *

Contribution by **Britt V. Pearson**
Director of Finance
Cerapedics, Inc.

In my experience, people possess very strong opinions regarding whether a small company is better than a large company, or vice versa, and the related pros and cons of each. I have experienced both, I appreciate both, and it depends on greater extending circumstances as to what I would prefer at any given point in time. Currently, I am at a small company but historically I have gone big. I went to a big university, started my career at the largest accounting firm in the world, and after leaving public accounting, went to work for a Fortune 500 company. What I have found that a large institution "teaches" you that a small institution inherently cannot is that the individual needs to seek out and work with other talents. It is more than a nicety, it is a necessity; the difference between getting by and succeeding. It is such an important skill that I no longer accept a job position based on the job description but more importantly, on whom I will be working with and who I will be exposed to.

After leaving public accounting for private industry, I was reviewing assorted job offers trying to make a decision. One option was a highly paid, highly titled position, with a company that provided amazing benefits. The company was solid and the position was secure. It was the standard type of position that every company has, needs, and has more or less perfected at least in terms of definition.

The second option was with a company that did not pay as well, particularly when taking into consideration the local cost of living; it required relocation to another state; the position title was generic and even considered "lowly" by some standards. The interesting part was that it was a newly created position in a freshly appointed team.

The third option that I was sincerely considering was with a company that actually was in my field of expertise. It was a small start-up software company that paid well, had the lure of the all-powerful golden "options" that everyone in my Silicon Valley career upbringing had lost themselves to, and the attraction of autonomy in the position.

The first two companies themselves were very similar—both were Fortune 500 companies and outside of the fact that they were different industries, there was not much to distinguish one from another. Neither of the industries was in my area of expertise, which I admit worked to spawn an interest in me. The second and third positions allowed me to define, create, and cultivate the actual appointment.

On paper, the first opportunity was nice but didn't have the draw that the second and third opportunity boasted. The second opportunity was attractive but included a significant drawback in the relocation to another state. The third opportunity was seemingly perfect. It contained the best aspect from all of the options, at least on paper. When really unearthing the position, I would be exposed to one other individual on a consistent basis. Ideally, we should seek out mentors in all arenas—not just at work. Realistically, this is neither feasible nor practical. This position and the related undertaking was one of those instances where it would be both unfeasible and unpractical. Only having real mentorship and interaction with one other individual was a considerable obstacle, greater than relocating.

In the end, I took the second position. This position afforded me the ability to work with a multitude of bright minds from all across the organization. While I developed the team, I was able to work with the Controller, several Directors, and HR. While I developed the program, I continued to work with the Controller, several other Directors, Regional Vice Presidents, and numerous other management team members. Working in the capacity that I did, and with the people that I was exposed to, when a major project was initiated, I was the first person many people and many teams thought of to bring-in. While working on this project, I was introduced to and worked with, among others, the President, Chief Financial Officer, Chief Operating Officer, and Legal Counsel; not to mention the external consulting firms Partners, Senior Managers, Underwriters, Lawyers, and Analysts. After spending significant time with and around these various team members, a position focusing on international operations came up, and my boss at the time was asked if I could be approached regarding this opportunity. This was a big switch for someone from the accounting/finance team. The company had almost 60,000 people working for it. My office laid claim to a quarter of those. I was singled-out because I had sought out mentors in various departments, requested to work on special projects and teams with these individuals, and thus I had become ingrained amongst these talented professionals.

*　　*　　*

Contribution by Brooke **Ann Etzel**
Senior Customer Relations Administrator
Fox Sports Net Broadcast Media

I grew up in the Midwest with honest, hard working entrepreneurial parents who enriched my life with their strong work ethic. Looking back, it makes sense that my first college job after leaving the nest was working for a coach, Coach Leonard Hamilton, and his coaching staff at the University of Miami. These coaches became role models to me and others because they were some of the best college basketball coaches and recruiters in the country. They lead by example exhibiting good character, hard work ethic, and they were men of their word. These role models had to be on top of their games physically, mentally, and emotionally while being grounded and taking public criticism. Among their many attributes were problem solving and delegating which I continue to use in business today. Because of this amazing experience I know it is important to lead by example, try to be professional at all times and surround myself with others I look up to. I also know that it is vitally important to always respectfully regard confidentiality at all times when working under or with great leaders, and never disclose personal information.

Each day since this experience I have tried to keep an open mind, be cooperative, work effectively with my business team and strive to perfect my position by using positive past experiences to problem solve in daily business life. I learned it is important to stay physically fit, to stay strong mentally and always strive for excellence. If I fail and things do not work out, I do not give up. Instead I become more aggressive by working longer hours, getting up earlier, and reorganizing my priorities.

The assumption to "seek out and work with other talents" is a vital part of the current professional working environment. Yes, experience does help you get ahead and yes, the more experience you have the more marketable you can become, but in order to be successful you must recognize and learn the correct behaviors to imitate in order to be more effective. I work with talented people and have found you must seek out the best possible example of these mentors because no one is perfect. Recently I learned that before saying or acting on a decision I must think about the outcome, talk things out with co-workers, get new ideas and try new things and some of the time sleep on things before coming to a conclusion.

My entire life has continued to be about surrounding myself and working with professionals who demonstrate desirable attributes that enhance my ability to problem solve, delegate, have a strong work ethic and exhibit strong character. I accredit my success to diverse experiences and the ability to know what works well, from people in my community, teachers, professors, coaches and mentors.

I have had to pick and choose what I take from these experiences and I am thankful for all the time spent, things learned and opportunities I have had. These people who I have shared memories and past experiences with have shaped the person and professional that I am now. The knowledge I learned along the way from those quality experiences proves that this assumption, about seeking out and working with other talents in order to become a better person and professional, is true.

*　　*　　*

Contribution by **David Jara**
Senior User Experience Researcher
Financial Services Industry

Introduction

I am always amazed whenever I watch sports on television; I am in awe at the level of coaching that is involved in high caliber professional sports. These athletes are highly skilled, in top notch physical condition, with few peers in the global athletic talent pool. In spite of this, they are not beyond coaching and instruction, with coaches clearly being shown providing advice, encouragement and direction. These coaches often have more professional experience, knowledge about their teammates and competition, a third person perspective, and detailed knowledge about specific athletic mechanics.

If these professional athletes gain from coaching and mentoring, how much could you enhance your own career by finding a trusted circle of advisers and mentors? Corporate life may not be as glamorous as professional athletics, but I would argue that it can be equally, if not more, demanding on our lives. In order to thrive in this environment, we need the help of experienced and wise guides who have faced similar situations successfully, as well as the opportunity to learn from their mistakes.

The Benefits of a Mentor

Working with a mentor has some important benefits that should be pointed out. Hopefully these will provide the needed motivation to both seek out a mentor and commit to making the relationship a success.

1. Everyday Advice

Your mentor should provide tangible benefits to your everyday working life. They should be able to provide you with a shift in mindset or direct skills that can help you perform on the job better. Often times, a shift in perspective as provided by a more experienced colleague can have tremendous benefits on our daily working lives. These are the kinds of contributions that you should expect of any mentor within a relatively short period of time.

2. Networking

Your mentor could be a very valuable source of professional connections. If your mentor has been at your company for a length of time, he may know individuals across the organization from previously collaborating with them on projects. As needs arise in your career, this network could be very helpful in solving issues that your mentor is not directly equipped to fix. Your mentor may even have close relationships with executives in your organization, which could be beneficial under various circumstances.

3. Potential Funding Resource

Your mentor may have access to a budget that might be relevant to your career. As your relationship progresses, she/he may see your work as a corporate investment that is sure to provide a return. She/he will know you well and will be confident in your skills and the types of projects that you would thrive in. This is a closely related benefit to social networking. Since your mentor may not have access to funds, he may have close relationships with other decision makers who do.

4. Discussing Work and Life Issues

Your mentor may be a good person to talk about the issues that are associated with balancing your career and your personal life. She/he may have some tips, tricks, and wisdom from experience, since they probably continue to deal with these issues themselves.

<u>Choosing a Mentor</u>

Choosing a mentor can be a bit stressful. It sometimes can feel awkward, almost like asking a date to the prom in high school. Keep in mind that you are not the first person to ask for a mentor in your organization, and regardless of the decision of your potential mentor, they will likely feel honored to hear your request. Don't take it personal if you are rejected, since it is most likely not for personal reasons. Your potential mentors are also very busy, balancing their work and personal lives; they may not be ready for the responsibility and commitment that mentorship involves. Here are a few tips to help you choose your mentor:

1. Build on an Established Professional Relationship

If possible, you should avoid the "cold call" mentor request. These have a high probability of failure if the potential mentor does not know you very well. Your mentor wants to know that there is a reasonable chance of success with his/her efforts and that time spent with you will be used wisely. The best mentoring relationships often form organically. You might already have a natural relationship with this person and sometimes go to this person for advice, or at least would like to. Even if you have a preexisting relationship, you could benefit by formalizing your mentee/mentor relationship.

2. Get Along

There are all sorts of personalities in our workplaces. Sometimes one is not better than the other in various circumstances. These various personalities can be what make working with others interesting; however, in a mentor relationship, you should try to find someone whose personality you are compatible with and whose company you enjoy. You should anticipate having occasional difficult conversations and disagreements. Your professional relationship needs to survive these in order to thrive.

3. Form Expectations

As you pursue a mentor, you should eventually discuss the expectations that you have for one another. This can help avoid hurt feelings and damaged relationships down the line. Some of these expectations are not necessarily positive or negative in their own right, from my perspective, but you should have a shared understanding.

- Will there be a formal agenda for the meeting?

- What times, days, and frequency works best?

- How are cancellations viewed? "I know we are all busy" or "you keep letting me down."

- Will the meeting be in person or over the phone?

- Are electronic communications acceptable? How often? What is the nature of these communications?

4. Explore Corporate Mentoring Communities

Some companies have an official mentoring offering where you can be paired with a compatible mentor. You can often learn more about a potential mentor through the site and set up your own profile where potential mentors can see more about what you are looking for in a mentor. Many times these official sites have their own guidelines, which may be helpful in building shared expectations for the relationship.

5. Establish Goals

In the initial stages of you mentoring, you should start to build goals with your mentor that you can both target over the coming months. This will help you gauge the effectiveness of your relationship and help you both make adjustments as time goes on. It is probably also a good idea to have a quarterly review to talk about what is working with the relationship and what you should change.

Internal vs. External Mentors

Mentors do not have to necessarily reside within our own organization, and I think it is particularly helpful to build a network of advisers both within and outside of our own organizations. Mentors outside of an organization provide a different perspective, which can be more valuable in certain situations, such as the decision making process for a career change. You may not want to discuss this with an internal mentor for privacy reasons. External mentors can also help you validate advice. If they work in a different company or industry and their perspective resonates with an internal mentor, chances are better that you are receiving good guidance. One of the benefits of avoiding "burning bridges" when you leave an organization is that some of your colleagues or supervisors can serve as mentors as you transition to a new company.

If you find the right mentor and build a good relationship, it could lead to significant benefits over the course of your career. Your mentor/mentee relationship will take effort on the part of both parties in order to thrive, but the benefits make it well worth your time. Even the number one people in their skill can benefit from a coach/mentor; I think we could all use a mentor in order to exceed in our own performance expectations, and in order to have a more fulfilling career.

*   *   *

Contribution by **Ericka M. Berti**
Project Manager
Healthcare Industry

In the perfect world, a person would have no weaknesses and would have all the answers to anything that came their way. An individual would have a solution for every situation they ran into. The situation would be handled with great finesse. Unfortunately, we all know that there is no perfect world. With that being said, how does one acquire the "toolkit" necessary to survive in Corporate America?

I realized at an early age, my early twenties, that if I work with successful people, I could learn from them and hopefully be successful one day. By working closely with different types of people and different types of talent, I was able to learn skills what would help me in the future. I learned that if there was one skill I was weak at, go seek out someone who is the best at it, and let them mentor you. You may not become as good as the person is, but guaranteed you will know more than you did before you sought that person out.

Throughout my career, I have tried to align myself with a variety of talent to make myself diversified. When I started as a help desk technician, I remember having discussions with other technicians who were on Level two and Level three support. I figured if I wanted to move to the next level, I needed to know what they know. Some were open to the opportunity to mentor me, others didn't want to bother. You can read a book on how to troubleshoot a particular component, but when it comes down to a real life scenario, a seasoned technician is going to be a better resource than your text book.

I am now an IT Project Manager. I guess I always knew that I wanted to manage technical projects from the time I was finishing my Bachelor's degree. It all started when I first met a current friend of mine. He was a polished PM whom I hoped I would get to work side by side with one day. I needed to learn what he knew. I wanted to align myself to someday be able to manage a multimillion dollar project and call it a success. I was given the opportunity to be a part of his project team for our Senior Project. He took his time out to share his talent with me and it has proved to be beneficial in my career. I was taught a discipline that will stay a part of my toolkit for as long as I am employed.

As a team, you need to have people that are diverse in their talents to be effective. Not every person will have the same experiences. Not every person will be great at one given item. As a team, everyone works together. My talent may compensate for something a team member is missing. And another team mate may have something that I cannot understand or am not good at. If you work together, you can accomplish your goals as a team. One of the very first projects I was assigned to in my career was a migration. The technology was new and there was no manual for it. I was given a CD to install and was told to figure it out and that I would be supporting the solution going forward. I was given a resource and we were told to work together. This individual who was assigned with me was amazing at the administrative details. She was able to create a database to keep track of everyone's credentials and automate the account creations for our end-users. She became a lifesaver because she mainstreamed all of our clerical work by the click of a button. I was envious of her talent. What I didn't realize was that we were a team. I was the individual who was able to learn the product inside and out, the nuances, the errors, all of the problems and bugs with the solution. While she took care of the administration, I was training our technical staff and crafting the technical documentation for future troubleshooting. Had we both had the same talents, the project would have failed. It is imperative that a project team contain various talents.

There are so many positive outcomes of working with different talents. Although it may not be obvious in some cases, you are developing the tools necessary to be successful in today's job market. I have been called a chameleon; I take that as a compliment. Having worked with different talents and continuing, it enables me to blend in when necessary and adapt to many situations as needed. Do not be afraid to approach an individual and ask them to work with you. You may get the skills you need for your next endeavor and maybe even a friend!

*　　*　　*

Contribution by **Louis Bing**
Analyst
Goldman Sachs

Goldman Sachs has long been known for its culture of openness, teamwork, and excellence. I learned firsthand during new-hire orientation exactly how much working relationships were emphasized. From the daily networking cocktail parties to the team building simulations, it was clear Goldman Sachs was instilling in our minds the value of great work-place relationships.

When I arrived for my first day of work following the two week orientation, I was placed in a one on one meeting with my team leader, Brittany. Again, there was plenty of emphasis on seeking out help from those around me. I learned I would be having one-on-one meetings with her each week, as well as meetings with upper level managers and vice presidents. In addition, Goldman Sachs assigned mentors to all of their new hires, making sure that all new employees received the benefit of learning from the best. This was a stark contrast to some of my previous work experiences, where it seemed like upper level management had no time to waste on the lower level workers. Instead of always wondering "Is this a good time to ask a simple question to my boss", I could freely schedule meetings with talented upper-level managers who were always more than happy to give any feedback or advise they could.

It may seem like common sense that the only way to get better in something is by learning from those who are experts. Luckily for me, I was in a place where mentoring and team work was part of the work culture. No amount of college classes can prepare you for Corporate America. I remember how lucky I felt to have a talented coworker, Robert Goodman, teach me the nuts and bolts of the workplace. To me, the reason why Goldman Sachs is still standing today while former investment banks have crumbled in the midst of the financial crises is because of this spirit of learning from the best. I've always considered myself a fast learner, but it would have taken me weeks to learn what I could in a day when working with the right people.

*   *   *

Contribution by **Ahmad Noordin**
Senior Manager
NorthShore University HealthSystem

A phrase that I often use is "great minds think differently," and it holds true in sports and in the corporate environment. Similar to a sports team, a corporate team needs to consist of players with a diverse set of background and experience. I have gained this perspective after working for various Fortune 500 and not-for-profit organizations. A corporate professional must proactively seek to be in a diverse team because that will be the winning team.

Some corporate professionals seek to work and partner with those who have similar interests and skills. This is the safe choice but unfortunately to be successful in the corporate world and in life one needs to come out of the safe zone and find those individuals who possess different talents. A team player is one who knows his or her own talents and understands the talents of others in his or her team. If you lack technical skills, instead of forcing yourself to learn technologies that may not interest you, the smarter route is to partner with someone who possesses those skills.

Some corporate professionals feel they can learn everything and do everything. This is impossible and in addition to working hard, one should work smart. There is a time when you have the ball and must score. Then there is a time when you must pass the ball and let someone else score. Putting one's ego ahead of the success of a project or a team can be detrimental to one's career and one's relationships with his or her peers.

A leader is always trying to create and sustain a team that has varying skills and specialties. Exceptional leaders are not those who are good at everything. Exceptional leaders are like talent scouts, doing their research and keeping their eye out for someone else who is talented in a certain science or field and bringing that person into the team.

In conclusion, I would like to give you a challenge: write down the name of members in your team (colleagues and subordinates) and try to identify their talents. Who is a good supervisor? Who is a good collaborator? Who is more organized? Who is more patient? Once you have created your list, you can utilize it the next time you have a project or initiative and need to involve those who have talents that you yourself might not possess.

*   *   *

Contribution by **Michael Podemski**
Architect
Fortune 100 Insurance Company

"Build relationships" was one of the best tips that I learned from one of my mentors. This advice sounds pretty simple, right? It is, but it's the type of relationships that you need to develop. Don't just add people to a contact list, but identify reasons why that person can contribute to your development. I have discovered over time that I built all of my relationships based on people that develop me as an individual.

Every year you work on your personal development plan where you begin to identify your strengths and weaknesses. You may list on-the-job training, workshops, and one-on-one mentoring as options to remedy your weaknesses. Many people fall into this trap where you spend all of your time focusing on your weaknesses. At the end of the year, you may improve slightly or never at all with your weaknesses. This leads to frustration with your personal development.

Instead, I propose that you fine-tune your strengths and ignore wasting your time with your weaknesses. This statement has saved me many years of frustration with my personal development. Let me explain how I approach my personal development plan with a few examples.

While I worked in our enterprise operations group, I had to develop and deploy a weekly scorecard based on operational metrics for our enterprise applications group. This was not a difficult task based on my experience with metrics and reporting. However, I knew there were better ways of creating the reports to explain the metrics. That's where my colleague came into the picture. My manager had recently hired someone to create metrics and reports for our entire operations group. Most people just sent him the requirements for their reports and he ran them. I did that too, but, at the same time, I wanted to learn more. Over the course of a few months, we partnered together to create the next version of our enterprise applications operational reports. Leadership was extremely happy with the results. My reward was the additional skills with metrics and reporting that I was able to gain from my colleague's experience.

As a new manager, my director expected that we understood our monthly financial reports. His expectation became my next priority. I had some basic training in accounting and financial analysis; however, I needed a crash course fast. Instead of taking an online course about our monthly finances, I used my network. I knew someone from our finance department that was able to sit down with me and discuss our monthly financial reports. Since he had generated these reports in the past, he was able to provide me with additional insight that could not be replicated in an online course. Not only was I able to discuss our monthly financial report with our director, I was able to highlight key trends that illustrated our performance.

I hope these examples illustrate the importance of building your relationships with colleagues that can aid in your development. It is also very important to recognize and thank these individuals when they assist with your development. You never know when they will tap you on the shoulder to ask for your assistance with their development.

*   *   *

Contribution by **Nina Chavda**
Sr. Usability Analyst and Information Architect
Ingenix Consulting

Working with others outside your realm of expertise opens up doors in so many different ways. For one, you are building relationships. No matter what background a person might have, that person is a contact and you will never know when or how that contact might come in handy. They might help out within your current role, or can be used as references as you move on to future roles.

After learning about what others do and their experiences as they achieved various goals, you might realize that their experiences have something that is either more appealing or less appealing from what you are currently doing. As you begin to narrow down what interests you, these contacts may guide you to opportunities that you may have never considered before.

If I did not take interest in other talents, then I would not be where I am today. I started out of school with a finance degree and tried out the investment banking and mortgage company routes, but was not happy. So from there, I took a job at a large telecommunications firm doing some financial analysis. Even after being promoted for all my effort, I still was not satisfied. I spoke to other groups within the company to find a role that might be more appealing. Unfortunately, I didn't have much luck, but some co-workers suggested I try going into consulting because I was still young in my career and would be able to travel around to different clients in order to explore new opportunities in various corporate environments. I was advised that having such exposure will help to figure out, ultimately, where I wanted to be.

Taking their advice, I began work at a large-sized IT consulting firm. I had a couple strategy roles while there, but the bulk of my work was more information technology based. I was not too thrilled with the idea of becoming a business analyst from a business school student, and crossed it off my list of things that might have interested me. Trying to find more opportunities within the firm, I came across a project that I was really passionate about. It involved building a website and my role was to complete the design. My manager at the time saw how much I really liked that type of work and forwarded me to a division within the firm called the User Experience Group. Most people in this group had master degrees in human interaction design. I did not have any real background in design, but because I was interested in learning more and had a good reputation within the firm, they gave me a chance to develop in this field.

After being an apprentice to a manager within the group, I learned the basics around user centered design and began building my own portfolio of projects within this niche. I developed skills not only in creating deliverables in the field, but in how to sell my expertise to clients. Using that knowledge, I interviewed for my current job. Even though they were looking for someone with both industry and educational experience, they gave me a chance to speak with them. Because of my portfolio and the professional skills I attained while working in the consulting firm, they trusted that I was a good candidate for the position and brought me on board.

Taking myself as an example, you can easily see that the more talents you work with, the more opportunities open up for yourself. Networking is everything in the career world and you never know who will have the connections to help you get to where you want to be. Learning more about other talents will help build relationships and spark interests in areas you probably never knew existed; it will ultimately take your career to new heights, which you may not have been able to achieve otherwise.

*　　*　　*

Assumption #5:
Ignore Evaluations

So far, the assumptions have been more or less gentle on our stomachs. Yet I do believe that you are ready for the next few assumptions that follow. This assumption can be a bitter pill to swallow for some, only because the assumption is so bold in and of itself. Like we've said before, be prepared to challenge your personal assumptions when you read our assumptions.

Good Talents have figured out that annual performance evaluations mean little to nothing and should, for the most part, be ignored. You read that correctly; you should simply ignore your performance evaluations. I have seen far too many talented people take their annual or quarterly performance appraisal from their boss too much to heart. Talents know that the performance evaluation or appraisal is worth taking a peek at, but not worth taking seriously by any means. They understand that every organization performs their evaluations differently, so you could be a low performer in one organization and conversely considered the cream of crop in another organization.

I recall a former boss of mine doing my performance evaluation one year. After being seated in a room, he told me that he had spoken to teams that I worked with. He continued that I was doing well in all areas and was pleased with my performance. He then politely told me that he was giving me a lower rating in an area because he was required to put something "bad" down for me. He explained that he had to show that I was going to improve on something next year. His exact words as I remember were, "I mean, I have to put something down."

Let me add further clarity. In general, when your organization is doing great and your department's fearless leaders have a nice big budget to work with, then you will likely get a fairly good review and a respective merit increase. When your department is on a cost cutting mission, you should get ready for an average to ugly review with a below inflation merit increase. Inflation being the average increase or decrease in the cost of living. Your organization will try to keep you in pace with inflation. Unless you haven't already figured this out, your annual inflation-type raises are not really raises. We will talk more about this subject in a few minutes. Over the years, I have found that, generally, my performance evaluation was a reflection of the mood of my organization.

Look, as a Talent, you will know where you stand before the performance review. Talents rarely ever worry about what their performance evaluations say. They may note a thing or two as learning opportunities; however, the rest can simply be ignored.

Allow me introduce you to . . .

Contribution by **Cherry Worring**
Sr. Financial Analyst
American Airlines

Performance Appraisal is an overrated, outdated company tool used today in evaluating an employee's performance. In today's job market, managers tend to rely on this tool more often than in the past. It is very common in today's economic downturn, as in downsizing, that performance evaluations be highly used as a major contributor to whether or not an employee is to be released, laid off, or asked to seek a transfer somewhere else.

I currently work for a billion dollar corporation with more than 80,000 employees. Within this 80,000, 5,000 are management and of this 5,000, 1,000 are its senior level management, Vice Presidents, and Executive VPs.

We have an outsourced company that created a performance evaluation tool for each work group and only management is required to complete it. Included in the Performance Evaluation form, are a "Self Evaluation" and a "Goals", section that are departmentally specific.

After each employee completes the form, his or her manager then evaluates each employee based on the prior year's goals and accomplishments and both the employee and the manager's evaluations are reviewed and compared.

Every year managers cringe when it's "Performance Appraisal" time. It is the manager's time to confront his/her direct reports. Appraisal, is defined more as a positive gesture than a negative one, it is rooted from the word "praise" which means to "admire or to appreciate." From my observations, I believe that the company's goals in conducting these yearly sessions seem gearing towards criticism more so than to praise. If this is not the case, then why do manager's cringe when it is "Performance appraisal" time?

Mary, one of the managers in, let's say, XYZ department had a disagreement with her boss on a personal issue a few months back. The disagreement was resolved that same day and both had a great working relationship as the year passed by. Mary was productive and was very well liked by her colleagues. Her boss even recommended that Mary would be placed on the promotion list when allowed.

Performance evaluation started the beginning of the following year. When it was Mary's turn for her performance evaluation with her boss, Mary's disagreement with her boss the prior year was brought up in her appraisal.

Mary's boss documented their disagreement and a detailed discussion was permanently placed in Mary's performance file. Not only was Mary surprised, but she was also upset and hurt that her boss specifically mentioned an incident that she believed was a personal issue between her and her boss and was not job related.

Mary felt uncomfortable and unsure if she wanted to continue to work in this department. She started being distant with her boss and she started working at minimum effort. Within a year, Mary chose to report to another manager. She basically lost trust and respect from her prior boss. She felt she was micromanaged and she was completely paranoid of the way her boss managed her.

This is a great example on how a majority of ineffective managers conduct their performance appraisals. Managers should never include personal issues in their reviews with their subordinates. They should stick with only job related issues, as part of the performance appraisal session. This often results in poor manager-employee relationship, decreased work ethic, and morale issues. These often times result in poor department effectiveness, leading to huge turnover rates.

I believe that eliminating yearly performance appraisals would not hurt an organization. I suggest that the ff be used to create a better atmosphere amongst employees in each department.

- Constant Feedback

- Weekly/Quarterly reviews—only job specific

- Employees should be given a chance to have a meeting with their manager to reestablish manager-employee relationships.

- Open door policy at all times

- Personnel file review—each employee should be entitled to see what is in his/her personnel file

- Constant interaction and rule out personal disagreements

I am sure that performance appraisals have helped corporations weed out the poor performers. But, why wait a full year? Why wait a full year if the same issues will be brought up again anyway? Why not conduct one-on-one meetings immediately instead of waiting until the following year?

The traditional practice of performance appraisals is almost like the old fashioned, traditional child rearing practice of the 1930's. In the past, psychologists, caregivers and physicians, advised parents to call on children's mistakes and bad behavior right away so the child knows that what he/she did is unacceptable. Whether the child continues to behave inappropriately or not is up to the parent to punish the child in the right way. The child is not heard and his/her feelings are not taken into consideration. This not only sways to distant themselves to their parents, but it follows unresolved issues between parent-child relationships. If not recognized, I believe that it will eventually affect the child psychologically.

Generations have tried and failed and I believe that continuous recognition and praise followed by strategically well executed reviews –whether parent-child or manager-subordinates, will in the long run result in better interpersonal relationships.

This applies to direct reports. If managers are willing to confront an issue immediately, then the employee has a choice to either get him/herself together or a warning will be sent for poor performance. Waiting for the yearly "performance appraisal" wastes time.

I believe that addressing the issue right then and there will provide a more productive workforce; it will eliminate a lag time of having a poor performer continue working for the firm. Performance appraisals as executed by major corporations today have not improved nor changed a company's employee's work performance. The yearly performance appraisals should be eliminated and replaced by continuous praise/coaching and counseling, appraisal, and reviews throughout the year.

*   *   *

Contribution by **Chris Bradshaw**
PlumLife
Chief Operating Officer

Be bold. Ignore your performance evaluation!

Very few organizations have valuable or valid performance evaluations. But, how can that be? Companies spend so much time and energy on getting these documents created, distributed, formalized, organized and tabulated! In many large corporations the evaluation methods, formats, and techniques are revised every few years. A lot of energy is put into training on how to perform evaluations, even how to sit and listen to the constructive criticism provided by your supervisor or manager.

There are techniques where you and your supervisor each do the same review of you, then sit across the table from each other. You quickly trade documents and each nervously read what the other one says, holding your breath, looking for the items of contention that will cause the meeting to be uncomfortable.

There's that 360 technique where everyone you've ever talked to gets to have an opinion. There's the ultimatum that everyone be spread out on a bell curve or the one where people get rated as a five or below. Another problem with annual reviews is: nobody can ever remember things that happened more than three to six months ago. It's a lot like "what have you done for me lately?" As you can see, a lot of thought have gone into creating processes for giving a message to employees about where they stand and how they are doing, yet none of them work.

No matter how good your evaluation is, it does not provide job security.

There are usually only two reasons people ever look at your file: 1. When they are trying to come up with a reason to get rid of you (getting your file "papered" for HR), or 2. When your supervisor knows nothing about you and looks back at what everyone else has written about you over the years in order to create a review that appears to have some substance.

Need some examples?

Take the case of an entire department that won the corporate-wide award for customer service. One person, especially, had been personally (with formal inter-company memos) acknowledged by almost every senior executive as to their prompt, exemplary, consistent level of support and service to their and the clients' needs. After three years of superior work, she had to step out of one meeting to take an emergency call from her ill mother. Guess what received the bulk of attention on her review? "Family issues are distracting this employee from their work." And what else? The entire department was eliminated when it was time for the company to cut costs.

There are many companies where the person doing the performance reviews have never even met the person they are reviewing. The employee is completely dependent on the reviewer contacting people who work with them on a regular basis and nothing getting lost in the translation. Major consulting firms are like this—seemingly arbitrary decisions are made about who "reports" to whom and the review experience can be night and day between supervisors. One woman was surprised to find an email telling her that her review had been completed, signed, and approved by someone she did not know or recognize; she hadn't even realized it was time for her review.

How about the fast-track, aggressive employee that knows all that the top 1% of employees in the company gets an especially large bonus. A previous boss had explained the entire process to her and explained what needed to be done to achieve that top 1% next year. By the time the next year came around she was excited and ready for the discussion. She had tracked and recorded everything throughout the year in preparation for this discussion. She worked diligently on preparing her review—backing up every comment with documentation, examples, percentage improvements, quantitative proof of the positive impact she had made in not only her direct areas of responsibility but also her positive impact on other departments and other employees. The end result? She had a new boss this year and he was philosophically against placing anyone in the top 1%.

Or, the manager who was given a champagne celebration by the ownership when her department's results caused the entire company to reach a revenue milestone months early. Three weeks later, after seven years of continuously getting raises, promotions, and commendations, on a Friday afternoon, she was laid off and escorted immediately out of the building. Why? The company needed a place for another executive to work while they found a new placement for him—and as the highest paid, most successful manager in the company, her job was the perfect place for him to go.

So what does all this mean? And, since we can't avoid the entire process of giving and receiving evaluations and reviews throughout our careers, what should we do?

We do them. We play the game. We take advantage of that time every year to sit back, look at ourselves and our careers. But, only in the context of our goals, our objectives and the accomplishments we create/created for ourselves. If you are lucky enough to have a boss that you enjoy, that takes the process seriously, then you may even learn something about yourself that makes the discussion worthwhile. But, this is not the place to spend your time and energy. Nor is it the place to find out or discuss issues that really do impact your success or failure in your job. Those are things you need to be looking at and paying attention to every day. Do you procrastinate? You knew that without being told. Do you have anger issues? Do you work well with your co-workers and other departments? Do you need more experience with one of the applications necessary for your job? Do you come in late every week? You know all these things. You choose every day to improve or do the least you can. It's not about acing a certain test on a given day once a year. It is about knowing where you're headed, knowing your goals and working continuously to achieve them, no matter what the process is where you work.

*   *   *

Contribution by **Dan Kesselring**
Consultant/Project Manager
Resources Global Professionals

The Intent of Organizations

One of the most important elements in the success of an organization is the effective management of its people. Performance assessment plays a critical role in identifying how well employees perform in accordance with the needs of the organization. It should also identify areas for improvement and provide the framework for employee development opportunities.

The Outcome of Their Intent

Unfortunately, many organizations merely pay lip service to performance management. Performance evaluations, the main focus and only outcome of performance management in these organizations, are usually required on an annual basis, if at all. In many cases, they are the only time employees receive feedback on their performance. Yet, performance evaluations and their accompanying rating often form the only basis for merit increases, bonuses, promotions, and the ultimate personnel decision—who stays and who goes. With so much on the line, why do so many organizations treat this so lightly?

There is a general disconnect between the organizational guidance provided by human resources, and the execution of that guidance by line management. In spite of the good intent by human resources, managers usually treat performance evaluations as an event, rather than a process. To be effective, employees should be assessed, counseled, and provided developmental opportunities on a regular and on-going basis, not just once a year. Managers are shirking their responsibility by not treating and developing their employees with more care and respect. It's no wonder that the most common reason people cite for leaving an organization is because of their manager.

Make the Evaluation Work for You

However, if you are a likely victim of a manager who does not take performance evaluations seriously, should you just ignore your performance evaluation? This would be incorrect. As mentioned above, organizations use performance evaluations to make important decisions about your professional future. Even if the performance evaluations do not accurately reflect the level of your performance, those decisions will still be made.

So how can you salvage something positive from your performance evaluation? Here are a few suggestions:

Even if not required, provide your manager with a self-assessment, outlining your achievements against any goals you set at your last performance evaluation. Also, include your goals and interests for the next evaluation period. Give your manager something good to work with. This is not a time to be bashful. Toot your own horn—don't expect anyone to do it for you.

Your manager may not provide any insightful comments on your performance evaluation. This indicates that he or she either hasn't been paying attention to your performance, or just doesn't want to expend the mental effort in writing such comments. Some organizations even provide standard cookie-cutter comments "for every occasion" that managers can use. However, these comments usually are so generic that they don't apply to any occasion. In this case, your manager is merely trying to meet the annual requirement with as little effort as possible. Don't let your manager off that easy. Read on.

If the performance evaluation form requires mostly numerical feedback (e.g. rating 1 to 5), ask why a particular rating was given. If no meaningful reason can be provided, then you know it was just a matter of checking off the boxes to get the evaluation done. If you don't ask, you may never know. You're a person, not a number, so don't let yourself be described by a number. If you're given an overall rating number, ask what you need to do to raise it to the next higher level.

In spite of the lack of specific manager feedback, stay focused on your role in the organization. During your evaluation session, ask what you can do to develop your skills or learn new skills that would benefit the organization (as well as yourself).

Following your evaluation session, subtly remind your manager periodically (e.g. quarterly) of the effort you are making in meeting your goals, regardless of whether they were manager-imposed or self-imposed. Be sure to document your accomplishments as they occur, so you and your manager don't lose sight of them. Otherwise, the next time you're evaluated, it will be only on what can be remembered, which may not be indicative of your real performance for the period.

If you are assigned a new manager during the evaluation period, review your goals with that person early on so that you can more likely ensure that your next performance evaluation will be a meaningful one.

The bottom line: take charge of your career. Don't turn it over to someone else in your organization, especially to someone who doesn't take it seriously.

*　　*　　*

Contribution by **Donna Horowitz**
Managing Director
POEL Consulting

While performance evaluations are often biased for many different reasons, real-time, honest feedback is critical to the success of a talented individual and he/she will seek it constantly from bosses, staff members, peers, clients, and others.

I had a boss, Jim, at one company who I had also known at my previous company. He was highly regarded at all levels of both companies—those above him, those at his level, and those who reported to him. Over time, I figured out that the reason was that he constantly sought feedback for what he did well and what he could do better next time. Although he responded to constructive feedback, he held on to his essence. He is an "out of the box" thinker, so while he sought the feedback, he did not worry too much when people criticized him for being a maverick, for crazy ideas, or things like that. In fact, he appreciated those comments.

As an example of seeking feedback, one time Jim had to deliver a message at a communications meeting with dozens of people about the need for them to do things differently than they had in the past. He knew they would not like what he was saying, because the new way would be harder, at least at first. Afterward, he asked one of his staff members, a friend of mine, to come to his office. Of course, she was worried that she had done something wrong.

She later told me that when she got there, Jim surprised her by asking, "How'd I do?" Specifically, he asked her about the clarity of his message and whether the delivery was well done. She and I were both amazed that a boss would ask such a thing. Most of the managers we knew were afraid that asking such a question would make them look vulnerable or less than perfect to their direct report. But he trusted that she would have a good read of the audience and would give him an honest answer (she was a pretty forthright person), and she did. I was impressed that he would seek feedback from such a forthright person because there was no doubt she would say what she felt, and how others were reacting. He clearly wanted true feedback from someone he respected.

When I finally got to work for him directly, I found out that all staff members had to write their own performance evaluation. Many companies do that now, but at the time, it was not common, and

I wondered how I'd know what to write. I wanted it to look good, but I'm certainly not perfect, and I knew he expected honesty.

When it came time to actually write the evaluation, I found it easy to do, and I realized that his good management was the reason. At the beginning of the evaluation period (about a year earlier), we had set clear goals with defined measures of success. Throughout the year, we held scheduled meetings where the only thing on the agenda was to discuss the status of the different goals, and any issues or potential issues. These were very constructive problem solving sessions. The meetings gave me the opportunity to ask for his support in terms of resources and/or advocating with higher ups (his peers) to smooth the path when things were needed from people in other departments.

I learned that he expected me to know what others were thinking about me and about my department at these meetings. Therefore, in order to prepare, I would go seek feedback from internal clients, from my staff members, and from cross-functional project team members. I found it helpful to get the input and knew I would continue to get the input even after I got a new boss. It often helped me identify issues early on and "head them off at the pass," rather than finding out about issues only when someone was so frustrated they couldn't take it anymore. It definitely helped my performance and my reputation, and did the same for people in my department.

At our meetings, Jim would tell me if he was hearing anything different from what I was hearing, or anything additional. We had honest discussions and he was able to coach me, especially for delicate situations. That's why it was easy for me to write my own performance evaluation. It was just a summary of discussions we'd already had. There was no new information at all. But the valuable part wasn't the one document; it was the whole feedback process. To this day, I try to use what I learned from Jim about getting continual, real-time feedback

Contribution by **Donna St. John**
Manager of Information Systems and Technology
Pride Solvents & Chemical Company

In my previous position with a large consulting firm, performance reviews were done at the end of every project by team members verses once a year by your boss. During my first post project review all the project managers sat around to review the team as a whole then by individuals. We had these great little packets that needed to be filled out for each team member rating them from unsatisfactory to exceeded expectations.

Two minutes into the meeting we were told not to rate more than three categories as exceeded expectations or we would lose the team member to another team. At the same time, we were also told that if we rated anyone as unsatisfactory they would remain on the team until they quit. Since this was my first review with this company I was shocked but waited till break to ask about the practice. It seemed the company suffered from team poaching, where highly rated employees were grabbed by higher ranking project managers to build monster teams.

Two weeks later when I had to go over the reviews with the individual team members it was a joke. Here I am rating my best performers as satisfactory just so I could keep them and having to explain that their pay rate had nothing to do with the review. We were not allowed to tell them about the rules. I had this one employee she was fresh out of college; this was actually her very first review ever and I had to rate her satisfactory, when she was one of the best employees I have ever had. Not only did she cry during the review, but she ended up quitting two weeks later to work for a company that valued her hard work. It did not seem to matter that she received a raise; the low rating was too much for her to handle.

I worked on a team with that employee two years later; she was now a lower ranking project manager. She approached me after the first meeting to thank me for trying to explain the game of performance reviews to her; she realized that in the end they really mean very little.

*　　*　　*

Contribution by **Jeffrey Phillips**
Software Support Engineer
Vizioncore

Let your work speak for you. Over the course of my career, this statement has become my own personal mantra. The company I worked for prior to my current employer placed extraordinary value on yearly performance evaluations. This company also set very high performance expectations for its employees, which made it somewhat difficult for some to find opportunities for advancement, or to earn significant merit increases based on yearly performance. With this in mind, I decided early on that the performance expectations I would set for myself would always exceed those set by departmental leadership. I decided that the work I performed would speak much more loudly on my behalf than some evaluation document ever could.

I was correct.

My decision to let my work speak for me allowed me to advance to senior level IT architecture and operations roles more quickly than any other employee in the history of this company. It helped me to earn the respect of my peers as well as the notice of senior IT leadership in the company. It allowed me to become an integral part of creating strategies and policy around server security compliance and change management initiatives. During my time with this employer, I never received a negative evaluation, largely because my own expectations far exceeded those of the departments for which I worked. I spent over nine years with the company and ultimately this decision helped me survive three layoffs that impacted many more senior employees than me. In the end, my departure from that company was my own decision to pursue another avenue in my professional development.

In my experience, defining one's value based on mostly generic evaluations is a mistake made by far too many employees. The value one brings to any organization lies to a large degree in that person's own hands. Striving to meet the minimum expectations of a performance evaluation is the equivalent of earning a 'C' when you could have earned an 'A' by extending a bit more effort. One part of the key to ignoring evaluations lies in setting individual performance expectations that far exceed those of the company, and/ or department where one is employed. The other half of the equation is to do the work necessary to meet or exceed those expectations. In other words, the concept of letting your work speak for you is much more than a notion. It requires high levels of desire, commitment, and dedication.

Desire means more than wanting to earn a certain amount of money, or holding certain positions within an organization. While aspirations to reach higher levels of income and position should be a large source of one's motivation, the type of desire being referred to here is the desire for excellence in whatever role you may find yourself. If you work in the mailroom, your desire should be to become the best mailroom employee in the company. In order to realize that desire you must commit yourself to learning, performing, and developing expertise in the various aspects of your role. You must show dedication to delivering the highest quality of work possible. This may mean long hours or otherwise going above and beyond to not only get the job done, but to get it done right the first time.

When you allow your work to speak for you, performance evaluations begin to hold less and less value. They become mere five minute mandatory yearly interactions between you and your manager that are for the most part ignored.

* * *

Contribution by **Len Salva**
NOC
MCI

Hark back to the days, as a child, when you played musical chairs at a birthday party. Did it matter if you were good, or bad? No. What mattered is where you were at that instant of time when the music stopped.

Today's performance evaluation process is very similar to that childhood experience. You could be one of the most productive, loyal, caring, astute employees an organization may have, however, if the music stopped and you were in the wrong place . . . see ya!

There is no "merit" in evaluations today. HR rules mandate that they must be done. Whether it's an annual event, or one where you have to update on a quarterly basis, the intent is disingenuous.

How often have you been told to "just get it done" when it comes time to fill out those self-evaluations? How often have these performance reviews been done post-haste? How often did you and your manager actually sit down and discuss not only your performance, but your goals and aspirations as well? My guess is, not often enough.

Remember the chairs? Every organization can only have a certain number of "high performers." The rest of us will be destined for that "meets standards" category. Meaning, we're breathing, we show up for work, and we don't make any waves. Even if you think you are doing one heck of job, that chair will more than likely be pulled away from you at the last moment.

The availability of chairs is dictated by what's really important: stock price and bonus monies available for the executive branch. Has the company earned enough net new revenue to meet stated guidance? If a company cannot make their numbers via top-line growth, the only other way to get there is cut bottom-line expenses. The more that has to be cut, the fewer chairs there will be.

Your direct management team has no authority to change the game. Edicts are sent downwards through the organizational chains where the rank-and-file managers implement said programs. There is no room for exploratory sessions where you and your manager can descent into a truly interactive session to exchange ideas or values.

The chairs are numbered, as you are. Evaluations are opportunities for companies to cut. You may be as stout as an oak, or you in fact may be driftwood, either way, it doesn't matter. What matters is where you stand in the organization. If you're not standing in the right spot at the right time, guess what, you won't have a chair to sit down in.

Do you still need to execute these evaluations? Of course; it's mandatory. However spend more time understanding your company and the underlying political environment. Who has clout and who does not? Who do you need to align yourself with? And whom do you need to separate yourself from?

When you used to circle those chairs, did you not always look to the group to see who was positioning themselves for the most optimal angle for a seat? Weren't you always on the lookout for those who you knew would pull that chair away from you without a second's notice? The game has not changed. Learn from your past to forge your future.

*　　*　　*

Contribution by **Lionel Roblin**
Vice President
SAIC

In many organizations, performance evaluations are simply a "check the box" activity. Everyone has to do it, so they do it and forget all about it. In other organizations, performance evaluations have an interesting way of reflecting the current economic state of the organization. When the organization is doing well, your evaluation will likely be a positive one. When the organization is not doing so well, everyone is scrutinized respectively. The point is: your performance evaluation is not a true reflection of you and you as a talented individual are better off ignoring most of it.

There are many reasons why a performance evaluation is rarely a true assessment of the employee's performance.

Most of the managers I have reported to viewed the performance evaluation of their direct reports as a time-consuming annoyance, taking time away from their real job. They saw no added value in the process and treated it as one of the chores of being a manager. They spent 15 minutes filling out the questionnaire and five minutes discussing it with me.

Depending on the type of questionnaire developed by the human resources department, filling out a performance evaluation questionnaire correctly may take a manager between one and three hours per employee and requires searching your memory and/or your notes. The discussion with the employee should in principle be a dialogue where the employee can ask clarifications, provide explanations, request changes, discuss the path forward, training options, etc. This could take another hour.

Most managers do not have that much "free" time and have no sufficient recollection or notes to make a correct assessment of a whole year of performance. Therefore, the performance evaluation will most often be just a snapshot of the employee's performance over the past several weeks.

Furthermore they felt (and often justifiably so) that they were useless; that they were carried out once a year to satisfy the company's requirements and justify the salary adjustments which, regardless, had to fit within the guidelines already provided by the finance department.

As a manager with fifteen direct reports, I tried to avoid these pitfalls. I believe that a clear and objective performance evaluation can help the career development of an employee and will help me in my own job and my company. I have to humbly admit that while spending more time than my own managers on the performance evaluation of my own direct reports, the pressure of urgent business demands have always prevented me from spending the necessary time.

Promotions are not made on the basis of a performance evaluation but on the appreciation of the people you provide support to and the availability of a position. None of my performance evaluations indicated that my performance exceeded the requirements of the position, I was however promoted three times in three years and eventually hired out of my company by a former colleague who offered me a higher position.

That is not to say that when a performance evaluation is particularly bad it should be ignored.

*   *   *

Contribution by **Miguel A. Velazquez**
Manager—Telecom Accounting
Verizon Communications

During one of the many employee assessment discussion meetings that I've held with people that I've supervised along my fifteen (plus) years, I noticed that the employee who I was meeting with looked a little tense. From the beginning I could tell that something was bothering her and it was clear that the meeting was not going to be a "smooth" one. I've always followed the practice of giving people enough time to read their performance assessment before meeting to discuss, because common sense dictates it is the right thing to do; however, in some cases "giving enough time" can turn into "giving too much time" and people can easily lose track of the objective of a performance assessment, as this story illustrates.

I started the interview with the individual described before by verbally providing the performance feedback in general terms; you know, the usual "this is what you did right and this is where I believe you can improve." To my surprise, she agreed with the verbal assessment and nodded in acceptance (and commitment) when I listed the actions that I believed she should take for improvement. I thought that I had initially misread the way the meeting was going to go and that it was going to turn out as a "smooth" one until I asked a standard (getting-ready-to-wrap type) question that I always use: Is there anything in your assessment that you don't agree or don't feel comfortable with? The person immediately said "Yes!", she flipped a hard-copy of the assessment that she had brought with her, that had been sitting on the table facing down, and I was able to notice several portions of bright-yellow highlighted text, which was nothing but a list of "language issues" that she needed to discuss with me. We spent over one hour going through the issues one by one while she made me explain why had I used specific words in each of the highlighted sentences and would request me to change them or reconsider them. Using basic negotiating skills, I granted some of the wording changes while I held a strong position on some others. She was not happy because she seemed to be determined to get the key highlighted words out of the written assessment. At some point, she even accepted that even though she agreed with the message she did not agree with it being documented in the assessment, in spite of the words used.

After several minutes (that felt like hours) of pushing and pulling on both ends, I realized that we were not getting anywhere. That was when she gave me a clue about what was going-on and, as a result, I came up with what turned-out to be one of the strongest arguments that I've learned in my career about performance assessments, and one to which I have recurred many times during performance interviews. I first asked: Why are you so concerned about the words being used and not about the message being sent? She replied, "Because I don't know who might be seeing this assessment." "Who do you think could be seeing it?" I asked. "I don't know . . . people in HR, or our Director [my boss], or even our VP . . . or maybe even an internal hiring manager sometime in the future if I need to apply for a different job in this company," she replied. My answer to her argument, as I recall, was something in the bounds of: "OK, first, why would people in HR care and, if so, do you think they'll have time to read employee assessments? There are over 230 thousand employees in this company! Also, do you think our VP has the time (or priority) to read people's assessments?" I concluded. "How about hiring managers?" she asked. "I'm sure they do spend time reading them for all the candidates in their hiring slot." Right there, that was the mind-changing clue about the view of performance assessments that she gave me. Being a hiring manager myself, I knew the answer to that, so I said, "I don't think so."

When hiring, we managers rely on verbal (not written) feedback provided by the immediate supervisors of the person and for that we just meet and/or talk on the phone. "As a matter of fact", I added, "I cannot recall a time in my entire career when I used a written performance assessment to try to come up with an understanding of how a person is performing, and that is not only for hiring but also for merit considerations, promotions, or for any other purposes I could think of . . . Firsthand knowledge and feedback is the practice." These are, in my opinion, very strong words and a fact to which a lot of people are oblivious. Large companies spend millions implementing performance assessment processes and tools to support them, and at the end these systems are reduced to minimal meaningful use, at least, for the actual development of people.

My next question in the interview story was key to the end of the discussion: "Do you think that John (our Director) needs to read what I write to know how you are performing?" I answered the question myself. "No, he doesn't. He knows form the day-to-day interaction with us and that is the same reason why no matter how much you make me change the wording of this assessment you will not change the perception that either of us have about what you need to improve." End of the discussions.

This was an important and eye-opening lesson for me. The discussion with this employee had made me realize that the only important sources of feedback that one gets are the good old-fashion day-to-day input from supervisors (when there is such input) and our own assessment of how we are doing things. Timely and candid feedback from a supervisor on a day-to-day basis is not always present; however, this is an issue related with a different assumption from the ones discussed in this book: Assumption #3: "You can either be managed or mismanaged."

I've seen organizations constantly "evolving" their performance assessment processes and tools. No two years tend to be the same. I have companies evolve from manual filling of template assessment forms to an intranet based tool that uses pre-set rating ranges and software-based workflow technology for the preparation, approval, share, acceptance, and filing of performance assessments. An interesting fact about these processes is that the system locks the ratings of the people, which are the mathematical drivers for determining merit and/or bonus ranges, long before the actual "write-ups" of the assessments have to be completed. In other words, the language of the assessment is usually prepared long after the numeric ratings have been locked. If you add the fact that for the two most recent performance years, because of what I believe are budgetary practices, a company has set a percentage threshold amount for the number of people that should be rated as "under-performing" as well as a limit in the number of people who can be considered excelling in their job; it is all now driven by these mathematical-formula limitations.

As a result of all this, and doing my best to adhere to the "process," I've found myself adapting the language of assessments to make them fit (or to justify) a rating that has long been locked and that, in some cases, was not even completely driven by the actual performance-based requirements of our group (because of the explained thresholds). I have to admit that there was a time when I was concerned about this but then I learned what I've explained (in the story of the "assessment-words pincher") about the true sources and uses of feedback; I now place more importance to providing/receiving timely and candid feedback on a day-to-day basis, and started caring a lot less for what is written in the assessment.

The wording included in performance assessments might be relevant from the legal and liability standpoint, but experience has taught me that written employee evaluations are seldom of relevance for the understanding of an individual's performance. So, go ahead and feel free to ignore your performance evaluation.

*   *   *

Contribution by **Naseem Malik**
Director, Global Sourcing
Terex Corporation

One of the more ubiquitous rituals in Corporate America is the performance review process. Having gone through this at several companies, I'd like to share my varying experiences at places like RR Donnelley, Navistar International Truck & Engine, Ariba (Free Markets) and others. I'll refer to the places I've worked at as Company A, Company B, Company C, etc.

The reason why it is a valid assumption that one can ignore a company's performance evaluation process is that, in most cases, integrity is not maintained. It becomes more of a popularity contest than an objective evaluation. The grand and lofty expectations of objectively quantifying how one lives the company's values and achieves superior results usually go by the wayside for any number of reasons. It could be an economic downturn or that things are humming along fine so there's no need to expend much effort on this mundane HR process. Or, it could be that you do not have the right chemistry with your boss and that will cause objectivity to suffer. However we choose to view it, more often than not it will turn out to be a subjective exercise.

At company A, I had an interesting experience, i.e., a complete reversal of fortune within the span of a year and a half. My first review was a few months after I joined and it was above expectations stating that I was doing great. Incidentally, the company was amidst unprecedented growth. Fast forward a year and everything had fallen off a cliff. Now that a precipitous decline was underway, nothing anyone did on the team was good enough and ratings plunged.

At company B this process actually seemed to be as painful for HR as it was for the employees. Interestingly enough, it didn't seem to matter whether the company was performing well or below par. There was no interest in making this a worthwhile effort beyond the perfunctory two-page form to fill out. What I found truly horrific was that most managers would simply put 'I concur' next to the self-appraisal done by the employees on the evaluation form. Talk about barely lifting a finger! All of this despite having an official 10-page guide on how to come up with 'SMART' (stands for: specific, measurable, attainable, realistic and timely) goals and assessing objectively.

At company C, I was told that I basically "walk on water." Now to be fair, this company had the most robust performance assessment process of all my former employers. Not only was everyone challenged to put forth 'SMART' goals, but they were public as was its tracking for all to see in our department. Once a quarter we had a one-on-one meeting with our manager to review performance and ensure we were on track and come up with plans if we were not. Now the fact that I was categorized as a high-potential and high performing employee did not do either me or the company very much good considering I was told all of this after I had given my notice to leave. Since my manager had already done my performance evaluation he wanted me to have it. While I appreciated the glowing words, it was unfortunate that it had to come to the fact that our company was in the middle of a merger with many people departing that they began the process of trying to retain their people. While I was generally aware that I had exceeded my performance targets and was given the periodic pat on the back, there wasn't any discussion of a career path or potential next roles during the course of the year.

At company D, I was told by a quirky boss that I was outspoken and that my sense of humor was perceived and construed as being abrasive. Since this was a dynamic, start-up environment, we all had revolving managers and direct reports. None of my other managers pointed out these particular traits as an area of improvement. Point being that my performance itself was not in question. As a result, I did not let one person's subjective view affect my confidence or style. In fact, in subsequent years and at most places, my sense of humor was usually singled out as an asset in building team rapport and business relationships.

At company E, in a course of a few months I went from being told that I have a lot more strengths than development needs to being told that I did not have a great year; just plain mediocre. What made this especially appalling was that in this instance leadership never took the time to come up with realistic and practical goals. When the company realized that there wasn't really any career path and wanted to save on bonus payouts then suddenly this annual performance evaluation ritual took on a lot more importance. Since goals were not reset or recalibrated during the year, this painful exercise in futility became all the more transparent for employees.

Having shared the above, do I think that the performance evaluation process is completely without merit (pun intended)? I would say probably not; however, I do not let these performance reviews define or label me. The value I have derived from these is limited to the extent that it helped increase my self-awareness. This in turn helped me improve myself and my team. While it may be tempting to write this ritual off completely, it would probably be unwise to do so. In most of my experiences, there is usually some sort of financial remuneration tied to this exercise. In some cases, you may find there is more at stake than you'd like and thus you have to ensure you go through the motions to the best of your ability. If for nothing else, take the opportunity for self-reflection and learning. Most of these performance evaluations have a self-appraisal section, and I felt that I owed it to myself to take the time and effort to elaborate on what I've accomplished, where I fell short, and what I wanted to achieve in the future.

There is one other aspect; I am cognitive and conscientious of when it comes to this ritual. And that pertains to my role as an appraiser. All the examples cited above have helped me learn what not to do in the realm of performance evaluations. And I have strived to incorporate these important lessons by trying to do the opposite while evaluating my team members. If leadership and team development is important to you, then there's no easier way to show your people indifference as to put forth a half-hearted and shoddy excuse of a performance evaluation. I admit that it is sometimes difficult to motivate oneself when the vast majority can't be bothered about this process. But, if it's done sincerely it will come through and, perhaps, even be appreciated.

At the end of the day, similar to other aspects of corporate life, this too is a trade-off. You do not want it to become an all-consuming and all-important yearly exercise. But you also don't want to be callous about it to the point that it has monetary consequences. Let's face it, when does one ever get asked to show their past performance appraisals to a future employer? This will probably never happen; at least this has been my experience.

*   *   *

Contribution by **Papi Valmond**
Key Accounts Manager
Chrysler Financial

When approached to write about an assumption that resonates with me, I was excited at the chance to contribute and chose Assumption #5 (Ignore your performance evaluation) with the hope that my story might help to improve someone else's corporate experience. In this excerpt I will share with you some experiences from my previous employer: The three most common career strategies, how these career strategies dictated your path, and how getting a promotion prematurely, based solely on a performance evaluation, can be a devastating career move. Sometimes even signaling readiness for a promotion prior to securing the necessary core competencies can lead you down a path of failure and may cost you time and money to remedy.

In my seven years of experience with a major automotive company, I have seen many instances that support the overall theme of this book. In that time I began to notice that I could classify the primary career strategies into three categories, the leaders, the supporters, and what I affectionately call the "chair blockers." The leaders were just that, they got into a new position, designed great strategies and changed the department for the better as they moved on. The supporters are those who made it possible for the leaders to lead, they knew the ins and outs of the bureaucracy and how to implement a good strategy. And lastly the chair blockers, people who have ceased to ascend for whatever reason (maximized potential, personal constraints, etc.) and are blocking the chair you need to sit in to gain valuable experience to contribute as a supporter or leader.

Immediately after noticing these categories, I noticed another interesting phenomenon. As the leaders continued to ascend, they would develop a preference for particular supporters who were integral to the leaders reaching their lofty goals. In either a feeling of indebtedness to these supporters or simply a desire to build a team that would continue to succeed, the leaders tended to "pull up" their supporters with them. At first glance, this seems logical, except for one thing, the supporters typically don't have the aptitude to rise as quickly as the leaders do, so you find people who lack the prerequisite skill sets in a particular area because they did a great job in another. The desire to move from a supporter to a leader combined with performance evaluations completed in haste can cause one to overestimate their own capabilities. It signals a readiness to their superiors without ever having taken on the added responsibility to gain fundamental analytical tools, knowing when to apply these tools, and the confidence to apply them, or for short, experience.

In one specific case, a colleague did just that. He pledged his allegiance to one specific leader and sacrificed all other objectives and relationships to appease this leader. In return, that leader took him everywhere he went including to assist him on a variety of projects with varying degrees of difficulty. As luck would have it, the leader left the company after 15 years. In that time, my colleague had managed to gain a great title and salary, but burned many bridges along the way. While burning bridges is one of the worst things you can do in Corporate America there is one worse; he had signaled he was ready for so many jobs in such a short time he hadn't developed the skills to commensurate with his salary and title. In working for the new boss he was found lacking the business acumen. When the new leader reached out to others, no one could vouch for him. Finally, he was demoted four levels in what I can only assume was professionally humbling and financially challenging. Even after proving mastery at this level he could never get from under the dark cloud that followed him to whatever subsequent position he took.

The moral of this story is two-fold. First and foremost, conforming to your performance evaluation and not a more realistic consensus of your strengths and weaknesses can set you up for certain failure. For many companies, a performance evaluation is merely a legal and human resources department requirement and not designed to help you navigate the corporate landscape.

Secondly, when choosing a career strategy, be genuine, be flexible, and always reinvent yourself. Whether you are a leader that depends too heavily on supporters, or a supporter that can't function without the comfort of someone else bearing the responsibility of decision making, be thinking of the next challenge and never get caught standing idle.

*   *   *

Contribution by **Tomi Davies**
Chief Executive Officer
TechnoVision Communications

I thought I would share two different stories to bring this assumption to life. In my previous role with a FTSE 100 retailing organization, once a year all employees' performance were "evaluated" by their line managers based on their role within the organization. Rob was a new graduate intake whose line manager was Joan, a long term employee who had worked her way up from the shop floor and became stuck in middle management. Rob's role involved a lot of technical details which were beyond Joan's grasp, unlike other areas which she supervised. She had, however, over the years, at the expense of other subordinates working in the area, developed a checklist of activities which she used as a system for conducting her evaluations to measure performance.

Rob, the "new kid on the block," decided to apply some of his newly acquired skills from a university to the outdated technical activities he was asked to perform in an effort to impress his employers. He managed to produce improved outcomes from his activities in significantly less time than his predecessors and even created documentation of his new approach to getting the job done. Joan's system, however, was based on ticking activities conducted and showed Rob only performing 40% of the ones she had on her list with her having no way of identifying that the ones not performed were no longer necessary with Rob's new approach. When performance evaluation time came along, Rob was surprised by his "below average" rating by Joan who told him "not to sweat it" and just make sure he did better at the job he was given by making sure he carried out "all" his activities. Rob's efforts to share his new approach with Joan proved futile.

Last year, Rob's company was contracted by the very same retailer to outsource the department which conducts the operations that still includes Joan as a supervisor. Had Rob not chosen to ignore the performance evaluation, he would probably still have been in the department reporting to her and trying to adhere to the activities list. Today, she is now one of his employees.

Aisha was a girl from Senegal who had managed to graduate magna cum laude in computer science and engineering from MIT. She came to work for us when I was heading the Strategy unit of a software engineering organization. She was put into a team headed by David an Irish guy who had learnt his programming skills, working at different computer companies in the UK. During her first year with us, which was in 2000 and the top of the dot com boom, Aisha like all of David's engineers, was rated five which meant "top of her game." The company's share price sky rocketed to well above $100 and the two founders who owned majority of the shares in the company became "billionaires."

Aisha, based on her performance evaluation, was of the opinion that her approach to programming, which resulted in longer delivery times than was necessary, was totally acceptable and the norm. No one, including myself, bothered to really review the staff evaluations even though we prided ourselves on developing our people. Within a year though the story changed dramatically as the dot com bubble burst and the market began to crash around us with the commensurate loss in share price. As the market situation changed, we as executives looked inward at capacity and how to get leaner and more efficient. As the performance evaluation period drew close, we informed our managers, including David, that the results of their evaluation would be reviewed by the Executive team. The same individuals who had been rated 4s and 5s just twelve months before were now rated 2s and 3s with Aisha's evaluation reflecting "cultural challenges" by David.

During the review, it came to light that for the two years Aisha had been in the company, no one had informed her that her code (the programs she wrote) were the least efficiently produced and always required rewrites by other programmers. This was due to communication difficulties between herself and David who confessed he could not understand anything she said. Unaware of her deficiencies and the subsequent evaluation, when Aisha was called to be told she was being made redundant as part of the restructure exercise, she thought she was being called to be given a raise. If she had ignored the previous evaluation and conducted her own assessment as a basis of self-development, no doubt she would have improved her situation before the axe fell on her.

Contribution by **Veronica Paz**
Controller
Trend Group USA

In my tenure with Arthur Andersen as an external auditor for several years, I received several performance evaluations, or "RATERS" as the organization had coined them; each one was from a different engagement partner and/or manager in the firm. The incongruity of the whole process is that everyone had a different rating for the same individual on the same category. One partner viewed my work as "exemplary" and "top notch," while I was viewed by other managers and partners as "above average." Some feedback provided was helpful to me in my development as an auditor, whereas other raters provided me with no additional information to help my growth. Such a broad range of discrepant evaluative feedback proves, in arguably most professionals' opinion, to be only marginally helpful in satisfying an appraisal of professional skill applied to any given assignment (and its associated tasks) based on such aspects as knowledge, efficiency, accuracy, and, most importantly of course, results.

At any rate, ignore your performance evaluations as those that did not rate so high did not obstruct me from getting double-promoted and running audit engagements smoothly. These merits were, in no small part, a direct result of professional skill, mastery of processes, procedures and their application toward achieving the desired results of any given assignment. The operative word is result. As implied above, evaluations are simply opinion-laden judgments and observations by others. Though even the most proclaimed "best-written" or "best structured" performance evaluations are said to be impartial, they are at best, a framework of evaluative opinion by others. Only to the degree that evaluations focus on (or completely isolate) results, the quality of such results and the relative efficiencies to which results are affected by professionals, are the true measurement tools for performance. If you believe in yourself and have the commitment to work hard and excel, then just pick and choose the advice you would like to take. Everyone has strengths and weaknesses; after all, you are your own best judge. Other viewpoints if constructive can help, but in business ignore your performance evaluations and you will still tend to do well if that is your ultimate driver. Focus on results, particularly since they speak for themselves and, by default, tend to render professional accolades which are based on measures; not opinion.

*   *   *

Contribution by **Sonia Clayton**
International HR Expansion Supervisor
Continental Airlines

The mere mention of work performance evaluations can be enough to send any employee into panic mode. Companies may talk all year about the importance of performance evaluations. Some use it as a motivation to get employees to work better/ harder/longer. Others use it as a threat to bully employees for undesirable behavior. And still other companies discuss performance evaluations only when it's time to complete them, seemingly forgetting about them before and after the fact.

Regardless of how different companies approach performance evaluations, business professionals likely worry about how much merit to give them, how it affects their careers and how supervisors handle the results. While the answers likely vary from organization to organization, the truth behind performance evaluations is that they may have less to do with your actual performance than you might think.

While no one can make a blanket statement about performance evaluations across all fields, companies and managerial styles, there are several overlying reasons why performance evaluations are flawed and why you don't need to live or die by your results.

Years ago, I worked for a company that provided SAP Documentation and Training Services. I functioned mainly in Brazil and other Latin American countries because I spoke Spanish and Portuguese fluently and was familiar with the culture and business processes. After a long period of time, marked by success in many assignments and ventures, I approached my supervisors about having a chance to work in the United States. I wanted to expand my skill set and have the opportunity to further my career. My supervisors hesitantly agreed to let me work for a probationary period.

After several months of working, wherein I gained several new high-profile clients, my supervisors conducted a performance evaluation to determine if I should continue working in the new capacity or return to leading the work in Brazil and Latin America. I received a surprisingly negative review considering the success I had experienced. According to the evaluation, I was not able to speak English well or perform the basic functions needed to operate successfully as an employee in the United States. As a result, I returned to my previous position and responsibilities.

I later learned that my supervisors manipulated my evaluation because they wanted me to stay with my current duties and pay and to avoid finding a replacement, since multi-lingual Business Developer Managers are not very easy to find. After receiving the negative review in May of 2001, I quit during the following month of July. Subsequently, I started my own company, Virtual Intelligence Providers, LLC (VIP) www.vip-global.com during the month September, just two weeks after 9/11. Currently, I work as the President and CEO of VIP, a global ERP implementation support operation, specializing in SAP Documentation and Training. Within the first two years the company became a multi-million dollar operation, and it is still running successfully after eight years, serving over 70 domestic and international corporations and public sector in the SAP Market and gaining new clients.

Needless to say, I was functioning especially well in the United States, speaking English, handling international operations, negotiations, and completing all of the tasks that I was not supposed to be able to do according to the negative evaluation I received.

My experience is only one example of how performance evaluations are not always accurate or important to regard. Several other factors also contribute to their less-than-successful outcomes.

Check the box.

Sure, there are some organizations that have developed a fair and useful system to complete the scheduled evaluations. They have a comprehensive way of analyzing an employee's track record for the year. They use the forms and interview to give constructive feedback. They gather input and ideas from the employee and provide an experience that is mutually beneficial for both the individual and the company.

In the majority of organizations, however, performance evaluations are simply a "check the box" activity. Few companies have invested the time or the money to create an effective system that can accurately assess an employee's performance and provide honest and useful reviews. Supervisors don't always like to take the time to fill out the exhaustive paperwork that often accompanies the evaluations and have difficulty thinking of specific examples to back up their comments. Since everyone has to complete the evaluations, often for legal purposes, they are recorded, then filed away and forgotten about—sometimes not even being reopened for the following year's review.

Chances are, if you work for a company that completes the evaluation questions with simple exceeds expectation, meets expectation, satisfactory, or needs improvement, type responses, your supervisors aren't putting enough thought behind the analysis of your performance to give it any further thought once you have both signed your names at the bottom.

Who is really being scrutinized?

When organizations are performing well, employees tend to be reviewed favorably. When organizations are struggling, everyone is scrutinized respectively. This leads some to ask what that says about the evaluation process.

In some organizations, performance evaluations have an interesting way of reflecting the current economic state of the organization. If everything is running smoothly and business is successful, the overall atmosphere generally is that of complacence and well-being. An employee's actual achievements may not be heavily scrutinized.

If a company is not doing well, upper management is likely to be criticizing every aspect of the business including accounting decisions, number of open positions, efficient functioning and individual employee value. Receiving a critical review during a time like this may not be an indication of an employee's effectiveness and accomplishments as much as a supervisor's need to prove that he/she is critically assessing and analyzing ways to improve business functions. Everything about the organization is being scrutinized, and individual assessments only make up a negligible portion of the overall picture.

So, the question comes down to what, if anything, should employees do with the results of a performance evaluation? In my case, it provided me with a crucial piece of information: the company's goals for my career and my goals for my career were incompatible. I was able to use that realization to my benefit and act accordingly. My experience was probably more drastic than most situations; however, the point is that a performance evaluation is not always a true reflection of an employee's performance. It can reflect a company's economic status or a supervisor's alternative need. It can be easily manipulated or politically motivated. It can be quickly thrown together and just as quickly forgotten, and when all is said and done, a talented individual is usually better off ignoring it.

*　　*　　*

Contribution by **Wei Fuh**
Senior Consultant
Deloitte LLP

We've all seen this before—performance ratings from a scale of "1 to 5" (or something similar), across a multitude of measurable areas. "1" stands for greatly exceeding expectation, "2" for exceeding expectation, "3" for meeting expectation, "4" for needing improvement, and "5" for needing serious improvement. After asking a few questions, we soon find that almost nobody gets a 1 for any area. That is just how it is.

I have been through the formal performance review at several companies, from public to large private companies, and I can tell you that performance ratings don't have much meaning behind them.

My first experience comes from my earlier years. Having just switched to the IT industry not too long before that time, my salary was relatively low. After working for less than a year, it was time for the annual performance review. My performance rating was a 2.

Having said that, my bonus was a decent amount, between 3% and 4%, and this was reflective of the company's well being in the previous fiscal year. My raise, however, was a whopping 20% increase. Since my starting salary was low, I was merely adjusted to reflect the industry average for those in similar roles.

My second experience is more recent. After about a year in a position, I went through a re-organization, where my team was absorbed by another group, and I also was given a different title. The performance review followed immediately, and I received a 3 this time. Even though the company was different, the performance rating system was more or less the same.

I ended up with a 6% salary increase, where as the company average was 4% for those in the same role. Again, with the re-organization, my pay was slightly lower than the industry average for the new title, and my pay was merely adjusted.

Clearly, performance rating systems do not accurately reflect the salary increase that a person should get.

*　　*　　*

Assumption #6:
No Raises, No Promotions, No Kidding

Every single Talent wants to be promoted. No Talent wants to be in the same role for a long period of time. We have already established that and that makes being promoted a very important milestone for a Talent. Yet, the caveat is that you are not to ask for a promotion. This may seem somewhat strange that you are seeking a promotion but you shouldn't ask for it.

You cannot demand a promotion and those who do will likely live to regret it. You might be able to aggressively bully your boss into promoting you by tossing around your accomplishments; however, consequences of a resentful promotion can come back to bite you.

There are a good amount of people out there who are harassing their boss to get promoted. Have you considered showing your boss all that you've accomplished and then asking to be promoted? I hope not, because that doesn't work. If you need to draft out a menu for your boss and ask for a promotion, it's too little too late.

Your boss and or your boss's boss are either aware of your contributions or they are not aware. If they are aware and feel that they want to recognize you, then they will. You do not have to map out your lifelong accomplishments, unless they specifically ask you to.

For a long time, I came to work and my boss and I had a one word conversation, "Hey." That's all we said to one another. I would say "Hey" and my boss would reply back with a "Hey." Guess how many times I got promoted at that organization? Forget promotions—my salary barely kept pace with inflation. My boss had little to no idea about my contributions and I was hoping that his mind reading capabilities would kick into effect any moment—they didn't. A few days before I left the organization, the VP of my department stopped by and wanted to understand why I was leaving? He said that I had been doing a great job and co-workers were very satisfied with my contribution. And then it hit me, of course, the better I performed at my current job, the deeper I was digging myself into my current cubical—I had trapped myself into a system.

We talked about being Trapped (by a system) at the very beginning. For those who are Trapped (by a system), a promotion goes something like this. You get a standard inflation merit increase and told that you are doing a good job and may now go back and take your seat. The unlucky ones get told that because they have done so well being trapped by their system, they will be made as the backup for another system. They are now well on their way to becoming *buried* by systems.

With Assumption #1 in place, who cares if your boss does not promote you? You have already taken care of that problem. You are in your current role to learning what you'll need to be successful in your next role. If your organization simply doesn't have your future role available, then go find another organization that does. If you are going to wait around for your organization to have that Team Lead, Associate, or Director position open sometime in the future—do it at your own risk. Do not get upset when two years have passed and your dream position hasn't opened up in your organization.

Well, if asking for a promotion is out of the picture, how about a raise? Sure, you may have your selection from the standard inflation rate. Would you like a 1.5%, 2%, or 2.5% raise?

The "I-need-a-raise" school of thought usually argues that "I'm doing my job better and more efficiently and should be rewarded with a material increase in merit because of this." There is a common misconception that we need to address here. When your organization hires you, they are taking your first year's performance and your subsequent year's worth of performances into account beforehand.

In an example, an organization might need someone to maintain the facility, file documents, proof contracts, design flyers, etc. They need someone to perform a specific function. You are there to fulfill that function until your organization no longer needs that function to be performed. You on the other hand are taking your first year's performance as a separate activity from your second year's performance. Do not make this mistake. If you need a merit increase, you will have to change your role to equal that to the value you are providing to what your organization is willing to pay for.

Having a corporate position does not shelter anyone from the laws of supply and demand. Think about it; your corporation is not sheltered from the laws of supply and demand; what could possibly make you feel that you can demand more money unless you change what you are supplying?

Now there is a difference between storming into your boss's office on a Monday morning asking for a raise because you need a new car and negotiating an increase in pay at an appropriate time, such as, when your contract is up or in an annual review. If you feel that you are delivering more than what you are being compensated for then you have a few choices.

- You can do nothing and complain internally. This is a popular choice. You become the guy everyone talks about at the office who keeps telling others that 'I don't get paid enough to do so-and-so'.

- During your next review, you can raise the awareness that you feel that you are delivering more than what you are being compensated for. I'll be honest—this is a tough one because if your boss doesn't already see that you're doing more than required and won't compensate you for it then you need to find another role, perhaps in another organization. And if you let this go on much longer, you are sending a message to your boss that it is okay to abuse you.

Most bosses are not evil and want to compensate you for your extra work, though the company may not be willing to provide the funds. So you either stop doing the extra work or find another role that will compensate you for your efforts. When you underperform most organizations are quick to make you aware of this. When you are over performing, you need to be able to do the same.

Finding another role is usually the best solution. It is possible that your boss might change your role and compensate you because you have taken on a new level of responsibility or workload—congratulations and my hat's off to you.

Since you have just discovered that you can take on more responsibility or workload, you have grown since you first took on your current role, and that is something to feel good about.

You will, however, need to find another role. This is because you have realized that you can do more and with each day that you continue to come to work, you will know that you can or are doing more and should be compensated for it. If your boss lets you know that you should stop taking on the extra responsibility because you will not be compensated for them, then you can choose to continue for personal growth or find another role that will compensate you for your abilities.

If you don't find another role or you willingly decide to stop performing that extra work, then be sure to not keep telling yourself that you can do more and that your boss or company is holding you back by not compensating you. No one is holding you back, except for yourself.

If you feel that you want personal growth and a merit increase, look for another role in another organization that will give you both. If you find that other organizations are not currently looking for someone to perform that role, then that is a clear indication that you are offering a service that the market does not care for—for the moment at least.

Although you may want to think, "I do so much, they can't afford to lose me," don't be surprised to know that everyone—and I mean everyone—can be replaced. So don't become angry at your organization for not giving you a raise; learn from the experience and hear what the market is telling you.

When you do get a raise or a promotion, you'll realize that it is because of the added responsibility that you've taken on. Individual raise percentages can vary on current economical conditions of your organization. When times are good, your organization will be more willing to give out larger raises; however, when times are bad, there is usually a tightening of the purse and your personal performance may have very little to do with your merit increase.

Allow me introduce you to . . .

Contribution by **Bob Gamble**
Learning Generalist
Wachovia

Unless you are doing more today then you did yesterday, it doesn't make sense to ask for a merit raise. If you feel that you are delivering more value then are being compensated and are not seeing a competitive wage, then you should find another organization that will pay you for your value because your organization is flat out telling you that they will not pay for the extra work that you are doing. We are all familiar with the concepts of supply and demand—you have the option to always test your demand.

To ask for a raise is essentially an attempt to breach the contract you have with your employer. When you first started at that particular salary, you agreed to produce a particular product or provide a particular service in exchange for compensation. The employer knew that he or she would need to make an investment in your training and indoctrination, but after that brief period, you would be productive. And that is what you are getting paid. This is not to say that your salary or hourly wage shouldn't ever increase—it should. But why it should increase may surprise you, and no, you don't ask for the increase.

First of all, I believe that it is a privilege to work. No one "owes" us anything. We are not entitled to a living wage. In America, we earn what we get, we don't demand it. The notion of entitlement is at the core of many of society's ills. The privilege to work in exchange for compensation wouldn't even be possible if not for the hard work and solid business practices of the men and women who built the company you work for. A business does not exist to provide you sustenance—not unless you own it.

Don't misconstrue this belief to think that I don't believe in fair compensation. I do. Not only that, but as a business owner, I am more than happy to give it to you. Very few business owners are greedy—far fewer than you may imagine, and if you feel that the owner or owners of your business are greedy, you shouldn't be working for them. If I am a business owner, and you can increase my profit by taking on more responsibility, don't you think I'd welcome you to take on that additional responsibility? And if I can make an additional two dollars by paying you one of them, don't you think I'd want to do that as well? And if you are that valuable to me, don't you think I'm going to compensate you well enough to keep others from taking you away from me? Therein is the answer to "Should I ask for more money?" The answer is, "no, you shouldn't." You should ask for more responsibility. You should ask for the opportunity to contribute more to the company's bottom line. You should ask for the opportunity to more strongly support your manager in the completion of his or her goals. You should demonstrate that you can increase profit and that you have increased your personal worth. The money will follow. It will follow when you show—with documented evidence—that you are more valuable than before, either at your evaluation or when you ask for an interim evaluation. It will follow when you let your network of friends and colleagues know what you're doing, and they can use you. It will follow when you can say to your manager, "I've been offered X salary from another company, but I do like it here, and I want to give you the opportunity to match it before I leave."

Another common misconception I hear people say is they deserve more money because they have gained a certain amount of experience. This may be true, but only if that experience makes you more valuable, as mentioned earlier. Too many employees claim that they have, for example, 10 years of experience, when in fact they only have one year of experience that they've repeated 10 times. Experience exposes you to new ways to solve problems, new perspectives on your business, new business acumen that you can apply. If you're not gaining those valuable attributes, you're not gaining experience, you're putting in time.

So, I implore you not to ask for more money. Ask for more responsibility, and then fulfill that responsibility better than the next person. More importantly, don't just do your job—grow in your job. The money will come.

*   *   *

Contribution by **Shalin Kothari**
Senior Compensation Manager
Schneider Electric

Some of the reasons an organization will provide an employee a pay increase is for merit, equity adjustments to bring closer to market, promotions or career development. An employee should not arbitrarily ask for any of these pay increases as a manger will provide them in its due time.

A merit increase is provided annually either at a focal review point or on an employee's service anniversary. In either case, it is based on the employee's performance during the last evaluation period, typically a year. A good manager will differentiate the increase based on performance rather than applying a peanut butter approach and evenly spreading the merit increase among all of his or her direct reports. An employee can always challenge the increase given if it does not adequately match up against his or her performance, but should not be asking for one on an ad hoc basis.

Likewise, in other situations, an employee should not be asking for pay increases. It is important for an employee to also understand that there are other elements of rewards other than compensation. Benefits, work environment and development are complimentary to compensation. An employee should look at the total equation of rewards and not just focus on pay. Compensation itself is not a motivator; it's the total reward package that provides motivation.

However, compensation can be a de-motivator if it not competitive with the market. Managers should be transparent with employees where they are relative to the market. It is also easy for employees to gather this information these days from the internet. Employees are typically paid below market if they are new to the position and do not have enough experience. Managers and/or organizations will gradually bring them to market over the course of a few years as employees gain experience. If an employee is experienced, a good performer, and not paid competitively, a discussion for an equity adjustment is warranted.

At the end of the day, if employees are asking for increases in general, managers will have the perception that they are money hungry, which may hurt the employee's overall career with the company. On the flip side, If an organization is truly being uncompetitive and are not willing to change its pay practices, its best for an individual to look for employment elsewhere.

*　　*　　*

Contribution by **Brad Wachter**
President
DefenseTalent.com

In times of economic and organizational stress, layoffs are a common reaction for companies that are attempting to reduce expenses and survive the storm. These chaotic times can spell trouble for those employees who have weak performance records or are in jobs that are non-essential. However, layoffs can provide opportunities for some savvy employees that know how to position themselves for the future.

Organizations are often inefficient in the act of carrying out layoffs. At times, the staffing cuts leave important work undone. Those who choose to take on new responsibilities and carry the load for those who lost their jobs may benefit. After the dust settles, those who are able to spot opportunity may find that they can increase their value to the organization by voluntarily absorbing additional responsibilities formerly held by those who have departed.

Look for mission critical work that has been left undone. Sometimes, layoffs eliminate employees who were performing work that is no longer essential to the business operation. It will do your career no good for you to pick up these duties. Look for responsibilities that you know are important to the core function of the business. These activities may have a direct impact on bringing in revenues, supporting clients, or producing the goods or services that are most important for the growth of the company. No matter what your functional expertise might be, there is always a way to work on things of value to the company. While working for Classic Residence by Hyatt, one young woman took the initiative to show up at executive team meetings in place of her boss who had recently lost his job. She was not expected to do so, but when she did she was accepted as part of the group and was able to act as a conduit of information to the rest of her department. This display of initiative and competence in discussing critical matters to the business helped her be named as a replacement for her boss. Even if she had not gotten the job, she gained valuable exposure to the senior team and learned a lot that would have furthered her career in the future.

Don't wait to be asked. The key to increasing the size and importance of your role without a promotion is to volunteer for additional responsibility or to simply start doing it without being asked. Move proactively to take on the additional duties. During my tenure at UBS, the best account managers would move to support the clients of a terminated colleague before those accounts were officially reassigned. If done right, when the reassignment was made it only made logical sense to leave the account with the person who had volunteered to play the interim support role.

Show that you are doing it for the team. It can be hazardous to your career to appear politically manipulative in your efforts to take on additional responsibility; however, everyone likes a team player. Keep your attitude positive and helpful and don't make others who might be doing less feel bad. If you make others look good at the same time you are positioning yourself for additional responsibilities; everyone will benefit.

Being proactive does not mean you don't need to be patient. Increasing the scope of your responsibilities takes time and you should not expect to be recognized for your increased value to the organization overnight. View your decision to seek additional responsibility as an investment that will require sacrifice on your part, but will pay off in the long term in the form of increased compensation, satisfying work, and/or authority.

Stay focused. Plan your work and work your plan and it will allow you to meet your objectives. It is important to understand that those around you do not have the same vision and set of goals as you, so don't let them be a distraction to you. If you stay focused on what you want, you will get it. It is in your control to get ahead in your organization.

*   *   *

Contribution by **Henry Motyka**
Consultant
Former Manager of Audit Technology
PricewaterhouseCoopers

If you have to ask for a promotion then perhaps you don't deserve a promotion nor should you get one.

Your work should stand out from day one. When you work, make sure you take on a little bit extra every day. You should, of course, complete every assignment on time and as well as you can, but there is more to it than that.

Promote what you have done. Make sure it is known in a way that is not bragging.

Get to know others in the department. Get used to passing around ideas in an informal fashion. You can impress others in the department by looking like you are always thinking of problems and you have potential solutions.

When you are going to meetings, always plan ahead. Think about what the issues will be and then think of possible solutions. When you get to the meeting, you can impress others with your knowledge and foresight.

Don't leave at 5:00pm. I once worked for a managing partner who was really big on that. Leaving at 5:00pm can make you look like you are a clock watcher. One day, there was a snowstorm. The managing partner announced that the office was closing early at about 2:00 PM. All my staff wanted to leave. I allowed them to, but I stayed myself. Sure enough, this partner came around checking to see who cared enough to stay and who picked up and left. The partner saw me working at my desk when everyone else had left. I think that helped my career.

When you do some of these things, you begin to stand out. In most businesses, the senior managers are looking for talent. They will probably notice you. When management jobs open up, they want to give them to people whose work they trust, who are reliable, who can think ahead, and who show initiative.

Often, they will ask you first before your yearly review. It may surprise you, but it should not surprise you. You prepared for that day many days before.

I started off on a financial software help desk in a large firm. The job was demanding and pressured, but I made it my business to put in extra time, treat every caller and customer very well no matter how badly they treated me, and I made it my business to work closely with others who were not in my group in the department I was in.

Sure enough, my boss sat me down and had a talk with me. I was a fairly green young person at the time. My boss said that the partners had noticed my level of work and would surprise me by putting me in charge somewhere. I was told to be aware and ready.

I was made supervisor of my group when my boss moved up to manager. My boss told me her part of the decision was made easier when my boss saw me working there to solve problems at 7:30 at night. I had gone "the extra mile". It was noticed.

They say management is always looking for talent, and I believe it is true. You can make their job easier for them and for you by exhibiting behaviors that say you care and are good for the company.

*   *   *

Contribution by **John Yavelak**
Senior QA Analyst
Global Payments, Inc.

There are two variations of this principle to consider; one, an indirect approach and the second, a direct approach . . .

1. Show your employer, indirectly, that you are ready for an additional role.

My first career position immediately after college was in trucking/ warehousing as a dispatcher trainee and then a warehouse supervisor. Despite my father's well-intended warning about putting in extra work hours for free, I threw myself into my job for long hours. I found out later that my effort was a major part of why I was re-assigned to the company's new warehouse operation opening in Jersey City, NJ. I continued to "over do" my assigned tasks as a warehouse supervisor. Next, the company sent me for computer training to learn to program their new computer, which opened a whole new world for me, the I.T. profession, for decades to come. The I.T. field would prove to be far more lucrative than the current warehouse supervisor I was. I didn't know then about the company's plans for computerizing their warehouse inventory. My working hours "above and beyond" what my co-workers did would open the door for a promotion for me. They retrained me (into a new profession) instead of bringing in an outside hire to do the job.

There are times to put in the extra effort even when you can't see or affect a direct gain from it ... In many industries, it will happen that when someone is diligent and already shows capacity for additional tasks, they will be the one selected by their employer as the one to re-train for higher or different responsibilities.

2. Show your employer, directly, by doing the additional role.

Years later in I.T. work, as I branched out into the Software QA profession in a major Telecom, our project grew into a company's core network rerouting system. Of course enjoying the QA role, I did all they asked. Our QA Test team grew. Without planning it in any particular way, I started to train new people. I was seeing the need and fill it, as the old saying in business goes. Wanting to grow more skills to be more employable, especially during the 1990's when telecom companies were downsizing, I took on additional roles, such as Process Engineering Team Lead, and others that opened the door for me to be promoted to Senior Member of Technical Staff. Many gurus of corporate politics preach to us in various journals about visibility and other practices that put us in the proper political position to be promoted. I don't agree with them. My experience (and others) taught me; first, show your employer you are already doing the higher level of work. They will acknowledge it later.

Another way of looking at it is that we don't ask for a promotion, we prove to our employer that we have earned it. Confidence is developed this way. They have it in us, and we have it in ourselves.

Wisdom in corporate politics is always important, but remember you don't need politics to get what your deeds have earned.

*　　*　　*

Contribution by **Melanie Hayes**
Certified Compensation Professional
Belk, Inc.

Do you believe in the "Promotion Fairy?" If you've been working extra hours, completing assignments, and running errands for your boss then just ask and she'll wave her magic wand—Instantly granting a promotion, complete with a corner office and a neatly wrapped executive incentive package, waiting for you on a mahogany desk.

This tactic may work in the Enchanted World, but does little to advance your career in the corporate workplace. Whether you ask the Promotion Fairy or your boss, chances are you won't move up until you have proven yourself capable.

When I began working for a major department store, my new job was, in my eyes, quite a step down from my former role of "CEO, Supreme Ruler & Head Bottle Washer." In other words, I had previously owned and operated a small business. The lure of affordable health care and paid vacations led me to try working for a large company. As I began my job search, I assumed that my experience, knowledge and skills would impress recruiters, and I would surely be placed in a management position right away.

The harsh reality was that most corporations want to fill management jobs with people who have had experience in a similar "big box" industry. I was offered the job of Sales Associate. Fortunately, I took the job. I knew that I would not be in this position long. I decided that since I had the drive, determination, intelligence and strong work ethics that would impress my boss, all I would have to do was wait for an opportunity to ask for a promotion, and I would work my way up the ladder in no time.

To accomplish this goal, the first thing that I set out to learn was the company culture. How were promotions granted or earned? I began talking to my co-workers. I met Nita, who had been the store's top sales person for five straight years. Despite this honor, she was obviously disgruntled with her job and the company. I learned that she had asked for a promotion whenever there was an opening, but had been denied each time. It didn't take me long to find out why. While she was well above par on generating sales and customer loyalty, she lacked the ambition to learn anything outside of her realm. She met her performance appraisal goals, but never volunteered to take on additional work, nor did she pursue any of the training programs offered by the store.

I decided that I must go out of my way to take any and every training course offered. I spoke with my manager and learned about how I could take computer based training classes, which would qualify me to work in more areas. I soon discovered courses designed for an area management trainee. I was not aware of anyone in the store that had this role and asked my manager if I could get involved in the program. Apparently, no one had pursued this in quite some time; no one that I spoke with at first knew what to do or how to begin. I didn't let up, and contacted the division human resources office for details. This act was dually fortuitous. Not only was I able to get the trainee position, but I also gained exposure to the managers in the division office.

I had been working for this company for a little over two months and was sure that I was now on the path to becoming a store manager within the year. I knew that I would get a promotion to an area manager when I completed my trainee program, which would eventually lead to an assistant store manager, then store manager. I thought I had my career path all planned out. What I had not anticipated was the detour.

Instead of the position of Area Sales Manager, I was asked to become the Administrative Assistant to the Regional Store Manager. "WHAT?!" I thought, "I don't want to be a secretary!"

The Regional Store Manager had abruptly lost his admin, and needed someone to help him out right away. I had apparently made an impression on him previously, and he asked that I take on the role—at least temporarily. I planned to refuse, but instead asked if I could think about it over the weekend.

One of my biggest concerns—other than the fear that I would be stuck in a position that I didn't want—was that I didn't have the skills that I needed to be an Administrative Assistant. I could not type and could barely even use a computer! In considering the "pros" to accepting the role, however, I realized that this position would make me visible to many levels of the organization. Additionally, it would be a terrific opportunity to learn more about the culture, politics, and expectations of the company. I bought a computer typing program on Friday afternoon and began to teach myself.

On Monday morning, I met with the Regional and explained that I was interested in taking the position, but that I was not a skilled typist. I had worked very hard over the weekend and was able to type enough to get me by. He was very supportive and assured me that he was willing to give this a try. I took the job, and ended up learning a great deal and was exposed to many of the executives that would inevitably assist me as I furthered my career.

A few months later, a human resource manager took a leave of absence, and I was asked to fill in and help out with her HR responsibilities. This was an area that I was strong in, having performed these duties as a small business owner. I was very pleased to help, even though it meant that I would have to do both jobs concurrently. At the same time, the company had purchased an HRIS system, and was working to train the human resource contact in each store. I was not very good with systems at the time, but was determined to master this challenge. Extra hours spent learning this system were rewarded when I was invited to help train others. I was eventually asked to represent the store-level end user in a focus group at the corporate office, and was able to help implement system changes.

Recognizing and mastering new challenges, along with creating a presence that made me familiar and memorable to the decision makers, became a pattern that led to many more promotions within the company. I became an Area Sales Manager, a Human Resource Manager and an Operations Manager. Two years after I began with the company, I was offered the position of Assistant Store Manager. It had taken a little longer than I had hoped to achieve, but I was on my way to my goal of store manager.

On the same day, I was also asked to join the Division office as an analyst in a new role to introduce an automatic time keeping system. Accepting this position over the assistant manager title would be a major detour from the path I thought I wanted. The analyst role would put me in a highly visible position and be quite challenging. No obvious career path led from this new position. There would be little instruction on what to do, as I would be expected to help to define the role.

I accepted the challenge, as I did with subsequent promotions as they were offered to me. Each position that I have ever had has afforded me the opportunity to learn skills and gain knowledge, training, and education that I might otherwise never have acquired. Each position has provided exposure to "decision makers" that have remembered me and helped me advance with the company. There have been roles that I would have liked to have taken on, but did not get. Missing out on these opportunities has taught me that I must never stop proving myself to those around me.

I try to live by the mantra "A wasted day is one in which nothing is learned." Instead of counting sheep each night, I think of everything that I learned that day. If I don't fall asleep before I've completed my list, then I know that I did not reach my full potential for the day.

In retrospect, there are ten basic axioms that have helped me as I've sought and received promotions. I impart them here in the hopes that it will make your journey easier.

- Know the culture of your company and understand the goals.

- Learn the language. Seek to understand the meaning of the acronyms and terms that are used.

- Map your options. Understand the chain of command in each operating area and what opportunities may exist in other departments.

- Know the decision makers. Who are the heads of the areas that you have an interest in, and how can you best make yourself known to them?

- Learn about positions that interest you. What skills or knowledge would be required to assume the role?

- Accept the detours. Don't be afraid to accept challenges that may differ from your ultimate goal.

- Get noticed. Volunteer, join groups or clubs, and serve on committees.

- Network with peers, both internal and external.

- Research topics that apply to your business; keep up with corporate results, reports, and news.

Share what you learn. This demonstrates a proactive interest and proves that you have the ability to lead others.

*   *   *

Contribution by **Ronald R. Dull (Ron)**
Vice President
Convergys

I have found that my greatest success in taking on promotions to the next level have been when I have effectively already taken on the additional roles and responsibilities of that next level. Recently, during a networking lunch discussion in which I was beginning to explore new career opportunities, a more senior colleague shared with me his insight that organizations are only going to hire you to do something that you have already done. While I do not believe that many "rules" are absolute, I have become convinced that this one career "rule" is indeed largely true and applies, whether you are looking for a new career with a new organization or for a new role within your current organization. Generally, you are going to be hired or promoted to do what you have already been doing and where you have already demonstrated success. This is particularly true in challenging economic times when the market is flush with strong talent. Organizations want and can take a "sure bet!"

For example, at a large business process outsourcing company for whom I previously worked, I was promoted to the Vice President level to take on the P&L and overall general management responsibilities for a portfolio of large, complex outsourcing and technology programs that included several of our largest and most well-known clients. This particular portfolio had struggled with low profitability, stagnant growth, and poor client satisfaction, and needed new leadership to continue to turnaround performance. About nine months prior, I had been asked to serve as an internal consultant to this portfolio to develop and execute a plan to turnaround the portfolio by working with the existing leadership and support team. Over those nine months, the project and collective team began to make steady progress in improving profitability and client satisfaction. When a new division President entered the scene and wanted to refresh her leadership team, it became apparent to her that I had already taken on a large portion of the key responsibilities required to successfully manage this particular portfolio, i.e., leading the ongoing improvement of a complex set of business process outsourcing services. Her decision was relatively straight forward to promote me and formalize my title and responsibility for what I had already largely been doing in the prior nine months. I did not have to ask for the promotion. It came naturally.

Given the core assumption of "never asking for a promotion," you might become skeptical that you will be able to truly take on dramatically different roles from what you are currently doing. I do believe, particularly in trying economic times, you do need to be very realistic about your capabilities and what you can truly take on in terms of additional responsibilities—short and long term.

I continue to be eternally optimistic about my own and others' abilities to achieve and succeed at new and increasing levels of responsibilities. The "lessons learned" for me in this area have been several-fold:

> 1) Set out realistic goals and "stepping stones" for the roles and responsibilities for which you aspire. Although there are certainly success stories for those who have completely broken into new roles without any prior relevant experience, this is an

exception. Create a path for your desired role that allows you to build toward that role with building blocks of additional responsibilities from that which you are doing now.

2) Work within your current role to take on those additional responsibilities that get you closer to that desired role. Volunteer for new assignments. Assist peers, including your manager and your manager's peers, in value-add activities that build toward the next formal role for which you have a goal. What can you do in your current role to get to what you want to be doing?

3) Identify ways in which your contributions can be measured, quantified, reported, and acknowledged. Not everyone will be interested in seeing you succeed to the next level. Develop champions who recognize your achievements and contributions. Have a balance on securing these champions.

Your primary focus needs to be on executing and succeeding—not in promoting yourself; however, I do believe that executing and succeeding may not be enough in all situations—and you need to ensure that your contributions are quantified and recognized.

*   *   *

Contribution by **Sarah J. Peacey**
Manager
KPMG, LLP

Shortly after starting my new role with a large public accounting firm as a Senior Associate, my manager left the firm. This provided for a unique opportunity. I wanted to be promoted to a manager and I knew that I had the ability to successfully perform the job, but I didn't have the title or previous experience. I typically take a direct approach when I want something, so I went straight to my boss and told him that I wanted to be a manager. He told me that I had to prove I was capable of the role by already doing the job and also to be perceived by my peers and other executives to be at a manager level.

Over the next year, I initiated a three step plan to transform myself and become a manager. The first step was to meet or exceed the productivity and performance goals for my current role. I did whatever it took to complete my projects with the highest level of quality, even if that meant work longer hours, evenings and weekends.

Secondly, I did a lot of research. I needed to act the part of a manager, so I attended seminars on professional dress, personal branding, and executive presence. I observed what other managers wore to work, then went through my closet and upgraded my wardrobe. I purchased a few suits to wear anytime I had a meeting where clients or executives would be present and got rid of any clothes that didn't fit right or showed signs of wearing. I tried to learn how I was being perceived by others and what I could do to change or enhance those perceptions. I also researched the role itself. I talked with people who currently held a similar position and I worked closely with my boss to understand what the expectations and criteria for success were for someone at the manager level.

The third step of my plan was to do the job of a manager. I knew there were risks involved with this step. I often thought to myself, "What if I do all this work and I still don't get promoted? I will have wasted all of this time, and now I am doing two jobs but only being paid for one." It was a gamble but I felt it was worth the risk. I asked to be included in management meetings and calls to learn more about the business. I volunteered to help my boss complete reports and asked to work on other special projects that would give me more visibility to executives. I also took roles in extra-curricular organizations within the company to expand my leadership, teamwork, and project management skills.

A little over one year after initiating my plan, I was promoted to manager. It wasn't because I asked for the promotion, but because I was already performing the job duties and acting in the capacity of a manager for six months, so they knew I could handle it.

*   *   *

Contribution by **Shane Cox**
Harvard Business Publishing
Manager, Talent Acquisition

On graduation day almost every college graduate thinks they can conquer the world. They have big ideas and they are hungry, driven, and eager to make their mark on the world and they think they know it all, but the reality is they do not. I know this because I was that college graduate. Early in my career I thought I should have been promoted within six months, but I was not. It was not because I did not give 200%, but rather it was because I needed time to understand business and learn about how business is conducted. I was impatient and I thought I deserved a promotion right at that point in time. Promotional opportunities were scarce from my perspective because I was viewing a promotion as something someone gives me.

I worked in the financial industry for numerous years and in the last twelve to fifteen years the financial industry has been very turbulent. I have been in companies that have merged and re-organized and I have even been laid off once in my career. You ask yourself with all these changes that are happening in the business world, how do I grow within a company? How do I get promoted? How do I succeed? These answers lie within you.

Keep an open mind and be a sponge. Learn as much as you can in each position you hold and take the initiative to make things better and more efficient. Take advantage of the services and benefits a company offers you during your employment with that company.

The second professional position I held I was an Administrative Assistant for a large HR department at a Fortune 500 company. This company was acquired about eighteen months from the time I started at the company. Within the eighteen months I went from an administrator to a junior recruiter without a formal promotion. I took on several different tasks and was open to traveling to different offices to help out the department. I worked late, did not complain, and did not get paid for the extra hours I worked. I had a supervisor who was willing to give me opportunities to expand my skill set because I was flexible, open minded, and willing to go the extra mile for the department. I was the "go to" person for my group and they knew that they could count on me when they needed an extra set of hands to complete a project. During this time I took advantage of the generous tuition reimbursement benefit and I went back to school to get my Masters degree.

After two years at this company, I was unsure of my fate due to the acquisition, so I took it upon myself to pursue another opportunity. I was offered a job at another finance company as the only Recruiter. This company had a long history in the Mid-Atlantic States, but was new in the New England states. Again, in this recruiter role I took on numerous responsibilities outside the realm of my duties, which never went unnoticed. This company grew and expanded and I was a contributor to the success of their expansion.

I have done and learned a lot in my career and I have been exposed to small businesses and big businesses. My success was a journey. One that was not always easy, but very fulfilling. What I realized later in life is that the Administrative Assistant position that I held early on was the catalyst that put me on the path to success. You have to work smart for what you want. I was focused and determined and also gave of myself to get me where I wanted to be. My career led me to becoming an expert in a segment of my field and also afforded me the opportunity to speak at a national conference that was held in New York City. Within six years of starting my career, I was able to become a Vice President at a boutique financial services company. Now, I am working in a different industry because I continue to be a sponge and want to learn something new and different. The position I am in now is allowing me to build on my skill set even more. I am taking a chance, challenging myself and stepping out of my comfort zone. I am one to go after the promotional opportunities. I do not wait around for someone to give it to me. One of the most important things I learned is that I hold the keys to my success . . . no one else does.

*　　*　　*

Assumption #7:
Open up-openly teach anyone willing to learn, what you do at work.

Whenever I've mastered a skill at work, I try to find some way of passing on my knowledge. This is something every Talent tries to do. I may either teach a co-worker how to do something or write down steps on how someone else can do what I did. Openly teaching others is extremely important and the benefits are so great; I am convinced that this is a must.

Let's talk about what happens when you don't openly teach others what you know. You already know of the concept of Trapped (by a system). This is the #1 reason why you ought to openly teach someone else what you do at work. You know that the trap exists and you should make a deliberate effort to be on guard.

Did you know that your organization loves experts? Yes, it's true. And you also know that one of the best ways to prove that you are an expert on a subject matter is by being able to teach someone else about that subject area. When you create a mechanism to pass on your knowledge, you prevent yourself from being Trapped (by a system) and become regarded in your organization as someone who is very competent.

The third, and equally important, reason for openly teaching others what you know is that you will have more leverage when trying to learn something from someone else. Like we said before, many people in a corporate structure are afraid of teaching someone what they do because of job security. You can take their fears away by teaching them something you do or know. And when you need them to teach you what they do, they will be more inclined to do so.

Allow me introduce you to . . .

Contribution by **Ali A. Gowani**
President
The Gowani Group

I fondly remember having a meeting with my former manager, Nick, many years ago. Nick is a smart man; he had interned at NASA and then ran his own company before him, and we started to work together at a consulting firm. In a meeting, he was coaching me on why we had to facilitate a concept of operations demonstration for the Vice President of a multi-billion dollar aerospace and defense company. Nick was telling me that we had to make the VP understand the purpose of the scorecard and how it operates. We needed to show the VP that what we are proposing can help his company stay on schedule and deliver under budget. I did not understand what Nick was saying because, quite frankly, most of it was over my head; however, I paid attention and tried to understand as much as I could.

One thing I did not realize when Nick and I were meeting was that we were meeting in a war room. A war room is essentially a big room with one long table and white-boards on all the walls. The purpose of the war room is to get all hands on deck to find a solution to a problem. Usually, the two partners and sometimes the senior manager would be situated in the war room. The fact that the meeting between Nick and I took place in the war room was important. Even though the partners were writing a proposal for other projects, I am sure that they were listening to the conversation between Nick and me. This made the partners realize that Nick was not threatened to share his wisdom with a neophyte. Nick would openly share what was in his mind and he would bring anyone under his wings and show him, or her, the inter-workings of the business.

One thing that I continue to do and promote within my company is the notion of sharing ones knowledge with each other and coaching people in the company. It is well known that when a person can teach someone a skill, then he has mastered that skill. Furthermore, when senior leadership sees a person openly teach others the secret to his or her trade then this shows the senior leadership that the person does not care to safeguard his secrets. It also shows that people who do this are secure in their own right and know they have the knowledge to be successful. This knowledge can never be taken away.

To this day, I think about that meeting and all the other meetings Nick and I had, where he shared what was going on in his mind. He was never obliged by our consulting firm to do so nor by the partners on the project. He did this solely to make me understand and be successful. And in turn, the least I could do is mention his name to others and promote the type of a business leader he really is.

* * *

Contribution by **Alexander Sultan**
Senior Associate
KPMG LLP

My first "real" corporate job was with an international management consultancy, where the culture was not your typical up-or-out model. It was not unusual to see a Consultant stay in their role for 3—4 years before they would get promoted to a Senior Consultant. Likewise, you would see Senior Consultants get stuck in their role and never get promoted to Manager. As such, I had a desire as an ambitious Senior Consultant to get promoted to Manager in two years. My career limiting mistake was asking my Senior Manager in the middle of my second year if I was up for promotion. I still remember his response to me, "you do not ask to be promoted, you get promoted when you are ready." At the time I did not read between the subtext of the message, but the rule of thumb was you got promoted when management felt you were ready.

When I walked away from that meeting I hadn't realized my faux pas. I had asked for a promotion before I had proven to them I could handle the work and leadership responsibilities as a Manager. As one can guess, I got passed up for promotion after my second year and then my third year. At the time I could not understand why I was being passed up, because I thought was meeting all of the requirements of a Manager. My Senior Manager taught me a valuable lesson, which was you always want to know what the next level entails before you attempt to get promoted. When you ask to be promoted you could be prematurely signaling that you are ready, before you have begun to perform at the next level. After you ask to get promoted, your management may assume you know the all of the requirements and leadership skills needed to successfully perform at the next level.

At the beginning of my fourth year, I decided to meet with my mentor regarding this situation since I had a new Senior Manager. My mentor gave me some extremely valuable advice. He suggested I sit down with my Senior Manager and identify tasks, duties, or projects that I could lead or take over. The premise was if I invested time in learning what my Senior Manager did and helped them by taking small tasks off their plate, I could ultimately free them to pursue other opportunities. He also suggested I have a conversation about promotion with my Senior Manager focused instead of asking how to get promoted, but what skills and tools I would need to be a successful Manager. The premise here was I should learn the criteria I would be judged against when promotion meetings occurred, and start demonstrating those skills often and early so that there was a track record of sustainable performance. His last suggestion was for me to find champions like him to do the word-of-mouth socializing to other Managers and Senior Managers, rather than me conveying my desire to be promoted directly. The premise here was other people talking about what a great job I am doing and how I am functioning as a manager is more powerful thank me doing it.

I took onboard my mentor's advice and actively spent the entire year trying to learn what my Senior Manager did, and help them take over some of their duties. This allowed me to learn skills I would not have typically learned as a Senior Consultant. I volunteered to take on tasks that in turn taught me business development, project management, and financial management. I volunteered to lead up small projects, co-founded an Asian Pacific American Forum for my coworkers, and eagerly helped lead different company committees whenever the opportunity arose. I also built strong networks within my management ranks and across other delivery groups to span my network of champions for when it would come time to discuss promotions. However, the most important thing I did was ensure all of the extracurricular tasks did not negatively impact my existing client work. As my mentor pointed out, if you cannot successfully complete your basic work, then you will never succeed as a Manager who has to multitask.

In the end, after my fourth year I was promoted to Manager and I think without my mentor's guidance and advice, it would not have been possible. I still to this day tell other colleagues of my story, so they can learn from my life lessons. When I hear them discussing whether to ask management for a promotion, I always relay the same advice my mentor gave me. At the end of the day, I think my mentor said it best, "do not ask, do."

*　　*　　*

Contribution by **Beth Becker**
Global Meeting Services Manager
MicroTek

About ten years ago, I was working as the Corporate Real Estate Manager for a Fortune 500 technology company that was going through yet another re-organization. During this restructure the role of Travel Department Manager was eliminated and a wonderful and talented Travel Manager was released from the company.

This was a shock to us all. And was especially shocking to me when I learned that the responsibility for managing this multi-million dollar department was now going to be shifted over to me!

Now, keep in mind that ten years ago I had zero experience managing a Travel Department. In fact, the only thing I knew about corporate travel was the telephone extension for the onsite agent who booked my flights, and I usually had to look that up! What were they thinking?

Not only did I have no experience in this area but I had some pretty big shoes to fill as well! I knew that if I wanted to be successful in this new role I would need to learn as much as I could about managing a Travel Department—and quick!

Fortunately, I had a good working relationship with the departing Travel Manager and she was kind enough to share her wealth of knowledge, internal processes and even her industry contacts with me. This crash course in Travel Management gave me a base understanding of the industry and our current relationships and contracts and helped me get through those first few months of transition.

Yet, the next year represented a huge learning curve for me, and I quickly realized that I still had a great deal to learn. Knowing that the previous Travel Manager had found a new position nearby, I called her up and made her a little proposition—If she would agree to act as my "lunchtime" teacher and mentor I would buy her lunch at the local restaurant of her choice. She agreed, and we spent many lunch hours together during my first year in this new role.

Her generosity and willingness to teach and openly share her knowledge and experience with me helped me to be successful in my new role, and for that I will always be grateful.

And, as life would have it, several years later she was employed as a Travel Manager for a large Telecommunications company that was going through reorganization. During this reorganization, she was asked to take over management of their Corporate Facilities Department; something she knew nothing about. But, she immediately knew who to call!

*　　*　　*

Contribution by **Christy Nicholas**
Senior Financial Analyst
RTI Biologics

Some of the most dynamic people I have met are constant learners. They are never happy at their current level of knowledge, but continue to soak up the data, ideas, and processes around them like a sponge. I am one of these people.

I truly believe that any moment not used is wasted. If you are not actively enjoying, creating, learning or doing, then you have lost that moment of life forever. You cannot retrieve it, you cannot change it, and you cannot make it more meaningful.

With this paradigm in mind, I love teaching others. I have been saying for years that the best way to learn something is to teach it to someone else. Your student will ask you questions you may have never thought about, explore areas you have never bothered researching, and come up with solutions you've never considered.

For several years now I've taught accounting at our local community college at nights. Simply on a part-time basis and only in the summer terms, but it offers me insights every time I teach it. The classroom is full of new, bright faces, eagerly soaking up the data and ideas I offer to them. Well, perhaps not eagerly—this is accounting—but I do my best to make it interesting and applicable to the real world. Occasionally, I've even managed to convince a student to change their major to accounting, and I feel well satisfied with my efforts.

When you translate this into the workplace, you may come across several different types of reactions. You may have a surly, stolid co-worker, happy with what he's doing, and not interested in newfangled things. You might have someone just uninterested, or you could have the eager learner.

There are really three ways of learning—auditory, visual, and kinesthetic. There are many journals and books written on this subject, but most people learn with a combination of all three ways. I'm primarily a visual learner—I prefer maps to directions, and picture a word in my mind before I spell it. Others might prefer lectures, or working a problem out themselves to seeing a slideshow.

I highly recommend writing a process task list for the person to refer to and keep. This removes some of the burden him/her, and allows him/her to see the process as a whole. It also empowers him/her with the ability to make notes directly on your page, making it theirs as it were. There is a reason editors like changing anything submitted to them—it tastes better after they've added their own "pinch of salt."

Some co-workers are unwilling or unresponsive, and do not wish to learn something new. If this passing of knowledge is at the direction of a superior, you must do your best to make the process painless. The task list mentioned above takes much of the initiative off their shoulders and onto yours, and it should make the pill easier to swallow. A bright attitude and patient demeanor will help. Do keep in mind that not everyone learns things easily, and some people require several passes to learn a process or idea.

If you come across a co-worker who is simply noncommittal about the learning process, the task becomes somewhat easier.

I usually start off by letting them know when the task needs to be done (i.e., once a month after accounts payable is closed), to whom the results need to be sent, and how long it should take them. Keep in mind that you probably do the task much more efficiently now than when you first started it, so try to convey this. "When I first started, this took me about three days every month, but now I am finished in an afternoon." This lets them know that, while it may take them a long time, that won't always be the case.

If you are lucky, and come across a co-worker who loves learning, your task is easy. The thing to watch out for here is over-eagerness. Steps can be missed if you don't have them written down clearly, and having written documentation of what you have taught is always a good way of covering your bases.

Our current office has recently had a spate of activity in shifting responsibilities as the result of a merger with another company. We had six people coming into a fifteen person department, so supervisors shifted, responsibilities changed, and occasionally personalities clashed; however, after about six months, everyone settled down into their current positions, with a minimum of fuss. I credit much of that success to the strong lead management has made, as they thought long and hard on the disposition of work and talent. Much more of the success I give to the people involved in that disposition—the employees themselves.

What happens if you teach someone what you know, and then are replaced by them? It can happen. I worked for one privately-held corporation as an Assistant Controller. The Controller taught me what to do while she went on a well-deserved vacation. She had worked tirelessly for this company for five years—and then when she returned, she had been let go. Management tried to give me her position (at about half her salary, which was still higher than mine). I refused, as I saw how they treated their loyal employees.

It is possible that this can happen to you, but the best way to avoid this is to become an expert on something. Even if you have taught the basics to someone else, you are still the person with all the experience in the area. You are the "go-to" person. It could be Excel, or the phone system, or SEC guidelines—or even the coffee-maker. Don't discount the importance of caffeine in the office!

They say that it takes two people to make a marriage, but just one to break it. I agree, and believe this analogy can be applied to the workplace. It takes just one sullen person to make learning and growing difficult for everyone else in the department. The best way, in my opinion, to lessen this effect is to be the best learner, the best grower, and the best co-worker you can be, without regards to the other person's behavior. Perhaps they will learn by your example.

Learning and teaching are great gifts, and those that continue to do so will increase their future possibilities. Never limit yourself to what you now know—explore, dream, create, and rise to wherever you wish to be.

*   *   *

Contribution by **Clare Cooper**
Owner
Aircoop Technologies

In a previous job with a large consulting company, I had an opportunity to build a team from the ground up in an area where I was a resident expert. The company was beginning to use a centralized support model to try to gain efficiencies by allowing teams to support multiple clients. My team was made up of mostly new hires as this position would give them the opportunity to learn the ins and outs of the consulting world in a fairly "safe" environment. At the time, I took this position,

I was at a cross roads with my job—I was burned out with the typical project/engagement and was wondering what my next step should be. The thought of changing companies had crossed my mind a few times but I decided against jumping ship order to see what this role would bring.

The new hires always seemed to have a certain type of energy. They are not jaded by the consulting world and are eager and willing to do whatever it takes to prove themselves. Their energy re-infused me and reminded me why I loved and chose consulting as a profession—it's the opportunity to truly help people.

As each team member rolled on, I would spend a fair amount time with him/her and would teach them what I had learned about the software over my years. I especially focused on time saving techniques and procedures. I also showed them how they had the base tools to solve any problem. Not too long after that, several of them were showing me programs/procedures that they had written to shave time off routine activities as well as different means they used to accomplish assigned tasks. Because of the constant give and take, we as a team became more and more fine tuned. We were even starting to get some attention worldwide. Several offices started requesting that we train some of their staff. Thus, our team started adding an international flavor which only helped us get better. For instance, since we were starting to bring in trainees, some of my more experienced consultants began to brainstorm with me about how we could structure the team slightly different so it took on more of a college feel. We would create "core areas" where everyone had to be proficient and then added in "electives" or different areas where team members could focus. This kept training exciting and allowed a person to learn what was needed to support most clients within a relative short period of time.

During the course of building the team, I added several experienced consultants to help me manage the new hires. It was one of these consultants that I had begun grooming to take my place as I knew I needed to start planning for my next step.

Most people in the company did not think of her as management material since her career path was not that of the traditional consultant. During my tenure in this position, we worked together to get her hard and soft skills to where they needed to be. She had the heart and desire to better herself even in areas that were not second nature. I probably learned more from her than she did from me. She helped me realize that although I loved this company and my current position, I had lost the passion I once had; and it was time for me to test the waters elsewhere. Thankfully, I could leave with a clear conscience, because I had helped train her and helped her get promoted. I could hand off the team to her knowing that they would be in great hands and that they would continue to grow. This freed me to find that spark I had when I first started working. I have since opened up my own consulting company and haven't looked back yet.

* * *

Contribution by **Dawn Mc Rae**
Accountant
Global Financial Services Company

Training a fellow employee or employees should not be seen as a diminishing job security. The experiences enable me to show what I know and not believe that the employee or employees will know more than me or will move up the career ladder over me. As a consequence, I love to train and I am aware that many professionals will not share their knowledge. Many professionals are obsessed with showing their fellow employees minimal work due to job insecurity. I am sharing the steps I used as a professional or in my daily life. Self improve and continuous training is one of my strongest beliefs and it's a gateway to life. After leaving school, I started my first job and I would like to give credit to my immediate manager, Mrs. Fontanell, who put me through three months of on-the-job training and I am grateful to her.

The world has grown more specialized and many experts try to make themselves indispensable through information advantage, whether they are administrator, accountant, lawyers, or financial advisors, to name a few job classifications. Their knowledge and experience that they acquired are used as an advantage to be hired. Modern life is linked to an incentive that exists through ones moral, social, and economic belief; however, sharing wisdom is better than having the knowledge and choosing to hold on to it.

In order to retain quality employees in your team you must be willing to teach what you do at work to anyone who is willing to learn. Accepting to work for a company is a major obligation and whether you consider yourself a loyalist to your employer, there are definitely some sorts of standards you would aspire to such as team player, conscientiousness, which is largely defined by the job itself. Associates in the business place sometimes find themselves filling several roles at once and have become a problem in micro business. This I will argue can be a pervasive problem if you are not willing to teach what you do at work to someone who is willing to learn the basics on given responsibilities and roles. I found it effective in my work and life and believe this should be done, for you can see the by product. My open policy of teaching what I do on the job is rewarding. Taking on this role allows me to make sure that what I am teaching the person is accurate. My obligation to the job in terms of the roles and responsibilities are always greater than my obligation to myself. Unselfish efforts are one of the best gifts you can leave in the work place or give to life. Therefore accomplished people in particular should be more willing to help be a guide or, mentor. This culture has driven the fear in many employees that they should never openly teach anyone what they do at work. The trend is due to the fear of losing their job; they believe its job security. While teaching willing employees on the job sounds straight forward, it requires several pieces of functional decisions. Whereby, you should do an analysis on the bad and good situations, seeing how you will disseminate the information.

The following are my basis for making the decision to train.

- Why train? It enhances the colleagues and the company; It helps the associates to effectively understand the function.

- When you train, you build a team.

- What you gain is concerted team effort.

- Who benefits? Everyone gains, including the company.

In life, you are forced to cope and consider many avenues while navigating the professional world. You must take into consideration the consequences of failing to give of your best, while encouraging others to do the same. It is a good practice to teach someone what you know, so it will transcend in the workforce to improve someone else's knowledge and skill set. The measures of substandard work are now prevalent with increasing scrutiny and accountability in the wake of so many scandals that are coming to light. Employees are now subjected to increasing compliance and security requirements, and it is changing the face on how you will be perceived.

Investing in another employee promotes clearly defined objectives and expectations for both parties. An effective team is built through the sharing of knowledge. Sharing information allows employees to set great standard for themselves and lead through the virtues of the job and not by the merits of the job title. Teaching someone what you know can make an employee do a better job, increase productivity and, in many cases, their confidence. I have found this approach highly effective, while creating a reduction in staff turnover, stress-free environment, and it is a guaranteed savings to the company. Cross training an employee or teaching them what you know adds value to the company and you. In sharing with an associate, they become knowledgeable in what you do and understand your function on the job.

Unless you take yourself out of the equation, you will not be able to analyze why you must teach someone what you do at work. Showing what you do is one of the most profitable investments you can make and will have far reaching results in the corporation. Management must emphasize cross training, which makes a parallel with co workers while helping to set them in the same direction that the company has for their objective. Personal performance is great, but it can harm a company when an employee becomes invaluable. If that worker gets sick or opt to leave, you have a crisis of not knowing what the person does; thus, you are stuck with cross training an associate in a short time. The integrity of teaching is creating resilience and it's invaluable.

I am pretty sure we have all had to do some business either in person or on the phone and you might have spoken to more than one employee and each person gave you a different answer to the same question. Do you want to work in a company where it is known for poor customer satisfaction? Remember that an organization is a team and working as a team will always benefit you in being efficient. Effectively representing your company in that way will build the business and better job security.

Always remember that taking the time out to train associates who want to know what you do will prove credibility for the long run and show a direct representation of your belief about the company. Never think about compromising yourself by choosing not to train them properly; it reflects your inability to work in a team. This does not mean, however, those employees who choose other options lack the accepted standards to management. Employees must realize that accepting a job and its responsibilities has to go beyond self interest. The job gets done more efficiently through imparting knowledge and skill sets. Perhaps you can encounter the great benefit in choosing to teach someone who is willing to learn instead of creating an atmosphere of "when I leave it leaves with me." The world is built on someone who started it first; someone else came along and improved on it. Would you like to be a part of that?

*   *   *

Contribution by **Jawed Valliani**
Project Lead—International
Abbott Laboratories

Earlier in my career, I had a great opportunity to be a part of a professional development program in which I worked in three distinct, eight month, technology assignments across the company. Not too far removed from University, naturally I was younger than mostly everyone in each department that I worked in (with the exception of the interns, of course). Here I was, the quintessential "sponge" on each project I was assigned to, hungry for knowledge and experience, trying to live up to this program's hype and learn as much as I could. I encountered some individuals who were quite forthcoming about their role in their respective organizations and the job they performed. On the contrary, I also interacted with certain individuals who closely guarded the knowledge they possessed. As I desperately probed these individuals to understand the big picture, I vowed to share as much I could should anyone take an interest in what I did in the future.

On my last assignment, I worked under a certain supervisor who just happened to be an alumnus of the program I was in. We swapped stories about our experiences and over the course of the next eight months I proceeded to pick his brain about his job. The knowledge I received from him enabled me to secure his position once he moved on to business school. Some time later, I was in a position to manage an employee from the same development program. I remember being in his shoes: curious, ambitious, and confused all rolled into one. Remembering the vow I made years ago, I ensured he had a meaningful and knowledgeable assignment, and taught him as much as I could about what I did. Not only did I have a hand in developing this individual, as he gained skill in handling certain aspects of my job, this freed up my time to pursue other interests. I was able to participate in more strategy and planning with my manager, as well as hone my management skills. By teaching him what I did at work, I was able to let go, take a step back, and further my knowledge about other areas of the business. Having to teach someone, in great detail, what you do ultimately hones your own skills. If you are able to shift your responsibilities to them because of the knowledge transfer, you are then free to learn something new. In my case, it was a win-win situation for all, and it improved my standing as a senior member of the team.

It is said that knowledge is power and that the more we possess, the stronger we are. While this premise may be true, in my experience it was clearly beneficial to transfer the knowledge (and power) to someone who was eager to learn because it made me even more powerful!

*   *   *

Contribution by **Louise Carley Lewisson**
Services Director
Kronos

I want to keep moving forward in my career, which should be no surprise to most people. And to do that, I need to find a successor and surround myself with talented people who can help me get to the next level.

So for those reasons, as well as to pay homage to the managers who helped me, I need to ensure that I enhance the knowledge of my peers and my team to improve their skills so that they can do it too.

My first job was in a library, and it was a very short time after I had started working as a lowly library assistant that my manager could see that I had what it takes to be a manager one day. At that time, libraries were notoriously short staffed and my first manager could see in me some skills sets that she felt would be of use in a management position, and she had faith that I could do the job. It also solved her problem as she was going on maternity leave and did not have a suitable replacement. So she took a chance and started to spend weeks with me, showing me what she did, who to go to with any issues, and how to handle various people so that I was equipped to do the job well.

I was put in charge of the library for three nights a week, from 5:00pm until 9:00pm. I was in charge of a staff of eight people, and I was barely twenty-one years old. But, I did it, and I was good at it. However, the reason I was good at this job was because she had made the time to transfer the knowledge she had accumulated in her five years of being a manager to me, in a condensed management 101 course.

It was a win-win situation for both of us. I got a chance to spread my wings and she solved a pressing staffing problem.

Since that day, for various reasons, I have always made it a point of making sure others know not only what I do, but why I do it. Anyone can teach someone how to create a budget or how to give a presentation to senior management about accounts that are past due. Yet more important to me, when working with people, is why this is important? Why do we need to do this? What can the creator get out of doing these documents? What are the personal and/or business benefits?

By enabling others, you enable yourself both personally and professionally. There is nothing better than to mentor someone and then see them go off and be successful. You get a sense of pride like a parent seeing their child off into the world. And they take a piece of you with them in their skill sets. And, like my relationship with my first manager, they may refer to me when talking about how to handle an irate customer or how to handle a person who is performing below par, by talking about how I handled a situation.

What some people also don't realize is that, by sharing information by teaching others what you do and why you do it, you build an incredible sense of trust and loyalty with your team; Once that trust is established, these people will go to the ends of the earth for you because you treated them as equals. You made a point of expanding your relationship with them to become their trusted advisor. Knowledge is power and by making them more knowledgeable, you have made them so much more powerful, and that, in and of itself, makes them feel indebted to you. Not indebted in a way that you can abuse them or take them for granted, but they are indebted to you because they understand that you acknowledge their professional worth and potential.

I often find that when I am explaining why I made a decision, or going through with someone how I came up with an approach, I also get valuable feedback. In many cases, the person you are working with makes a suggestion as part of the knowledge sharing process that enhances your approach. One of my mantras is that I don't always have the best ideas and so one of the many benefits of teaching is that the teacher can often learn from the student.

My success as a manager, and as a leader, is to never stop learning and evolving. Learning from others, taking certain parts from certain people, and using these things to supplement your own knowledge and skill sets should be part of our everyday approach to work. Even taking one thing and adding it to your "toolbox" of knowledge is worthwhile because you can then pass it on to another person, as can they, and so on.

Some of this knowledge is not always something that you can hold, read, or view. One of the most valuable things you can teach others is an attitude or an approach to a problem. Sometimes the value and wealth of sharing knowledge is not in the deliverable but in the positioning of the deliverable. The words and body language you use when dealing with a difficult situation, in many cases, is so much more important that the actual resolution to the problem you are solving. By working with others to explain why you are delivering the message in this way, or how you organize your approach, is something that cannot be taught and needs to just be experienced.

Furthermore, some of this knowledge is specifically what you don't do, and why you don't do it. One of my key messages is always to uphold the decision of someone on my team, even if I don't agree with it. If a customer goes over one of my team members heads and looks to me to refute the subordinate's decision, I very rarely do this. Why? If I do, I make my team member a toothless tiger. I am, in one swoop, removing their power and credibility so that later on the customers will know they can always bypass their actions and come straight to me. So, I never do this. The list of what I don't do is just as long as the list of things I do—So don't forget to share the things you don't do, as well as share the things that you do.

One final thought: knowledge is power, but shared knowledge is far more powerful. The sum of many is worth far more than the sum of one. Share what you know. Embrace the idea that you are leaving a legacy that empowers people.

*   *   *

Contribution by **Marcie E. Thomas**
Account Executive
Gables Corporate Accommodations

By nature and design, I am a supportive person who puts relationships first. Although this self-described personality trait has shaped my personal life's purpose, it has also attributed to the advancement of my career. I think of teaching others as a learning cycle, with the ability to change one's business perspective, and as a growth process. In past times, I have been given the daunting task of "teaching" a co-worker a process or their specific job duty; however, the mere notion of teaching has produced a less-than-desirable outcome of what was anticipated. Therefore, I would like to think of teaching more as sharing information with others instead of merely instructing their actions.

As an example, I was once complimented by an assistant in my department regarding the number of accounts I closed in a single month. After which she asked me the question, "How did you achieve this level of success?" My answer was not brief nor was it self-congratulating, and I found this to be the perfect time to share the big picture with someone who wanted to learn. Initially, I thought this was an opportunity to "connect-the-dots" for an effective work flow. So, I began to share the structural elements of business operations starting with our delivery systems and concluding with internal and external customer relations. The first item on my agenda was to ensure she fully understood how her position, as well as others in the company, directly affected my performance as a top producer. Next, I proceeded to explain a step by step process on how to keep performance thriving on any level, and how this should be a shared business goal. The interesting aspect of enlightening others with valuable insider knowledge of any trade is sharing how you arrived at your proven and successful destination. In sharing these experiences, in terms of successes, is to highlight a strategic methodology for learning. What is important is that when someone is willing to learn, an environment must be created for that individual to learn. This environment can be produced from sharing real-world examples that had positive and negative results in order to build upon realistic outcomes. In my experience, this appears to engage the listener to learn effectively and, often times, change their prospective regarding being taught. Furthermore, when sharing these often undisclosed strategies, I discover what motivates my personal business successes.

As I reflect on the countless times that I have freely shared my techniques, some would say that I'm too forthright with this privileged information. Yet my opinion is to the contrary, I take great pleasure in obliging others, with willingness to learn, what I have created into best practices for personal success. What most people don't understand is that the competitive edge is acquired from the questions you ask, not the questions answered. Sharing my skills and talents will never diminish my ability as a top performer. When I share with others what I have experienced, it opens a new understanding to what can be achieved, and how to derive a new level of success. I like to think of this as my personal cycle of shared business implementation.

*   *   *

Contribution by **Matt Bell**
Managing Partner
Pacific Rim Capital Equity

Working as a project manager and consultant for many years, I have to be careful what questions I ask and how I ask these questions. Some workers are intimidated when asked about the details of their jobs. Due to job insecurity, lack of skill, or lack of knowledge, some employees are reluctant to discuss their job responsibilities or teach others in order to improve job mobility.

When I began working at a Fortune 10 global technology company, there was a considerable amount of emphasis focused on teaching and mentoring others about specific skills sets. In addition, the learning tool known as a "lunch and learn" was used to develop specific skills. The theme was always that, if the project manager or other key resource had to be redeployed, the team would have the skills to reallocate resources and continue without a business interruption. I was very much in favor of this policy as I believed this process made me a better project manager, and focusing only on job security would limit my learning and development skills. Because of this process, other team members would better understand my role, and I would receive feedback from them regarding opportunities to improve operational and technical processes. The "lunch and learn" tool was utilized on a weekly basis to review areas of interest, and core competencies in various practice areas (such as documentation, technical analysis, and communication skills). Again, the theme was to insure that everyone on the project team had a clear understanding of what everyone else's role on the team was. I focused on mentoring everyone on the project manager's role so that anyone could step in and fill my role if needed.

Every team member had an in-depth understanding of the project manager's processes and responsibilities. By utilizing the "lunch and learn" tool and mentoring about the project management role, my skills and responsibilities, as well as my performance, where completely transparent to the project team. I frequently focused on communication skills due to the fact that many technical team members limited their roles because of a lack of confidence in their writing and overall public speaking skills. By sharing what the project manager's responsibilities are, regarding communications, I was able to imbue my technical team with considerable confidence that everyone could develop the writing and public speaking skills needed to move from a limited technical role to being a project manager, leading the team, and interacting with clients.

By developing this philosophy of promoting, mentoring, and training other employees in the role of a project manager, the ability to become a more productive and responsive employee becomes easier. Additionally, by not worrying only about job security, team members can focus on developing skills that will permit all team members to be more versatile and become more marketable. Given the current economic climate, it is more important than ever to share and mentor your skills, to maintain best practice skills, and to focus on learning new skills. Focus on teaching others what you already know and what will help others improve career and personal development.

*   *   *

Contribution by **Matt Shefchik**
Senior Consultant
The QTI Group

When I started my career in compensation consulting at the fifth largest professional services firm, I was responsible for coordinating our salary survey practice. Although I was learning a tremendous amount from the experts I worked with, I was trapped in that role until I could pass along my knowledge to someone who could take over my work.

I came into the organization and immediately began working in administration, analysis, and publication of the compensation and benefit surveys that the organization did for our clients. I had good teachers, I was open and willing to gaining more knowledge, and I learned quickly. My client contact skills, interpersonal communication abilities, and detail-orientation shined in this role. During my time, the survey practice grew, our processes were refined, and technology enhanced. I was efficient and successful at my job.

That feeling of success quickly turned into discouragement and monotony as I was pigeon-holed into handling all survey work without the opportunity to work on different types of projects and grow my skills. When you are good at something, more of the same comes your way.

I had been working on the surveys for over a year and half before budgets allowed us to add staff and I had the opportunity to train a new member of our team, Tom, who was well suited for survey work. Tom was eager to learn the processes, gain insights, and learn the helpful tips and intricacies of what I did. Tom was pretty much glued to my hip; he shadowed me while talking with clients, doing data analysis, and proofing reports. I unloaded as much information as I could onto him.

After six months of training with Tom, my workload finally allowed me to do more work outside of the survey practice. By this point, I was the one eager to learn and take training from the experts around me. I was able to work on a slew of diverse projects with different client. Then, through retirements and turnover, I quickly added greater and greater responsibility and oversight for the consulting practice.

Because of my actions, management saw talents in me to do other things; more diverse, high-value, projects, but it wasn't until I had the opportunity to train another member of our team that my career accelerated. Now, I'm leading a consulting practice and a major reason for my success was the opportunity to train someone to do my job.

*   *   *

Contribution by **Thomas Juli, Ph.D., PMP**
Managing Director
Thomas Juli Empowerment Partners

My passions have always been sharing information and empowering people. Not too surprisingly, teaching has played an important role in my career. Be it as an economics instructor in college, professional ski and snowboard instructor and coach, or in the in the world of consulting in IT and project management. The ability to teach gives you at least two unique opportunities. First, you share your knowledge, your experience, and your expertise with a wider audience. Second, you learn by structuring your thoughts, receiving feedback from your listeners, and witnessing your advice in action.

The first dimension of teaching—sharing your knowledge and expertise—is the most obvious. Teaching takes place in all kinds of places. You may teach in a class room, recommend a solution to a problem to your client, or speak at a conference. The location may be part of the teaching concept, but it is not necessarily at the core. Teaching styles differ as do the audiences. In this sense, teaching by itself is multi-dimensional. You do not need to look for the right location or opportunity in order to teach. Chances are, your immediate environment offers you ample opportunities to teach by sharing your knowledge and expertise.

The question arises: is teaching critical to becoming an expert in a field? I strongly believe so. Let's look at the second aspect of teaching—the learning aspect. Before you teach, you need to structure your thoughts. This by itself constitutes a learning process. In addition, receiving feedback from your listeners about your presented pieces of information adds to your knowledge bank. Furthermore, seeing your words turn into action (be it a solution you recommended to your client or the demonstration of a new skill) tells you how practical your expressed ideas may have been. Teaching allows your ideas to become reality, and thus may tell you to what extent they are practical. That being said, how much you learn from your own teaching is up to you. For example, if you do not embrace feedback, then your own learning effects may not be very substantial. However, if you are open to feedback, welcome, and request it, chances that your teaching activity will honor you with a wonderful learning experience are much greater.

There is really no excuse not to seek an opportunity to teach. Teaching as described above can take on many forms. It need not be in a classroom setting. Talking to your client or peers, too, is a form of teaching. By teaching, you are exposing your thoughts, ideas, knowledge, and expertise to the outside world. They may be accepted or challenged. Either way, if you seek feedback from your audience, you can learn more about the viability of your ideas. This is vital if you want to excel in your profession. Phrased differently, I claim that you cannot excel in your profession unless you share your knowledge and expertise with a wider audience.

It was my passion for sharing information and empowering people that has led me to a career in consulting. During the last ten years, I consulted for various companies in the telecommunications, banking, energy, medical, and public sectors. At first sight, this may have nothing to do with teaching, but the truth is that teaching is playing a central part of any kind of consulting on at least two levels. The first being actual consulting activities, and the second level consisting of formal presentations for clients at conferences, or in publications.

To me, consulting consists of at least two parts:

1. Analyzing a problem and finding a solution

2. Communicating the solution.

Both parts are equally important. If you cannot explain your solution, there is no need to become a consultant. Having said so, it is crucial that you teach. You need to be able to translate your findings into a language that is easily comprehended by your client. Furthermore, you want your client to understand your suggested solutions to the extent that they accept, embrace, and live them. This may be referred to as "empowering your clients." Empowerment goes beyond mere teaching. The teacher becomes a coach who strives to enable its "students" to apply their newly-gained knowledge in everyday life. Thus, empowerment takes teaching to the next level.

Teaching in consulting is not limited to giving advice to your clients. The second level of teaching in consulting is reaching out to a wider audience, e.g., internal trainings, conferences, or publications. Not every consultant may feel comfortable speaking in front of a large crowd and this is okay. There are plenty of other venues that provide excellent opportunities to teach, share, and learn. For example, attending internal round tables; the idea being to share experiences, identify best practices, and learn from each other.

Soon, I started talking about my own perspectives, which encouraged me to seek a wider audience. Though daunting at first, going public turned out to be very rewarding. When you speak to a large audience at a conference, it is virtually impossible to predict the outcome. You need to set a tone and articulate your thoughts in a way that is easily understood by most, if not all, of your audience. This in itself makes you a better communicator both inside and outside of your consulting world.

It is one thing to know a lot or be an expert. It is another thing to communicate your knowledge to the outside world. When you are able to talk about your expertise and share it with others, you open the door to a unique learning opportunity that, as a consequence, strengthens your expertise even further. Teaching gives you the chance to be challenged and then prove your expertise. The combination of sharing and learning makes teaching a most rewarding experience. At the same time, it helps you excel in your profession. This is why teaching has, does, and will always play a prominent role in my professional career.

*　　*　　*

Contribution by **Thomasina Tafur**
Senior Manager
Federal Express

They say imitation is the highest form of flattery, and I would agree. So, any time someone asks me how I achieved certain goals or milestones, I always share my ideas and why they work for me and my teams or clients.

An example of this was when a former peer at FedEx asked me how I was able to maintain 100% compliance on deadlines for my team, yet have little to no re-work or misunderstandings when it came to my projects. I then took out a document called "My Basic Expectations." The document outlined in great detail what my individual expectations were of every team member. It was a living document so it evolved from time to time. I also had each employee sign it under the clause that they understood these expectations and agreed to them. Believe it or not, my teams loved this document. They knew exactly what I expected from them. They also knew I was open to suggestions and modifications if necessary. My peer read it and asked for a copy so he could emulate it for his team. It came as no surprise that the copy he gave his team was mine, verbatim. That's okay with me in this case, as it was an informal document. I do not condone plagiarism at all. As it turns out, the document was so successful that all Seniors Managers were asked to create something very similar and all of our teams became more productive.

I believe most people resist sharing their ideas or roles for fear of not getting credit or losing some kind of "mystical value" within their organization. There are a number of reasons why this is illogical. First, you can't patent an unfinished idea. For you to formally claim an idea it needs to be well thought out. This is not only the case legally, but also informally within businesses. If you have a great idea, develop it, document it, and then raise it to the powers that be when the time is right. If not, share your idea and let someone else make it happen. It's important to look out for yourself, but you also need to think about what is good for the organization. Most people are good about giving credit to those who helped. Also, giving feels great! Secondly, if you truly do add value to your organization, then cultivate the ideas you like best and allow someone else to cultivate some of your other ideas. Over time people realize who the real brain child is behind projects. Also, I'm a big believer in karma. In all my years at FedEx, I never played politics—all my promotions happened due to a great track record.

*　　*　　*

Contribution by **Wayne Anderman**
Managing Partner, Business Services
Anchor Capital Resources LLC

Setting the Stage

I was the Vice President of operations and sales management in charge of California and Colorado's regional branch of a mutual fund and financial advisory company. This company was owned by a bank that became one of the largest asset management firms in the world. My division was located in the west coast headquarters of the firm on a floor below the Western Regional CEO and President's offices. The firm had grown to a significant size throughout the 1990's and 2000's via many acquisitions and was now a behemoth of strategic company fits from banks, mutual funds, brokerages, family-offices, and asset management companies to trust and custody as well. Well over a dozen regional heads from almost every company of the bank's portfolio of businesses were located in the building that brandished its logo in the downtown financial district. My background prior to this position was in the big brokerage houses, not banks.

Act One

On a large geographic scale, the regional CEO and President held a quarterly meeting, known as "The West Coast Strategy Committee". Well over two dozen senior and mid-level executives of the company's various institutional and retail divisions, hailing from states located throughout the western region, met in southern California to review their performance for the period. These were both retail and institutional based business line representatives. Our mission was to share success stories known as "wins", explain what our particular business line did, teach each other how we did it, and create synergies between our businesses. This took place in an all day session around a large conference room table. There were enough chairs in the room and seating was on a first come first serve basis (with exception of the CEO chair at the head of the table). This was significant as during these meetings we were all students of our colleagues' various businesses while simultaneously we were all teachers of our own business line expertise.

It was a level playing field, with business conducted on a first name basis. Senior management understood the importance of a top down approach, with buy-in at the loftiest levels to developing "learning leaders", and to replicating the process with our most prized asset: the employees who are in direct contact with the client. It was recognized that those employees and those contacts were the life blood of the firm. In the weeks following the meetings we taught our business models to each other's client relationship managers (RM). This enabled an RM to request a client's permission to make an introduction to another business line if they identified a client need and possible solution.

It was a brilliantly effective environment which defined our regional branch as a leader in cross-unit business development (a.k.a. silo-busting), revenue growth, and as a successful model of a learning organization for both officers, and our employees. We were able to deliver value-added services from other units by identifying solutions to problems outside the scope of our core business with the client while exceeding the clients' expectations by reflecting a strong awareness of their business needs. Human resources played an important role in facilitating the bridging of many of the gaps by helping management and employees understand and navigate the professional and cultural differences of each type of business. HR was essential in enhancing communication and understanding across an ever-growing and diverse system of people and business lines. In effect, they transferred their field knowledge to the committee, and we carried that to our people.

Eventually an annual event known as the "Company University" was created. Hundreds of employees from the various cities and states on the west coast attended this all day and dinner event. Dozens of "learning leaders" in thirty-minute class room sessions talked openly about their particular lines of business.

Act Two

The second paradigm of openly teaching what we know to others brings us to the local level of my experience. Once more in the regional CEO's conference room on the floor above my office, a half dozen officers of private wealth management, private banking, business banking, private mortgage, and high net worth brokerage firms met monthly in what was known as the "Western Region Private Client Group". What we had in common was the type of client we dealt with: the individual investor and their need to protect and grow personal and (in some cases) business wealth.

Each member of the group shared the knowledge of where our core competencies lay, the value propositions that we offered, and how we assessed the needs of the client while compliantly doing business. We took that knowledge and, in meetings in our respective offices, illustrated what we had learned from each other by teaching it to our people. We followed up by sending our reps from our individual divisions to meet with each other in after work functions, and encouraged them to schedule time in each other's offices during the week to continue this process.

Across the company we grasped the opportunity granted by our new knowledge and delivered business opportunities on behalf of our clients to our sister divisions. The more our people taught other employees outside our "silo" about our knowledge base of investments and how we can help their clients, the more we learned about other types of banking our clients might need. The proper introductions were made in order to benefit our clients. It helped bring their business, sometimes spread amongst many competitors, under one roof.

Encore

My employees were soon able to operate effectively without my interference other than mentoring based on specific cases from my own experiences and, of course, regulatory oversight. They achieved levels I could not have led them to if I had dictated what to do and how to do it. I shared my knowledge, and in many to most cases they improved on it. In the end you are only as good as the output of the team you lead, so make certain the input is there for members to do what they do best. In my case, the increased competencies of my team freed me up to move on to other projects and keep the unit on the radar.

Private Banking knowledge for one financial advisor determined a career move to another premier institution in that field. Another representative found commercial and business banking was their forte, and transitioned into branch management. I firmly believe that these career paths were enriched by the shared knowledge experiences, both between ourselves and with other units.

The operations assistant I hired at the beginning of my tenure, whose guidance helped me manage over one billion dollars in assets effectively and responsibly, came from a big commercial and business banking background. She taught me everything she knew. Her knowledge enabled me to build and manage in a system that was quite foreign to me, even after fifteen years prior experience in the financial industry. I also taught her what I knew. She currently is the operations manager of an institutional money management firm in Los Angeles which was founded by one of the senior executive officers who taught me how to better teach others in those strategy meetings I mentioned earlier. I recently founded my own consulting firm working alongside a family enterprise rooted in three generations of sustained success.

Knowledge is not a finite and quantifiable package of information. It is a dynamic and changing source of perspective molded from what is perceived by one individual and then related to another, who may be exposed to it for the first time. What we teach anyone is our perspective, and how they choose to use it or apply it becomes the foundation of their own base of knowledge. The important thing is to teach, both openly and gladly.

*   *   *

Contribution by **Joan Finley**
President
Joan Finley Inc.

Over the years, I have found the most enjoyment in my work, when I am inspiring others to do their best. As a management consultant with the Big 8 until it was the Big 5, I defined my success as providing the guidance and support to my clients to achieve their aspirations. A hallmark story is focusing on doing what I could to transfer my talents and know-how in leadership, management, and strategy through matrix management to a Senior Vice President's leadership team of VPs in Operations, Customer Service, Technology, Marketing, Product Development and Sales. My primary role was to provide program management leadership and as I grew to know the challenges each of the leaders were faced with, I provided them my consultative advice in the ways each of them uniquely could apply it. Through this approach, they learned how to manage risk, manage their SVP, and get things done pragmatically through others. They sought me out, eager to share their challenges and learn how to apply planning, prioritization and "big picture" communication techniques to their leadership and management repertoires.

I learned their business, their various management styles—as leading and managing a sales team is very different than executing leadership of an operations unit. The trust grew across the group of VPs as we collaborated to drive results across our teams versus separately competing. We provided as a united front at the weekly update sessions with the SVP. We met the first milestone, implementing on-time and on-budget. We achieved the second milestone, with application of "scope change management" as priorities and market demands shifted and we shifted with them. We achieved the final implementation on-time and under-budget—thanks to a spectacular team effort!

Throughout the program, I was continually pinching myself, as I knew this may be the best it would ever get as far as career positions are concerned—being adopted into an international bank's senior management team, sharing our strengths, and complementing each others' weaknesses. We celebrated milestones together and, in the end, I reluctantly turned down the offer to join this great "once in a lifetime" team of courageous and humble leaders. I am one of the few who has learned first-hand what it means to share my experience and leadership while, at the same time, being in a place of humility. I learned what international business is about—as I proudly saw my client promoted to EVP of an international bank; one of the few women to be positioned in such an important and influential role.

*   *   *

Assumption #8:
Never Fall in Love

We can all be pretty competitive when needed, and when we are working for a well known organization, we have a tendency to do some name dropping. Name dropping is exactly what it sounds like—you drop the name of your company in conversations with other people, primarily other corporate professionals. You're talking to your third cousin on your mom's side, whom you meet once a year, and you say "Yeah, well I work for So-And-So, I'm sure you've heard of them." You laugh it off knowing full well that the only purpose of that statement was to give you an ego boost. There is nothing wrong with an innocent ego boost every now and then. The problem reaches an unhealthy level when you have genuinely fallen in love with your company.

When you start to genuinely fall in love with your company, you start making significant personal sacrifices to the organization in hopes that the organization will reciprocate. Sometimes your organization will reciprocate and other times, it will not. When your organization doesn't reciprocate, you will start to build resentment. For example, you take your laptop on your honeymoon and field a few problems while out of the office. Your significant other is not pleased by your decision; however, you love your organization and want to make sure that everything is running smoothly. Six months later, its performance evaluation time and you get a standard inflation bump in your salary. Or your child is sick one day and needs to be picked up from school early, but your boss appears to be frowning when he gives you the early leave. All this time you were thinking that you'd be treated like a rock star because of that big sacrifice you had made on your honeymoon, and now it appears that instead of being treated like a rock star, you are having rocks thrown at you.

I don't hesitate one bit in wearing my company's hat or t-shirt, or in showcasing their luggage on public transportation. However, you can be sure of one thing—I am not in love with my company. You see, I do not dislike my organization or bear hostility against it. I like the organization I work for, and if I didn't, I would go work for another organization instead.

What's important to know is that a Talent does not fall in love with the company that he or she is working for. Instead, a Talent falls in love with the opportunity that the organization is providing him or her. This opportunity could be anything, from working in a thriving environment with other Talents and industry leaders, to a chance to learn something new. Also, you must keep in mind that you can always try to find the same key opportunity elsewhere if it is no longer available in your organization.

Above all, don't badmouth your organization because the opportunity went away. We should all remember that this is just business and your company needs to think of survival first. Your company must think of what is best for everyone, including the investors.

I'd like to introduce you to some friends who have personal experience with the idea of not falling in love with your company. I hope you'll allow them to share their unique experience and I'm sure that there is at least one additional piece of knowledge from each of them can apply to your current situation.

Allow me introduce you to . . .

Contribution by **Christian Nascimento**
Senior Manager, Deployment Planning and Reporting
Comcast

In 2004, I joined the Wilmington, DE-based MBNA (at the time, the largest issuer of credit cards in the world) as an Assistant Vice President. This banking organization was well known locally for its distinct culture—more jaded people called it a cult. The fact was that this organization did an excellent job of indoctrinating people into its way of thinking.

Because of the bank's close proximity and relationship to the University of Delaware, the organization recruited a large number of graduates each year, many of whom stayed with the bank for years and years and, in truth, expected to make their entire career there. Additionally, their call centers were located in areas of Delaware that did not have many other career options. Add to this the fact that this bank paid higher salaries than most other local companies, offered a more robust benefits package (including a large number of vacation days, and a pension), and provided a unusually high number of amenities (several free employee fitness centers, dry clearing, an arcade and even a barber shop), and it becomes easy to see how they developed a very strong feeling of employee loyalty. In truth, a large number of employees fell in love with the company, and believed that the company loved them.

Soon management made the decision to merge with an international banking giant. Employees were stunned. Many of them had assumed that they would be with the bank for their entire career, and ignored the warning signs. They now put themselves at risk of being laid off, especially if they were in areas that would be redundant once this global giant completed the acquisition, such as HR or Accounting. In addition, by not getting ahead of the curve, they now had to face more competition for the limited number of jobs locally.

The employees had so much loyal to the bank that many employees ended up hurting their careers. It's unfair to blame either organizations because the merger was good for the shareholders. However, I hope that it serves as a cautionary tale against falling too much in love with your employer.

*   *   *

Contribution by **Craig L. Chapman**
Sr. Network Engineer
Northrop Grumman

In today's world where the "Old Garde" is always on the lookout to punish those who challenge the status quo, this little piece of advice is one you should always remember. It is my earnest hope that sharing my experience with fellow Talents will help them to avoid the same pain that I suffered.

As a corporate professional, the chance to be employed by one of the largest defense and governmental contractors in business sounded very appealing. What happened next was totally insane. After my hire as a 6 month contractor (a trial period that is standard with larger companies), I began to notice that the Old Garde was more interested in sitting around and milking a paycheck than in performing their jobs and therefore showcasing themselves as a Talent. In an environment such as this I quickly stood out. My boss at the time, we will call him Stan, was very impressed. Stan wanted to speak with me at dinner the second day I was employed. In that meeting Stan expressed to me that some of the older members of the team could do simple tasks but what was needed was a Talent that could lead this team. After a nice discussion on how to achieve that I went to work. I began calling meetings that no one thought I had the authority to call, challenging the Old Garde's decisions and attempting to show them that keeping pace with technology and the skills needed to use it are a good thing. This resulted in my joining the ranks of full-fledged employees a full month before they planned. Sounds great, right? I thought so too. Shortly after this Stan and I spoke again about my performing so much higher than the rest of the team. In this discussion Stan stated that he spoke with upper management and they too had noticed my performance and that compensation would increase by a specific amount in one month. I was ecstatic and understandably so. Unfortunately, things were going to change—Stan soon left the organization.

Now my team had no leadership and no drive. I did what any Talent would—I stepped in and led the team. Senior management approached me and recognized my effort and stated that they had something to tell me. The discussion that we had was similar to the one I had with Stan. Then management told me that the increase amount was going to be %50 of what Stan and I had discussed. I mentioned my concern about this discrepancy and that Stan had mentioned an amount double that. Upper management assured me that it was an honest mistake and one that would not happen again.

I was excited to be working for this company and let it slide. They say hindsight is always 20/20 and, looking back on it, this is the point where I should have recognized that I was in love with the company. Soon a manager for my team was found, we'll call him Jim. Jim saw my drive right away. I was able to get extended technical education and a greater understanding of management. Jim set a meeting for me at my 6-month review. Jim informed me that my Talent had been noticed and I would be promoted. Jim also stated a set raise that was going to happen. Jim said that the raise would be a certain dollar amount . . . I got a funny feeling and asked him to get it in writing from upper management. Jim was unable to do so, and again the raise or compensation increase came in at less than 50% of the amount discussed. It was at this point that I began my plans to move to a new employer.

I kept thinking that if such a thing was going to happen again I would confront management and deliver my resignation in person. I spoke again to upper management about my concerns and again for the second time they brushed my concerns away. So I began my search by networking and talking to colleagues. Jim noticed this and asked why I might want to leave, I told him about the lies that he had told me and what upper management and I had discussed. Jim was defensive and chided me for my attempts to be treated fairly and compensated for my work. I began to lay low. It was the following February (year-end review time), when Jim and I again had a discussion on compensation. Jim stated that the raise I was going to get would be $10,000. I expressed my concern that upper management would not follow his recommendation. Jim assured me that he had spoken to upper management and they had come to this agreement. I thanked Jim and began planning my move. I was not going to let this happen again. Sure enough, in early March Jim called me into his office and told me that my compensation increase had "gotten messed up". Jim insisted that it was not his fault. At this point I thanked Jim and delivered my resignation. I informed Jim that I was no longer "in love" with this company and wouldn't be with any other.

My fellow Talents, beware love is a strong emotion that can blind you to reality. Don't let it happen to you.

*　　*　　*

Contribution by **Frank T. Mitchell**

It was a Wednesday afternoon when I received the invite for a fifteen minute mandatory meeting with my boss for the next morning titled "staffing". Needless to say, it was not going to be easy to wait out the next 12 hours or so until the meeting. I then found out that everyone on the team had a meeting scheduled. We started to reach out to each other one by one to see who knew what. The word had spread that there was going to be a "Reduction in Force". That's right, by the end of the next day it became apparent that not all of us would continue to be employed at the number one company in our industry.

The rest of that afternoon and into the evening, I could not help but think what I could have or should have been doing differently. I am a dedicated Human Resource professional, and I've spent a considerable amount of my career in the Staffing Business—I had seen this type of thing happen to countless numbers of people and even to myself a time or two in the past. Those experiences had equipped me to deal with the remainder of the evening, and even to encourage some of my peers. Needless to say, now was not the time to try to figure out what I could or should have done differently—that is something that I should have been thinking about all along. In the next few paragraphs, I will explain to you the one thing you should never do: "Fall in love with your current employer."

I didn't say don't love what you're doing, or don't like who you're doing it for, just don't think that your current employer is the only one that can utilize your skills and talents.

Back to my morning meeting with my boss the next day. The first words out of his mouth were "You're fine, your job is safe." He then proceeded to tell me what characteristics I had that made me incredibly valuable to the organization; some I knew, and some were actually news to me. This was refreshing to hear because it quickly became apparent that the things that had kept my job safe were the same things that would have, and continued to make me attractive to the competition. I learned a very important lesson that day. Because of the strong working relationships I had built with certain individuals I had advocates in the room who were able to vouch for my skills when my name came up in the staffing meeting. They were proud of not just my work, but also how I interacted with others, as well as other leadership qualities.

I can remember one of my former peers, let's call him Dennis, saying after he had learned that he would be severed "What am

I going to do now? I have given my whole life to this company." I remember thinking to myself; does he really think that his life is over because he lost his job? Dennis had poured so much into his current employer that he forgot to take time out for himself. He did not network outside of the company, so he had no idea what was actually happening outside the company doors. He had been there for so long that he didn't even know the names all of our competitors. It had been quite some time since Dennis had graduated with his degree in the field, so his knowledge was not as up to date as it could have been if he had refreshed his learning with some recent courses.

I am going to outline a few simple things you can do to keep yourself marketable within your industry and current company without falling in love with your employer. However, before I do, I think it is important to define what I mean when I say "falling in love with your current employer." I am not saying that you should not like your current employer. In fact, I believe it is imperative to hold similar core values. What I am saying is that when you fall in love you begin to think that it is the only place for you, which is a very dangerous mental place to be in. You actually start to lose value, become less innovative, and even lose your sense of drive. So I am not saying don't love what you're doing, just don't fall "in love" with who you are doing it for. With the current economy and job market being the most unstable it has been in the last four decades, you should have numerous examples right around you of folks who have lost their jobs through no fault of their own. At any time this could be one of us.

Here are a few simple steps which I believe will let you see your stock rise inside and outside of your current employer if you implement them:

> 1. Network within you current organization. Networking is very important on a daily basis because you can meet internal resources to help you accomplish your daily tasks more efficiently. So, next time you are in the break room getting

your daily dose of coffee, and that same person you see every day walks in, formally introduce yourself. Discover what department they work in and at a minimum identify how your two departments interface with each other if at all. It is always easier to reach out to a warm contact when you are in need of some help.

2. Always know what you're working on and the way it relates to how your company makes or saves money. This is extremely valuable when talking to internal and external clients. This allows you to help others understand how you fit in to the way the company works. When others know what you do it automatically increases your value.

3. Have an industry perspective. What this means is you should always know what others in your industry are doing. Having this knowledge will give you the ability to act as a consultant within your current organization. This is an extremely valuable skill to acquire. I always recommend attending industry events and building a network of peers that perform a similar function at another company. I would also recommend subscribing to an industry magazine that covers your discipline. This will allow you to gain a global perspective within your industry every thirty days.

By following these few simple steps you won't need to fall in love with your employer, but beware . . . your employer may fall in love with you.

* * *

Contribution by **Lila Asante-Appiah, PHR**
Sr. Mgr., Corp. HR, Training, and Org Development
Broder Bros. Co.

After thirteen successful years at my first employer, post college, I was forced to come to the realization that being consistently rated an "outstanding achiever" just was not quite good enough for me. I was, by all accounts, loyal, hardworking, tenacious, and a high performer/achiever. All of these admirable qualities served me well, with one exception. I was devoted to the organization almost to a fault. I never once entertained the idea that the organization would not be as loyal to me as I was to it. In a moment, I will give you a little bit of background on my experience with company "X." First, however, let me share the bottom line, which is to never fall in love with your company to the point where you are not prepared to move on when circumstances call for it.

I began my career with a major retailer through an internship program. Immediately upon graduation, I was promoted to a management position wherein I was responsible for monitoring profit and loss, managing a large staff, overseeing procurement, and merchandising for a five million dollar department. Through my remaining twelve years, I was offered opportunities to work on various mentoring and diversity committees that offered me a great degree of exposure. I was considered a high potential (HIPO) employee and was promoted several times, moving from store to store within the District. All the while, my performance evaluations were outstanding and I was pleased when I was promoted to work on the District staff. My new position was far reaching in that I was responsible for managing and directing training and education efforts for 4,000+ employees, district-wide. I was extremely loyal, to say the least, and never considered leaving the company. With my solid record of performance, why would I ever consider other opportunities outside the organization?

Four months into my new position, the District Manager called me into his office and offered me a District HR Manager position! Finally, I was being recognized for my hard work, loyalty, and contributions over the last several years. The only hitch was that the position was in another state, several hundred miles away. I was exuberant and crushed all at the same time. After several discussions with my husband, we decided that we were not yet ready to relocate our family. I was beyond disappointed, but I knew it was the best decision for my family. Instantly, or so I felt, I was no longer considered a HIPO. My position was eliminated roughly two months or so after I declined the position. The organization had always placed a heavy emphasis on relocation. Basically, employees (including those once labeled HIPO), who were not in a position to relocate were also not considered for additional opportunities.

That experience was a wake up call for me. I had come to the realization that the company that I loved decided that I was no longer worthy despite my continued dedication. Essentially, I had made the grave mistake of falling in love with my company to a point where leaving was painful and appeared impossible. Were all my years of working there and honing my skills and management competencies for naught? In my heart of hearts, I knew that I had acquired many valuable talents that I could fully utilize somewhere else. Nevertheless, I panicked as I thought about going out into the business world to look for other employment. In the end however, about two months later, I resigned and moved on. It was by far the best decision of my entire career. My only regret is that I did not leave sooner to pursue my passion.

It is critical that, as you spend your days adding value while working tirelessly for a company, you never lose sight of your goal, which is to gain valuable skills and continue to improve your talent. Keep in mind that companies undergo changes continuously and some of these changes may not necessarily benefit you. Finally, yet most importantly, always prepare yourself for the next chapter in your career.

Contribution by **Mario Sanchez Carrion**
Marketing and Branding Professional

As somebody who has worked for the same company for the last twelve years, I understand how easy it can be to get used to the comfort zone of a familiar environment. That kind of stability, though, is anything but typical. In fact, government statistics show that about one third of the workforce changes jobs each year.

While many people switch jobs to take advantage of better opportunities, mobility is also a by-product of the general business environment. For example:

The rapid pace of technology can render products, companies, and entire industries obsolete very quickly.

Globalization may allow new, more agile, competitors to enter the market and challenge the status quo.

The economic climate can take a turn for the worse and force companies to downsize in order to survive.

At the same time each year, the competition for good jobs gets fiercer. This year alone, 1.5 million people are expected to graduate from college, around 20% of them with business degrees.

Our current reality teaches us that job security is an outdated concept. The fact that our situation may change at any moment means that we must always stay relevant. Unfortunately, having an updated resume is not enough to stand out from the crowd any more.

These days, standing out from the crowd means having a strong personal brand. Personal branding is basically the art of effectively articulating and communicating our skills, personality, and values so that others seek us to help them solve a problem.

Building a strong personal brand is now easier than ever thanks to Internet tools like blogs and social networks, which have taken the traditional notions of marketing and networking to a whole new level.

Here are a few pointers to help you build your personal brand:

- Find your center of gravity

- You will be more successful if your job fits your abilities, experience, interests, and values. Can you answer the following questions?

- Do you prefer a structured corporate environment or a more entrepreneurial one?

- Do you prefer to work with products or services?

- Are you more comfortable with consumer or industrial products?

- Do you like to delegate and manage people or are you more comfortable in the role of individual contributor?

- Is your goal to take on different functional roles over time, or to become an expert in one of them?

- Are you willing to travel, or do you prefer to work from one location?

- Are your company's products in tune with your values?

- What are the things that you are really good at?

- What do you need to improve?

Even if you consider yourself happy with your current job, going through this exercise will provide you with a good reality check.

Develop an elevator pitch

Put together a short statement, or "elevator pitch," that concisely communicates what your personal brand is all about. A good elevator pitch should answer these questions:

- Who are you?

- What problem do you solve?

- What makes you the best?

- What is your call to action?

For example:

"My name is John Smith and I have ten years of experience providing customized commercial lighting solutions to international clients. I deliver value through a mix of strong product knowledge and technical abilities, proven sales and marketing expertise, and life/work experiences in three different continents. For more information please visit www.johnsmith.com"

Register your domain name

It will only cost you about $10 a year and five minutes of your time to secure your very own online identity. Go to any reputable domain register and register yourname.com before somebody else does.

Yourname.com is your home on the web, and it can host your blog, samples of your work, presentations, videos, podcasts, etc. You can start by creating a basic page with some information about yourself (for example, your elevator pitch) and a way to contact you.

Use social networking sites

Create a profile on LinkedIn (www.linkedin.com) and add people to your network of "connections." Then, continue networking by joining different professional groups and using the "ask/answer questions" feature to showcase your expertise. Also, don't forget to get recommendations from former bosses and colleagues.

You can also create a profile on Facebook (www.facebook.com) and join communities organized around a region, a company, or a school. You can also network by joining groups organized around specific interests, products, and brands.

Twitter (www.twitter.com), a micro-blogging platform that lets you post updates of 140 characters or less, is also a good source of information and networking opportunities. You can get useful insights from the people you "follow," and bounce ideas off the people who are "following" you.

Start a blog

Get in the habit of writing regular articles in your area of expertise and publishing them in your own blog. You can easily set up a blog by getting an account with a hosting company that supports Wordpress, a popular blogging software. You can then ask them to help you set up your blog using your previously registered domain name.

<u>Help people</u>

- One of the best ways to network and showcase your expertise is by helping other people. You can:

- Put together short PowerPoint presentations and make yourself available to speak to professional groups and organizations.

- Participate and answer questions in different online forums.

- Write articles for magazines, newspapers, and blogs.

- Train/mentor those who are just starting out in your field.

<u>In conclusion</u>

If you love your company and enjoy your job, by all means work hard and bring your "A" game to the office every day. However, don't make the mistake of thinking that your current situation will last forever. Develop your personal brand instead. A strong personal brand is like insurance: you may not need it now, but if you ever need it in the future, you'll be glad you have it.

*   *   *

Contribution by **Mark Goloboy**
Director of Global Data Governance
Monster

When I was hired at a full service marketing agency, I was part of the new regime. My manager and his boss were both new, and were brought in to refresh the organizational chart. The executive team surmised that veteran employees were too comfortable, and there was a need for some fresh faces in the hallways. Many of the existing employees had been with the company for at least ten years. Processes had stopped maturing, and systems were becoming stale. The group hadn't kept up with the latest trends, nor were they willing to adapt.

Instead of replacing low performing team members, the executive team chose to bring in highly motivated Project Managers and Business Analysts with consulting firm backgrounds who were schooled in rigid project management methodologies. As a Program Manager responsible for implementing new systems and processes, this challenge was an increase in responsibility that was truly a step toward my CO-level goal.

As the new vision progressed, willingness to change was noticeable, at least on the surface. New employees were looking toward the future and it seemed like everyone was on board. Teams were collaborating well, and successful project delivery appeared to be the norm. But within months, the inevitable culture clash was palpable to all. The old regime started to miss deadlines, and, just like in the old days, assumed that their managers would come up with creative excuses so the clients wouldn't be upset. Veteran employees would help out their friends on other projects while ignoring their own customer's needs. This undercurrent of resistance was a nightmare to manage since it was endemic to the organization.

The veteran employees had survived management regime changes in the past, and knew they could wait out the change without truly embracing the process or looking toward the future. When a change agent attempted to implement a new process, the affected employees would complain until the decision was reversed and the change was eliminated. There was a constant fear that if one employee left, it would cause a chain reaction and the company would lose all of their talent. The apathy continued to permeate the workforce, and within a year the new Project Managers and Business Analysts with all their big consulting firm experience were utterly frustrated and exhausted from their futile efforts to change the culture of the organization. They were working hard to maintain excellent service to the clients, while internally the newer Project Managers were forced to rely on resources that were not committed.

As a Project Manager brought in as part of the new regime, I had a personal and professional stake in this culture war. Every day was a challenge. Clients were promised services that could not possibly be delivered. Timelines were set as a measure of success before project plans were even made.

The company over promised to clients and did not provide enough buffer for the schedule to slip. Unrealistic expectations and continual failure to meet milestones were a part of the routine. Predictably, the highly qualified subject matter experts and change agents from large consulting firms began leaving this toxic environment.

At first, the new hires appeared to leave for better opportunities. But as the months passed, people just left. Eventually, there was just one manager within the company who motivated me to keep working hard. He just might have been the most burnt out of them all, and I could see his departure was imminent as well.

My dream of success at what seemed like a stable company with growth opportunities for me had faded. I spoke with past colleagues and a mentor whom I trusted and they all concluded what I already knew. It was time to get out. As I look back at the company, I have to wonder what I would have done differently. I was sold on the idea that change would come, but it never did. In the future I will turn a more skeptical eye on new roles and consider the worst-case scenarios from the start.

*   *   *

Contribution by **Mike Levy**
President
Levy Consulting, LLC

The company is important, but so am I!

I totally agree with the ninth and final assumption of this book,
"Never fall in love with your company". I also think the company
never owes you a job for life. I worked for Hewlett-Packard (HP)
for 25+ years and to this day I have a very strong sense of pride
in the company and truly believe it's one of the best companies in
the world. When I worked for HP, I always gave 150% to my job
and to the company, and I have no regrets whatsoever. But one
thing I learned along the way is that nobody will ever care more
about me and my future than myself! I learned to understand
that employment with HP was not for the rest of my life, but is
for as long as there was real value for both the company and me.
I learned you can not possibly predict the future, but one thing
is for sure—everything is constantly undergoing change, some
things more than others. I learned that paying attention to the
needs of HP was just as important as paying attention to my own
personal needs and growth opportunities.

Only I can take care of my financial future!

A lesson I learned very early in life, was something my father
taught me. My father told me when I was growing up not to rely
on Social Security or your company to take care of you, and I
listened to him. So during my years working at HP, I put away
some savings and bought some stocks and real estate investment
property. I paid attention to my future financial situation and it
turned out to be a very good move in the long run.

I acquired the skills needed for working at HP, but also for what
I needed for the future!

Throughout my career at HP, I also paid attention to what skills
I needed to develop both to help HP as well as to help myself

in my future endeavors, whatever they might turn out to be. I knew those could include working for HP, working for another company, or even working for myself. A dream that I had from very early on in my life was to start my own company. So as I was developing my skills for my work at HP, I also considered how those skills and others might help me later in life if I decided to start my own business. As it turned out, many of the skills I needed to manage and work in a large corporation were actually very similar to those I needed when starting my own company.

I was laid off after 25+ years with HP. It was difficult and scary, but I figured out how to SUCCEED! I was not bitter. I focused on the positive, and I took control of my life!

I was never bitter about being let go, but I do understand being laid off can elicit feelings of anger and bitterness—you have to limit the time you spend dwelling on that. I have never felt that a company is obligated to take care of me in any respect. I never had the expectation that HP owed me anything. They never told me that it was a job for life. It was for as long as they had a need for me.

Finally I realized that I needed to make something happen for myself. That is when I decided to do something I'd always wanted to do but was too scared to try with a "good job" and "nice salary coming in". I started my own company. I had so much fun doing it I've since (in the last five years) started three of my own companies, and one for someone else. Looking back at the situation, I now think that my positive attitude and enthusiasm for my new projects and ventures might be part of the driving force behind my successes.

My retrospective

Looking back, I can safely say that I may never go back to working at any large corporation. Getting laid off gave me the opportunity to do something I had always wanted to do, but I was too risk-adverse to do. What I learned at Hewlett-Packard were basic skills, and the skills necessary to learn more. This was invaluable to me in starting my own company. If I ever work for a big company again, I guess I'll have to grow my own company into one.

*   *   *

Contribution by **Sandra Teague**
Advantage Employment, Inc.
President
University of Chicago
Booth School of Business Graduate

During my career, I have spent time working for others, and time working for myself. I've held jobs at different companies (both large and small), and I have started and operated several of my own businesses. I have made conscious deliberate decisions during each step along the way about where I would work, who I would work for, or what business I would go into. Each decision was made based on a combination of current circumstances, my current skill set, and my long term goals and objectives. That all changed dramatically for me just recently. For the first time in my life, I was laid off.

The company that I worked for was a small boutique staffing firm owned by a husband and wife team—I'll call them Sue and Bob. When I first met Sue, the company was flying high. In business only a short time, Sue had successfully brought in a significant amount of business, had built a staff to support that business, and was ready to take the company to the next level. Her husband Bob, who ran the 'back office' operation and managed the finances, provided great balance, and although he was not a sales oriented person, he provided needed resources and kept the place running. I was hired in as their first Director of Sales with responsibility to grow and oversee the sales team and to keep the company moving ahead. Creation of this new role made sense, and I was incredibly excited about the opportunity.

The culture at this young growing company was electric. Motivated by success, the owners gave liberal bonuses, lavish trips, and gifts to the internal staff employees. Customers were wined and dined. New business was celebrated. A very large long term project came in boosting morale even further. Everyone was working hard, and enjoying every minute of it.

Then came the rapid economic meltdown. The company held its own for a while. Growth slowed, but orders were still coming in. Then the end date of that large project, which originally seemed so far off, was suddenly looming. Other business then started to dry up. With major downtown employers laying people off left and right, the market for our service started to decline rapidly. The electric culture that was so motivating started to turn sour. Poor business practices and sloppy service that could previously be covered up by spending a few extra dollars were showing their ugly face. Disputes between employees were on the increase. Instead of mutual support, personalities clashed. It became hard to solve business problems and to work with customers due to the infighting within our own organization. The future started to look grim.

I knew where things stood and I was well aware that if things got much worse, my job could be in jeopardy. So I looked around and evaluated my situation. If the unthinkable happened, what would I do? Where would I work? What was different about my skills and experience now as compared to when I first started in my position? Quite a bit actually! I had learned about a different segment of the staffing industry that I previously knew very little about. I had the opportunity to develop and coordinate larger, more expensive marketing campaigns than ever before. On my own time and at my own expense, I obtained a professional certification that would validate the broad experience that I had built over the years in the field of human resources. I even started laying out plans for a "future" business that I would like to start.

Well that "future" came a lot sooner that I thought it would. Thankfully, I felt ready to receive it. Within a week, I had my new business idea solidified and was ready to hit the ground running. I enjoyed the time at my last company, but always kept an eye on what I was learning, what experiences I was gaining, and what my next move would be. Getting laid off was certainly upsetting, but starting a new chapter in my career far outweighed the negative. There are things about the job that I will miss: colleagues that I liked working with, and a fantastic office view, among other things. I realize, however, that there will be things to appreciate in my future opportunities as well. Looking forward to that is both motivating and exciting.

*   *   *

Contribution by **Scott Sutker**
Senior Vice President, Global Human Resources
Bank of America

There is nothing wrong with having a sense of pride about your organization. However, you must realize that your organization is separate from who you are. You must also recognize that your organization is constantly evolving based on the current and future economic landscape. While your organization may be the best in the world, it may not always be an ideal place for you. You must develop yourself such that should you need to walk away from your organization, you can do so with hope and confidence in personal and financial survival. If there is anything to fall in love with at your organization, it is the opportunity that your organization is providing you—the opportunity to learn and grow into being a Talent.

During the past 24 years since I graduated college, I have been fortunate to work for some great companies. I almost always received an "exceeds" rating and I take great pleasure in delivering results. I relate falling in love with your company to falling in love with your spouse. Over 60% of marriages end in divorce and with second and third marriages, only 20% remain happily married.[1]

If the odds of being in love with your significant other only has a 20 to 40% chance of success, and you have control over that situation, then how can you expect to have much more luck in with falling in love with your company? You could claim that divorce rates and falling in love with your company do not have a correlation, but I would argue that it does.

I consider myself a very loyal employee. I also know that, realistically, there are many outside factors which determine my employment that have nothing to do with my performance. Follow on for a summary of my last few jobs.

Organization #1: This was a small company (300 employees) that was in business for over 25 years. I was at the company for 9 years and was considered the top sales person nationally. In fact, one year, I sold more than the rest of the sales force put together. I was in a different league than the other sale people and usually won every sales contest. I really loved this company. I was an all star that exceeded expectations. Then, one Thursday afternoon, I was brought into a conference room and told that the company would be closing their doors on Friday. I was told to pack up my stuff and leave. And, by the way, we would not get our payroll for the last three weeks and our expenses would not be paid because the company was out of funds.

Organization #2: When the doors closed on my previous organization, this brought me in-house to implement the solutions I had been selling them. I felt really lucky that that I

---

[1]   Statistic taken from http://ezinearticles.com/?The-Costs-of-Rising-Divorce-Rates-Across-The-US&id=1003126

had great clients that immediately offered me a job. During my 7 years at Wachovia, I built various teams and created solutions that the bank had never seen before or expected. During my tenure, the bank continued on their quest of building the company by mergers. After one bad merger, my entire team was displaced due to budget cuts. As I was again a top performer and could show the financial impact I was making on the company, I was fortunate enough to be able to stay with the company another year in a consulting role. However, they later decided to outsource their HR department to a third party. I was really displaced then.

Organization #3: This is another great company. When I found out about previous employer was outsourcing their HR department to this organization, I decided to go ahead and join this organization. This was an interesting role where again I became a strong performer. I was the person that was assigned to the clean up the toughest accounts and make them work. When I joined this organization, there were around 12 project managers on the team. As time went on, the team went down to 3 project managers and I decided it was too risky to stay.

Organization #4: Again, I am very lucky to have a position with a great company like this. We are one of the strongest in our industry in the world. Again, I love my job. Also, I was rewarded a job title promotion in less than one year, so, I must be doing something right. However, I am also seasoned enough to know that there are many other factors that play into the company's decision to keep me, such as mergers, the economy, outsourcing, and company politics.

What I have learned is that you have to fall in love with what you do and not the company. You need to have the passion to do a great job but also realize that you can do a great job at any company. There are many studies about how Gen X'ers and Gen Y'ers think so much differently about employment then the older generations. They do not plan on staying in roles or companies long and they change jobs more often. Is this progress?

Contribution by **Sheila Wyatt**
Former Microsoft Human Resources Manager
Wyatt Groves Consulting

Don't fall in love with your company—you may lose the opportunity to grow.

Let me share with you what I have learned about this statement.

Many years ago, when I first entered the workforce upon graduating college I joined the largest bank in Washington state. I assumed I would be with that company for the rest of my career. The company had an excellent reputation and wonderful training and promotional opportunities. Everything seemed perfect. Little did I realize what the future would hold.

I stayed seventeen years with the company, and they were great years. But, along the way, the top bank in Washington State was acquired by a Fortune 100 financial institution, and while the new owners promised to keep their distance, it was only a matter of time before cost effective measures were put into place. The good news is that I survived a massive layoff, and went on to be the Affirmative Action/Diversity Manager for the company. In addition to that, I was given the opportunity to be Vice President and Manager of Human Resources for the Commercial Real Estate Group and work for one of the best leaders I have ever known in my working life. Life was good.

But things began to change. The people I admired most (including my boss), began to leave. The fun had gone out of going to work. We were now marching to a different drum, one much different from the one that I had come to know. So I began to consider the possibility of moving on.

Through a former work colleague, I found out about an Human Resources Director position for a small health care company. The company had grown to 185 people, and now needed someone to work with them on building the HR side of their business. I went from a sophisticated company employing thousands to a small company with great aspirations to grow. Their primary client was a well-known high-tech company located just outside of Seattle in Redmond, and they were growing exponentially. I thought I had found Nirvana; it was a company that was implementing a participatory management philosophy (which I believe in strongly) and listening to employee feedback. I thought I would be there forever. Life was good.

And just when everything was going great, I found out that my boss, the President, was having an affair with one of the two owners, and both were married. While they assured us (as they both proceeded with their respective divorces), that life would be the same and their personal relationship would have no impact on the business aspect of the company, the company culture began to change, and not in a good way. So, it was time to get out that resume, dust it off, and start looking for a new opportunity. Darn—I had hoped to be there for a long, long time, and do some wonderful things. Oh well.

Once again, through a former work colleague, I heard about a position available at a large wireless communication carrier. The position was responsible for employment in a 10-state region, and I had heard that the client group was great. I got the job, and came on board excited about working with some of the wonderful people I had met during the interviewing process. I brought on board a staff that had a high energy level and collaborated well with managers and candidates alike. We were a team in the greatest sense of the word. Again, life was good.

I was surrounded by great people, except for one person: my boss. She definitely was one who wanted to bring about change, but not in a way that we found conducive to the work environment. Unfortunately, she thrived on the chaos theory, and one by one,

I began to have my staff confide in me that they couldn't work for a woman who did not seem to have the best interests of the company and the employees at heart. So, again I said "Darn," decided it was time to update that old resume, and move on.

Through a friend of a friend, I learned of a Human Resources Director opportunity at a Fortune 100 high-tech company in the area, one that I would gladly add to my resume. I was hired by a great manager, had a challenging albeit large client group, and once again, I was in Heaven. I discovered it was okay to challenge the status quo, and was not penalized for doing it. I was surrounded by smart if not brilliant people who worked hard; for the first time in my life, there was very little dead wood floating around. Life continued to be good.

But then, by my fifth year, I began to get bored. The company was growing at a rapid pace, and it was becoming more difficult to be innovative and creative. The performance appraisal process paralyzed the company for a good part of the year (I am pleased to say that process has been simplified in recent years), and it was starting to feel like "same-o, same-o, been there, done that." Was it time to move on again?

One of my clients was the CFO, and he started talking about a joint venture between our company and a highly recognized global consulting firm. The concept behind this joint venture was sound. The position that I was being considered for was the Organizational Development Director. I would have responsibility for integrating cultures from 16 countries around the world. I would also have less of a commute, and I would be able to travel and work with diverse cultures (both of which I love). I was ready to sign up, and I did. Again, life was good.

Unfortunately, the company did not perform as well as it anticipated after the first year, and I offered up my position for elimination at that time. My greatest regret was no longer working with the great people I had met around the world. Fortunately, to this day, I am still in touch with many of them.

So what am I doing today? I am working with some very diverse companies who can't afford to have a Human Resources person on staff. What I love about this phase of my life is that I am providing them with valuable tools and resources that I have accumulated along the way, empowering them to act with common sense, compassion and courage. These are companies that want to make a difference and are not satisfied with the status quo.

<u>Life is good</u>

It's been a wonderful journey, but I know it is far from over. I look forward to what is ahead of me for the next 20+ years.

Here are some of the lessons I have learned along the way and offerings of advice for the next generation:

- Never say never. You may have found the place you want to be for the "rest of your life," but continue to be open-minded. Circumstances change.

- Embrace change. Don't be satisfied with status quo. Don't become stagnant. Continue to challenge yourself and to grow.

- Never burn your bridges. While I live in a very large metropolitan city, it is amazing how frequently I continue to come in contact with my past. Six degrees of separation is alive and well.

- Network, network, network. You may have noticed that every job opportunity I had opened up because of past contacts I kept in touch with.

- Keep the old job while you look for a new job. It is always easier to market yourself while you are currently employed.

- Never stop learning. I didn't realize the power of learning until I was in my mid 30's. Along with that comes recognition that you can learn from those who are older as well as younger than you. My 90-year old father has wonderful business success stories he continues to share with me; my 19-year old daughter has introduced me to Facebook and other social media that I am utilizing in my business. Knowledge comes from all different ages.

- Surround yourself with positive forces. By this I mean eliminate those who "drag you down." Keep in close contact with those who are as energized about life as you are.

- Practice humility. Nobody likes an egomaniac.

- Be a team player. Remember that there is no "I" in team. As the famous coach Paul "Bear" used to say, "If something goes wrong, I did it. If something goes halfway right, we did it, and if something goes really right, they did it." Isn't that great?

- Last but not least, don't fall in love with your company, because you lose the ability to grow. Isn't that where we started, but wasn't it a great journey?

*   *   *

Contribution by **George Moraetes, CISM, CGEIT**
Information Security Executive and Enterprise
Architect
Independent Contractor

There is no such thing as companies being loyal to their employees in today's business world. What matters most is that an individual be loyal to themselves and to their career they enjoy. I have seen many people work long and hard hours beyond the normal eight hour day without striking a balance with their personal lives. These people have a great work ethic, tremendous energy to excel, and they absorb knowledge like sponges in water and thirst for more but often fail to attain their goals. They have no direction, no plan, perhaps a vision but fail to put a plan in motion hoping their loyalty to one company will serve them well.

Many believe that good old hard work, going that extra mile to show their devotion and loyalty to an organization will enable them to be noticed and promoted, yet many find that is not the case, and for many reasons. There are consequences to this—people exert themselves hard for long periods of time becoming fatigued to the point where mistakes happen. The end result is they get burned out and discouraged. The irony of it all is the wasted energy spent working hard for a company but receiving nothing, getting no compensation in return for all their efforts. A pat on the back from the boss (maybe) is not going to help.

Smart individuals will have a vision and a plan to execute it to attain their career goals, if not with their current company, then with others. They must be able to recognize when it is time to jump ship and go to the next level in their plan. They also need to know what skill sets it would take to qualify, where to get the knowledge, and to have the all important people skills to climb the corporate latter.

One individual began his career as a Junior IT Analyst after graduating from a major university. His goal was to become a CIO at a large company. After 3 years he went on to become a senior IT analyst, with his tenure culminating as a supervisor in his department in the fifth year where he worked until his eighth year. In those years he mastered his job responsibilities and took every company sponsored training course to become a manager. He earned a Master's Degree along the way (paid for by the company) but was never promoted into a management opportunity. Frustrated, he began looking elsewhere and found another opportunity as a manager where he worked for 5 years. He was later promoted to Infrastructure IT Director where he acquired the business knowledge and skills he needed for his next step as a CIO. He found that opportunity at a new company where he works to this day. As a Vice President and CIO of a large corporation he has successfully attained his goal.

It is important to understand companies have their limitations, and individuals who want to climb the corporate latter need to recognize those limitations. Once they recognize these limitations, the next step is finding other companies willing to offer that next leap in their career plan which will culminate in achieving their vision.

*　　*　　*

Contribution by **Marcus Cadell**
Human Resources Consultant
ClearChoice Dental Implants

I had spent several years with a Fortune 50 telecommunications company with a global footprint and their culture implied that each employee had a job for life. The company had disappointing quarterly earnings reports for several periods, the chief executive had stepped down and senior executives stated that times were challenging. Employees thought that whatever the circumstance they would be taken care of by the company indefinitely. One morning the senior manager of our group called a last minute meeting and announced that they were going to offer voluntary severance packages over the next three weeks in order to trim costs. She reassured everyone that their jobs were not in jeopardy and that the objective was to have a 10% reduction in the workforce through voluntary departures. A couple of weeks later the senior manager called another meeting and this time in the presence of the Vice President announced that the department was going to combine with another leaving only 3 of the 15 employees with jobs. Afterwards most employees in the department were devastated, they could not understand how the company they were so fond of, most of them spent their entire careers with, could do this to them.

After the announcements I spoke with several employees about what they were going to do and most were not prepared for the future. One of the clerks working in our department Theresa had worked for the organization for 20 years in the same job. I talked with Theresa at length about her situation and she felt her prospects were more grim than most. The organization did have some skill development programs that offered ongoing training each year to enhance their skill set. Theresa took some classes but only took courses that did not enhance her technical abilities. After working for the company for 20 years she was still technologically challenged which made her very uncomfortable. The 3 employees that were selected to continue their jobs in the new department were very technically sound and Theresa was not one of them. I assisted her in putting together a resume as she had never had one before. In addition to that I recommended for her to take some Word and Excel classes as soon as possible to be considered for a similar paying job outside the organization. Theresa had been very proud of working for the company but was now forced to retire early or accept a lower paying job until she could have the same lifestyle in retirement as when she was working.

If Theresa had looked at her position as an opportunity instead of as an entitlement and been more proactive she could have extended her career with the company as well as been better prepared for her future. The lessons I learned firsthand from this situation was that an organization no matter how successful they have been in the past has to adjust as market demands change and as an individual you must create your own brand to be competitive. Other valuable lessons I learned from this experience were to keep up your skills, take on new tasks to gain further knowledge to expand your abilities, to lookout for yourself as the company will not always look out for you.

*   *   *

Building Talent

Building yourself as a Talent is, of course, a conscious decision. You have to *do* something about it, and do it regularly. You have to work with these assumptions to ensure that you are on the path to success.

What the Corporate Bold team would like to do is to offer you something that can help you build your Talent. We'd like to offer you some special resources that we feel will help you in assessing and building your Talent.

Please go to www.CorporateBold.com and take a look at some of the tools that are available to you. These tools are designed to help you get moving right now. We have personally selected these tools because we feel that they are the right tools.

You can, of course, find the Talent Assumptions that we've discussed here, which you can download for review or for sharing with others. We invite you to browse the Corporate Bold's Dictionary online for the lasted buzz words which you can learn and share. We highly encourage you to contribute to the dictionary as well. Connect with the contributors of this work and share your experiences and insights.

There are many more resources available to you right now and more will be added as they become available, so take advantage of them.

Starting the Journey

At this point, you and I need to start thinking about what we need to do going forward. If you have been able to challenge your past assumptions with the ones that we have outlined, then going back to the office is going to be thrilling experience. I suspect you will be able to walk around your office environment and actually see everything we have talked about in real life.

Remember to keep the focus on you and not get caught up in labeling someone else. I will reiterate that you should try not to hold hostility in your heart for your co-workers—those who are simply not aware that they are a **Talent** or those for whom it hasn't sunk in yet.

Even with the overwhelming evidence, it was difficult for me to challenge myself at first. The breakthrough that can be the result of challenging one's assumptions should really be experienced by everyone.

As you can probably tell that some of these assumptions (such as Assumptions #1) can be applied right away. Other assumptions may take time or need to be slightly fitted to your specific situation. Either way, you are now armed with these core concepts and you can actively participate in controlling your path to success. I encourage you to take control today! Work on the assumptions that stand out the most to you, first.

Friends, I hope to meet or correspond with you in the future. Additionally, you may correspond with any of the co-authors as well, via our website—www.CorporateBold.com. We certainly welcome the opportunity to hear about your personal experiences and insights and to gain as a collective community. Please share your experience with us and other Talents, privately or publicly, at www.CorporateBold.com.

See you back at the office!

Corporate Bold Dictionary

Career: A series of jobs, or projects, that you've worked on in a particular field.

Change: When you move on to a new, preferably preconceived, role at work.

Consultant: Someone who has worked on multiple projects and leverages what they've learned from those experiences to solve problems.

Dinosaur: Someone at your work who has been around for a long time, who has stopped seeing him/herself as a Talent, and is usually willingly **Trapped (by a system)**.

Historian: Someone at your work who has been around for a long time and likes to tell old company war stories.

Job: A short-term task that you perform to get a result.

Knowledge Broker: Someone how knows where to find certain types of information around your company.

Path of Opportunity: A process where you find and solve problems that benefit your organization as well as your development.

Quit: When you leave your job based on negative emotions.

Talent: Those developing themselves and solving problems for their organization.

Talent Manager: Those who work to develop other Talents.

Trapped (by a system): Stuck in a role because you are the primary person who knows how to do something (for example: administer a system).

Pitching a Tent: Staying in a job for an indefinite period of time.

www.ingramcontent.com/pod-product-compliance
Lightning Source LLC
Chambersburg PA
CBHW031821170526
45157CB00001B/141